Why Latin American Nations Fail

Why Latin American Nations Fail

Development Strategies in the Twenty-First Century

Edited by

ESTEBAN PÉREZ CALDENTEY
AND MATÍAS VERNENGO

University of California Press

University of California Press, one of the most distinguished university presses in the United States, enriches lives around the world by advancing scholarship in the humanities, social sciences, and natural sciences. Its activities are supported by the UC Press Foundation and by philanthropic contributions from individuals and institutions. For more information, visit www.ucpress.edu.

University of California Press
Oakland, California

Library of Congress Cataloging-in-Publication Data

Names: Pérez Caldentey, Esteban, editor. | Vernengo, Matías, 1968– editor.
Title: Why Latin American nations fail : development strategies in the twenty-first century / edited by Esteban Pérez Caldentey and Matías Vernengo.
Description: Oakland, California : University of California Press, [2017] | Includes bibliographical references and index.
Identifiers: LCCN 2017028439 | ISBN 9780520290297 (unjacketed cloth : alk. paper) | ISBN 9780520290303 (pbk. : alk. paper) | ISBN 9780520964525 (ebook)
Subjects: LCSH: Economic development—Latin America—History. | Sustainable development—Latin America.
Classification: LCC HC123.W59 2017 | DDC 338.98—dc23
LC record available at https://lccn.loc.gov/2017028439

Manufactured in the United States of America

25 24 23 22 21 20 19 18 17
10 9 8 7 6 5 4 3 2 1

For Osvaldo Sunkel

Contents

Preface

The chapters in this book were presented at the Eastern Economic Association Meeting in New York between February 27 and March 1, 2015. The objective was to provide a multidisciplinary view of the institutional turn in development and economics and how it does or does not illuminate the limitations of the current development strategy in Latin America. Our preoccupation is to go beyond the proximate or more superficial causes of underdevelopment in the region and, hence, discuss the endless failures of alternative development strategies to promote catching up with advanced economies.

Contributors

MARTÍN ABELES Economic Commission for Latin America and the Caribbean, Buenos Aires, Argentina

MIGUEL A. CENTENO Princeton University, Princeton, NJ, USA

AGUSTÍN E. FERRARO Universidad de Salamanca, Salamanca, Spain

KEVIN P. GALLAGHER University of Boston, Boston, MA, USA

STEFANIE GARRY Economic Commission for Latin America and the Caribbean, Mexico City, Mexico

CARLOS AGUIAR DE MEDEIROS Universidade Federal do Rio de Janeiro, Rio de Janeiro, Brazil

JUAN CARLOS MORENO-BRID Universidad Nacional Autónoma de México, Mexico City, Mexico

JEAN C. NAVA Princeton University, Princeton, NJ, USA

JOSÉ ANTONIO OCAMPO Columbia University, New York, NY, USA

ESTEBAN PÉREZ CALDENTEY Economic Commission for Latin America and the Caribbean, Santiago, Chile

ALEJANDRO PORTES University of Miami, Coral Gables, FL, and Princeton University, Princeton, NJ, USA

REBECCA RAY University of Boston, Boston, MA, USA

SEBASTIÁN VALDECANTOS Universidad Nacional de Mar del Plata, Mar del Plata, Argentina

MATÍAS VERNENGO Bucknell University, Lewisburg, PA, USA

1. Introduction

Matías Vernengo and Esteban Pérez Caldentey

INSTITUTIONS AND THE LIMITS OF THE CURRENT DEVELOPMENT STRATEGY

There are many explanations for why some nations grow to be rich while others are poor. And there are different views on why the great majority of economies, including the Latin American ones, remain stuck in between both poles without being able to compete with poorer economies or catch up to the rich ones.[1] The traditional mainstream explanation for the differences in economic development and growth across nations has relied on the neoclassical production function. The production function permits the decomposition of the rate of growth of an economy into the respective rates of growth of factor inputs (i.e., labor and capital) and a residual, total factor productivity, which represents the different forms of technological change.

Since growing by accumulating successive units of capital and labor is confronted with diminishing returns, a sustainable growth path can only be achieved through innovation and technological progress. This placed the focus of the analysis of growth—and of catch-up between countries—on technology, even when considering increasing returns to scale in capital and labor. However, besides insurmountable inconsistencies characterizing the specification of a production function (such as the fact that capital cannot be measured independently of prices and distribution, as pointed out in the Cambridge capital controversies), a large part of growth rates and differences in growth rates among nations cannot be explained by either factor accumulation, innovation, research and development, or technological progress (Helpman, 2004).[2] This key failure of mainstream growth theory opened the route to consider alternative explanatory variables and, in particular, sociopolitical factors including geography, culture, and institutions.

1

red Diamond, author of the best seller *Guns, Germs, and Steel,* is cor
..t to point out that, in part, technology is geographically determined; for
him, geography plays a central role. Culture has fewer defenders; most
prominently among modern economists is probably McCloskey (2010).
But the obstacles to that argument are even more difficult to overcome, not
the least because in modern times, countries with diverse cultures have
become developed, like Japan and South Korea (Acemoglu and Robinson,
2012). The Weberian Protestant work ethic would not help, in this case, to
explain relative development. It is important to note that culture does matter, even if it is not determinant, since different cultures produce different
types of capitalism, some more benign than others (Hall and Soskice, 2001).

The explanations of growth differences based on cultural and geographic
patterns lack the generality and universality required by neoclassical theory to argue that societies placed in different contexts and historical periods
respond, at the general level, to one and the same principle: utility maximization. This limitation has significantly contributed to consolidating the
institutional factor as the most promising mainstream line of research to
explain the central divide between the levels of development across different nations and historical periods.

According to this line of research, institutions are generally defined as
"the informal norms and formal laws of societies that constrain and shape
decision making" (Alston, 2008, 2). "Informal norms" are standard rules of
behavior that are unwritten but understood within a group or a community;
more specifically, the term refers to sanctions, taboos, customs, traditions,
and codes of conduct. By contrast, formal rules "are consciously designed by
humans and often codified in written form—examples are constitutions,
laws and regulations as well as property rights" (North, 1990, 97).

Within this view, the focus is placed on property rights as the crucial
"institution" that affects and enhances economic growth and development.
This responds to an issue of theoretical consistency: the definition and specification of property rights are required for the determination of an optimal
allocation of resources. Also, the "one concrete institutional element on
which all authors agree as a major determinant of economic development is
the existence of secure property rights" (Angeles, 2011). One of the most
recent statements of the view that institutions (and private property rights)
are essential for development and growth is Acemoglu and Robinson's
(2012) *Why Nations Fail.*

In the case of Latin America, the institutional approach to growth has a
long history, dating back to the failure of mainstream empirical studies
based on trade and protectionism to prove and illustrate the distortive and

inefficient nature of the state-led growth policies advocated by different governments in the region in the 1960s and '70s—which, by the way, resulted in the highest growth rates recorded in over four decades. The weakness of this economic argument led to a body of research and thinking termed the "new political economy," which emphasizes, in a way that is very similar to Acemoglu and Robinson's distinction between inclusive and extractive institutions, the rent-seeking character of government and government officials. Rent-seeking is portrayed as a wasteful, inefficient, and costly activity inherent to any regime based on strong intervention of the state in the economy. According to this line of thinking, government intervention transformed the main agents of production and growth, namely firms and entrepreneurs, into rent-seeking entities.

More recently, Engerman and Sokoloff (2000) have provided a variation on Acemoglu and Robinson's view of the role of institutions and property rights to analyze Latin American growth performance. For them, the point is that countries in the region with a high proportion of people in relation to available land would have, according to neoclassical theory, low wages—that is, low prices for the abundant factor (labor) and high prices for the scarce factor (land). In their view, then, societies with high population-to-land ratios developed institutions that protected the white elites and were, in general, less egalitarian. Property rights tended to be more insecure, and hence innovation and growth faltered. Institutions (property rights, essentially) were central, but so too was the geographic "good luck" of abundant land.

In this book, we argue that there are several key problems associated with "new institutionalist" arguments and, in particular, with the way they are applied to viewing and understanding Latin American development. For one thing, they provide a limited view of comparative historical analysis, failing to read and understand history on its own terms. An illustrative example is Acemoglu and Robinson's (2012) characterization of the Spanish and English colonizations as being extractive and inclusive, respectively, when in fact the historical record shows that both types of colonization were at times extractive and inclusive. Also, while examples of extractive institutions and poor growth performance would obviously come up in a study that covers such an enormous territory in terms of countries and time periods as *Why Nations Fail*, there are also major counterexamples that disprove their main arguments—for example, the contribution of property rights to the industrial revolution.

There is solid historical evidence showing that the usefulness of patents, copyright, and other forms of property protection for explaining growth is limited at best (Moser, 2013). Hoppit (2011) argues that in the case of England,

> property was often heavily taxed, frequently expropriated and, exceptionally, eradicated through redefinition. Such vulnerabilities did not diminish after the Glorious Revolution, they increased. . . . The scale of that expropriation was such, and the consequences so profound, as to undermine an important thesis that property rights became more secure after the Glorious Revolution, developed in a notable essay by Douglass North and Barry Weingast and now conventional amongst some 'new institutional economists'.

In other words, the Industrial Revolution can hardly be attributed to strong property rights in England. If one thinks of modern developing countries, it is hard to be sanguine about the notion that Western-style property rights in developing countries would be a sufficient condition for catching up.

Turning to more recent historical examples, the economic success of South Korea and some other Asian nations such as Singapore can hardly be said to be based on inclusive institutions. As is well documented, South Korea (as well as Japan), in an earlier period in history, used protectionism, exchange rate control and management, credit controls, and a mix of public and private initiatives to boost its real gross domestic product (GDP) per capita from U.S. $1,127 in 1961 to $28,875 in 2013, thereby changing from a middle-income to a high-income country (Chang, 2007).

Finally, the institutions emphasized by the new institutionalism and in *Why Nations Fail*, fundamentally property rights, are uniquely concentrated on the supply side of the economy, along with the generation of incentives for productive investment (to buy machines and equipment).

A different story about relative development could be advanced. Adam Smith, in *The Wealth of Nations*, argued that the division of labor, which was the basis of technological progress, was limited by the extent of the market—that is, by demand. According to Landes (1969),

> it was in large measure the pressure of demand on the mode of production that called forth new techniques in Britain, and the abundant, responsive supply of factors that made possible their rapid exploitation and diffusion. The point will bear stressing, the more so as economists, particularly theorists, are inclined to concentrate almost exclusively on the supply side.

In other words, institutions might be relevant—though not, primarily, the ones associated with the supply side, but rather those linked to the demand side, in Keynesian fashion.

Neoclassical economists, when discussing growth, always downplay the importance of demand. Structuralist authors with Keynesian tendencies, on the other hand, emphasize the role of demand-led growth. The dominance and persistence of Say's law, the notion that demand adjusts to supply, is behind the limits of the neoclassical account of the wealth of nations. Note that a demand-based argument for the wealth and poverty of nations implies that there are other institutions that matter for development. Poor countries that arrive late to the process of capitalist development cannot expand demand without limits, since the imports of intermediary and capital goods cause balance-of-payments crises. The institutions that allow for the expansion of demand, including those that allow higher wages to expand consumption and to avoid external constraints, are and have been central to growth and development. The role of the state in creating and promoting the expansion of domestic markets, in the funding of research and development, and in reducing the barriers to balance-of-payments constraints, both by guaranteeing access to external markets and by reducing foreign access to domestic ones, was crucial in the process of capitalist development.

In this view, for example, what England had and China did not was a rising bourgeoisie (capitalists) that had to compete to provide for a growing domestic market that had acquired a new taste (and hence expanding demand) for a set of new oriental goods, like cotton goods from India or porcelain from China, as emphasized by Berg (2004) among others. In the same vein, Latin American economies lacked an expanding market that would have forced domestic capitalists to produce and innovate in order to keep up with the competition. Latin American economies entered the world economy to produce silver (mining economy, Amerindian population), sugar (plantation economy, African American population), and other commodities for external markets. These were exploitation economies, less reliant on the development of domestic markets, typical of settlement colonies in the northeast United States or of the central countries in Western Europe.

CONTEXT, OBJECTIVES, AND OUTLINE OF THIS BOOK

Latin American economic development strategies have gone through significant changes over the past three decades, following the debt crisis and the "lost decade" of the 1980s. And yet, from the '80s to the present, Latin America as a whole has registered mediocre growth trend levels. The average rate of per capita GDP growth for the period 1980–2014 is 2 percent. This performance responds not only to the medium- and long-term effects of successive crisis episodes within the region—starting with Mexico's "tequila crisis" in late 1994 and culminating with Argentina's default in early 2002—many of which were the product of unsustainable balance-of-payments difficulties, but also to expansions that are, in comparison with other developing economies, short lived and less intense.

In the most recent period of expansion (2003–08), in spite of improved international conditions associated with higher commodity prices, greater access to liquidity, and external demand that allowed for higher growth rates (Pérez Caldentey and Vernengo, 2010), Latin America reached only a 3 percent rate of growth of GDP per capita, which is below that of all other developing regions (9.3, 7.0, 3.6, 6.6, and 3.8 percent for East Asia and the Pacific, Europe and Central Asia, the Middle East and North Africa, South Asia, and Sub-Saharan Africa, respectively). This expansion period did little to change the growth trend.

Currently the region faces more stringent external conditions. The slow-down in the external demand of developed economies and also of China, which had become a major trade partner for some of the economies in the region, coupled with the ongoing crash in commodity prices, has affected those economies whose production structure and exports are resource based. The transmission channels include not only the balance-of-payments difficulties, but also lower fiscal revenues (which, in some cases, far surpass those of other sources of public income), lower rates of growth, and even contractions in domestic investment (which is based on natural resources in many economies of the region). But the concomitant reductions in foreign financial inflows and higher risk perceptions have also affected countries that are not specialized in commodities. Far from being temporary, the current slow-down seems to embody a perception of protracted economic stagnation.

At the same time that Latin America faces a more restrictive external environment, other long-standing problems of the region—such as persistant poverty rates affecting some parts and some income strata of the region, high inequality (Latin America is the most unequal region in the world after Sub-Saharan Africa),[3] deficient education standards, and low productivity, among others—have become more visible and appear to be, if only at the discursive-rhetoric level, a more urgent priority for policy makers. This is not to deny that significant progress has been made in many different economic and social areas. However, these efforts—and, more importantly, their accompanying successes—have remained confined in scope and overall impact. They have not been able to generate the broad-based upgrade in capabilities needed for development (Paus, 2013).

Furthermore, the political shift toward democracy and the increasing importance of the rule of law as a guiding principle in civilian life that took hold of Latin American societies since the '80s, and more strongly in the '90s, has been tainted as a result of the more recent corruption scandals that affect many governments in the region. That is true even though corruption is certainly a structural problem that precedes the recent events.[4] Also, the rule of law and democratic principles have been undermined by the persistence of political instability and, in some cases, the sudden and illegal takeover of elected governments by judicial and mediatic processes.

As can be ascertained from the analysis above, institutions are an essential component of Latin America's development problem. We think that the new institutionalist view and the focus on property rights is part of the lack of success of mainstream policies that have dominated development economics in theory and practice in the past decades. We also think that given their importance, institutions deserve a broad, critical, and multidisciplinary approach, beyond the property rights approach, that could provide a basis for alternative policy recommendations. This, in essence, is the objective of this book.

The book comprises eight chapters, divided in two sections. The chapters in the first section highlight several key problems associated with new institutionalist arguments and, in particular, how the latter are applied to viewing and understanding Latin American development. In chapter 2, Carlos Medeiros contrasts the mainstream or neoclassical and the "new developmentalist" explanations for the successful development strategy in East Asia and the failure of Latin America, at least since the 1980s, with alternative heterodox views broadly defined as structuralist and connected with the Economic Commission for Latin America and the Caribbean and heterodox Keynesian perspectives. The author argues that both the neoclassical and the new developmentalist views have a tendency to de-emphasize the role of demand-side factors in the process of development and suggest solutions that require getting the prices right. Medeiros is also particularly critical of the so-called new developmentalist view according to which the main reason for Latin American underperformance was the macroeconomic policy adopted and the resulting real exchange rate appreciation, considered the main lever of manufacture exports, and economic growth. In his view, demand and the institutions associated with demand management are central for economic development, but multiple instruments, not just the exchange rate, must be used to promote growth, and the role of industrial policy has been neglected in Latin America.

In the same vein, chapter 3, written by the editors of this book, suggests not only that demand and the institutions that allow for its expansion are also relevant for the process of development, but also that the emphasis on private property as the main, if not almost the exclusive, role of the state in the process of development can only be inferred by distorting the historical record. The authors suggest that it is not the historical evidence, which would imply that there is significant space for a developmental state to promote technological innovation, but the preoccupations and requirements of neoclassical economics that have led to the institutional turn in development economics. The dismal productivity performance in the region is then tied to the current development strategy, which is still heavily influenced by the collapse of the state-led industrialization strategy in the early '80s, and the adoption of Washington Consensus policies subsequently.

Miguel Centeno and Agustín Ferraro suggest, in chapter 4, that two kinds of developmental failure are relevant for understanding Latin America's relative backwardness. They suggest that presidential interference tended to derail development programs, designed by career experts, that had run successfully. They exemplify their arguments with the Brazilian computer industry and the Chilean experience with a national developmental institution dedicated to industrial promotion. The authors suggest that autonomous bureaucratic institutions are central for development, but in Latin America the principle of supreme administrative authority of the president, established in several constitutions in the region, has had a negative impact on development institutions. In their view, if one contrasts the design of developmental institutions in East Asian and Latin American cases, the main lesson is that in the latter cases there is more interference from politicians.

In chapter 5, Alejandro Portes and Jean Nava review the theoretical and empirical literature leading to the institutional turn in the economics of development. They argue that sociologists have welcomed this turn as a vindication of their own ideas but have neglected two major shortcomings in the economics literature, namely (1) a failure to define institutions rigorously and to distinguish them from the real-life organizations that they underlie; and (2) a tendency to use nations as units of analysis in cross-national studies, neglecting intranational differences. They tackle these limitations through a comparative study of institutions in Latin America and one Southern European country with similar historical and cultural background. In total, twenty-nine institutions were subjected to one-year studies in six countries. Using Qualitative Comparative Analysis (QCA), the authors examine the combination of criteria leading to institutionally adequate and developmental organizations. Differences across countries and among institutions are systematically highlighted and discussed. Implications of the winning combination of determinants for a competent development institution, as uncovered by QCA, are examined. Multiple intranational differences show the inadequacy of treating countries as internally homogeneous as in past cross-national studies.

The theoretical and institutional discourse of mainstream economics analyzed in the first section of the book has, to a large extent, guided the policy prescriptions followed by Latin American governments over the past three decades since the debt crisis and lost decade.[5] Using empirically based analyses and specific source-case examples, the second section (chapters 6–9) provides critical assessments of this development strategy, identifies the future challenges, and presents alternative policy proposals to the ones that are currently being followed and implemented. While the initial chapters can be seen as discussing the deep causes of relative backwardness in the region, and engaging the new institutionalist literature that has dominated economics, the subsequent chapters deal explicitly with the limits of the current Latin American development strategy. The role of the cycles in commodity prices, the persistence of the balance-of-payments constraint, the possibility of the Dutch disease, and the role of the increasing integration with China, in particular the environmental consequences of Chinese investments in the region, are tackled in these chapters.

José Antonio Ocampo argues in chapter 6 that the decade 2003–13 was an exceptional one for Latin America in social terms and also, though less clearly, in economic terms. Growth slowed down significantly after the exceptional external factors that fed the 2003–07 boom came to an end. The unwinding of the period of high commodity prices and, to a lesser extent, of the expansionary monetary policy of the United States, has added new challenges. The major issue is the need to overcome the poor long-term economic performance that has characterized the region in the post-market reform period, particularly by adopting active production-sector development strategies.

In chapter 7, Juan Carlos Moreno-Brid and Stefanie Garry examine Latin America's economic performance in the past three decades with the objective of assessing whether it entered a new phase of strong and persistent growth with stabilization in the 2000s. Their analysis pays special attention to the changing roles of exports and investment as drivers of growth and to the region's performance in the fiscal area, the composition and dynamics of foreign trade, investment, and labor productivity. Their results indicate that, in general, the region has achieved important progress in macroeconomic matters, but it has failed to overcome major structural, long-term constraints linked to its balance of payments and, to a lesser extent, its fiscal performance. Unless these challenges are resolved, the region's long-term growth will hardly be favorable.

In a similar vein to the two previous chapters, Martín Abeles and Sebastián Valdecantos discuss in chapter 8 the return of the external constraint in South America. They suggest that South American countries transitioned from export-led growth before the subprime crisis to debt-led growth afterward. This, in turn, implies that the capacity of governments in the region to implement countercyclical polices to promote growth and social policies to reduce inequality depends fundamentally on the vision held by the international investor community.

Finally, Rebecca Ray and Kevin Gallagher look in chapter 9 at the sharp increase in social conflict and environmental degradation brought about by the recent commodity boom. The boom, driven by trade and investment with China, was concentrated in petroleum, mining, and agricultural sectors—sectors historically linked to environmental and social conflict. With some notable exceptions, Latin American governments have fallen short of mitigating these risks. Moreover, as the boom cools and Latin American economies slow, regional governments face pressure to "streamline" approvals for new export and investment projects, stymieing civil society's work of holding governments and foreign firms accountable.

INSTITUTIONS AND ECONOMIC POLICIES

Notwithstanding the combination of theoretical and empirical analyses with different emphases and approaches, this book provides a solid basis for the formulation of a coherent set of policy recommendations. First, the book argues that development policy cannot rely solely on purely economic factors such as growth and capital accumulation, or on social protection objectives. Development policies must also focus on improving the character and quality of national institutions. The most suitable definition of the term *institutions* as used in the different chapters is "blueprints specifying relations among role occupants in social organizations" (Portes and Smith, 2012, 4).

Second, this view does not imply that the main prerequisite for developmental take-offs is the establishment of set rules, such as property rights, to delimit the behavior and responsibilities of different economic agents and the spheres of action of the private and public sectors, so that market forces can optimally allocate scarce resources among alternative ends, as seems to be the case in new institutional economics. Contrarily, the institutional turn considered in this book advocates that the most important condition to promote development is strong, but flexible and dynamic, government involvement across a wide variety of areas—including investment, industrial policies and innovation, and education and other social policies—in addition to those that traditionally fall under the scope of public policies.

Third, this means that states and governments, rather than limiting their functions to those of mere "referees," regulators, or market plumbers, must assume the role of architects and market makers in the design and establishment of institutions.

Fourth, institutions, rather than focusing solely on the supply side (e.g., by changing incentives), must allow the expansion of demand to promote growth and development. In fact, the most relevant institutions to development are demand oriented. These encompass policies that include active production-sector strategies, the funding of research and development, ensuring the existence of markets for innovations and newly developed products, or overcoming external constraints by ensuring that the responses of international goods and financial markets permit the growth of domestic economies according to their potential. Demand-oriented policy means placing the focus on income and not on substitution effects.

Fifth, government involvement is not tantamount to centralized government. In fact, this book argues that developmental institutions and demand-oriented policies cannot work properly without bureaucratic autonomy. Bureaucratic autonomy means the establishment of a professional bureaucracy and public administration. Bureaucratic autonomy is counterposed to the belief that organizations are most effective, as a whole, if there is a clear and final authority for all important decisions.

. . .

Matías Vernengo is a professor at Bucknell University. Esteban Pérez Caldentey is senior economic affairs officer at the Economic Commission for Latin America and the Caribbean in Santiago, Chile. The opinions expressed are the authors' own and may not coincide with those of the institutions with which they are affiliated.

NOTES

1. According to World Bank data from 2016, countries that had a gross national income (GNI) per capita of U.S. $1,045 or less in 2014 are considered low-income countries. Countries (such as the majority of Latin American economies) with a GNI per capita of more than $1,045 but less than $12,736 are considered middle-income countries. Countries with an income per capita above $12,736 are considered high-income economies. Low- and middle-income countries are considered "developing countries."

2. There are also measurement problems, as suggested by Felipe and McCombie (2015), since total factor productivity is not really a measure of productivity and essentially indicates the weighted average of the rate of growth of wages and profits.

3. Comparable Gini coefficient estimates are available for 2010. In descending order, the Gini coefficients are 44.4 for Sub-Saharan Africa, 43.8 for Latin America and the Caribbean, 38.1 for East Asia and the Pacific, 36.0 for the Middle East and North Africa, 35.0 for South Asia, and 33.6 for Europe and Central Asia. See Alvaredo and Gasparini (2013).

4. It is also worth noticing that the more recent literature on the effects of corruption on economic development tends to emphasize its negative impact, while the older literature suggested that a certain degree of corruption greased the wheels of business and helped promote growth. Samuel Huntington (1968, 368) famously argued that "in terms of economic growth, the only thing worse than a society with a rigid, over-centralized, dishonest bureaucracy is one with a rigid, over-centralized and honest bureaucracy." From our perspective, the main problem with this literature is that it mostly deals with subjective perceptions of corruption, which may deviate from actual corruption, and that it does not address the issue of causality, that is, whether corruption causes lack of growth (or growth) or vice versa.

5. The causality between ideas and policies in Latin America is also the subject of *Ideas, Policies and Economic Development in the Americas* (Pérez Caldentey and Vernengo, 2008).

REFERENCES

Acemoglu, D., and Robinson, J. (2012), Why Nations Fail: The Origins of Power, Prosperity, and Poverty. New York: Crown.

Allen, R. (2012), "Technology and the Great Divergence: Global Economic Development since 1820," Explorations in Economic History, 49, pp. 1–16.

Alvaredo, F., and Gasparini, L. (2013), "Recent Trends in Inequality and Poverty in Developing Countries," Documento de Trabajo Nro. 151 Noviembre.

Berg, M. (2004), "In Pursuit of Luxury: Global History and British Consumer Goods in the Eighteenth Century," Past and Present, 182, pp. 85–142.

Chang, H.J. (2007), Bad Samaritans: The Myth of Free Trade and the Secret History of Capitalism. New York: Bloomsbury Press.

Cornia, G.-A. (2014), "Recent Distributive Changes in Latin America: An Overview," in G.-A. Cornia (ed.), Falling Inequality in Latin America: Policy Changes and Lessons. Oxford, UK: Oxford University Press.

Diamond, J.M. (1999), *Guns, Germs, and Steel:* The Fates of Human Societies. New York: W.W. Norton.

Díaz Alejandro, C. (1984), "Latin American Debt: I Don't Think We Are in Kansas Anymore," Brookings Papers on Economic Activity, 15, pp. 335–403.

Engerman, S., and Sokoloff, K. (2000), "Institutions, Factor Endowments, and Paths of Development in the New World," Journal of Economic Perspectives, 14, pp. 217–232.

Erten, B., and Ocampo, J.-A. (2013), "Super Cycles of Commodity Prices since the Mid-nineteenth Century," World Development, 44, pp. 14–30.

Felipe, J., and McCombie, J. (2015), The Aggregate Production Function and the Measurement of Technical Change: 'Not Even Wrong.' Cheltenham, UK: Edward Elgar.

Frenkel, R., and Rapetti, M. (2012), "External Fragility or Deindustrialization: What Is the Main Threat to Latin American Countries in the 2010s?" World Economic Review, 1(1), pp. 37–56.

Hall, P., and Soskice, D. (2001), "An Introduction to Varieties of Capitalism," in P. Hall and D. Soskice (eds.), Varieties of Capitalism: The Institutional Foundations of Comparative Advantage. Oxford, UK: Oxford University Press.

Helpman, E. (2004), The Mystery of Economic Growth. Cambridge, MA: Harvard University Press.

Hoppit, J. (2011), "Compulsion, Compensation and Property Rights in Britain, 1688–1833," Past and Present, 210, pp. 93–128.

Huntington, S.P. (1968), Political Order in Changing Societies. New Haven, CT: Yale University Press.

IMF (2014), Fiscal Monitor 2014: Public Expenditure Reform Making Difficult Choices. Washington, DC: International Monetary Fund.

Landes, D. (1969), The Unbound Prometheus: Technological Change and Industrial Development in Western Europe from 1750 to the Present. Cambridge, UK: Cambridge University Press.

——— (1998), The Wealth and Poverty of Nations: Why Some Are So Rich and Some So Poor. New York: W.W. Norton.

McCloskey, D. (2010), Bourgeois Dignity: Why Economics Can't Explain the Modern World. Chicago: University of Chicago Press.

Moser, P. (2013), "Patents and Innovation: Evidence from Economic History," Journal of Economic Perspectives, 27, pp. 23–44.

North, D. (1990), Institutions, Institutional Change and Economic Performance. Cambridge, UK: Cambridge University Press.

Paus, E. (2013), Getting Development Right: Structural Transformation, Inclusion, and Sustainability in the Post-Crisis Era. New York: Palgrave Macmillan.

Pérez Caldentey, E., and Vernengo, M. (2008), Ideas, Policies and Economic Development in the Americas. New York: Routledge.

———— (2010), "Back to the Future: Latin America's Current Development Strategy," Journal of Post Keynesian Economics, 32, pp. 623–644.

Pomeranz, K. (2000), The Great Divergence: China, Europe, and the Making of the Modern World Economy. Princeton, NJ: Princeton University Press.

Portes, A., and Smith, L.D. (2012), Institutions Count: Their Role and Significance in Latin American Development. Berkeley: University of California Press.

PART I

The Institutional Turn

2. Industrialization, Trade, and Economic Growth

Carlos Aguiar de Medeiros

INTRODUCTION

The long-term economic performance of Latin American and East Asian economies has aroused great controversy regarding development economics and development strategy. For the World Bank and neoclassical economists, successful economic trajectories (most in Asia) resulted from high levels of savings, free trade, enabling market institutions, huge investment in human capital, and prudent macroeconomic interventions. To paraphrase Tolstoy, all economic successes, like all happy families, are alike; thriftiness, good government, and prudent macroeconomics are their pillars. And each economic failure, like each unhappy family, fails (is unhappy) in its own way. This ideological diagnostic survived the contradictory historical evidence from East Asia, where strong developmental states (initially in Japan and then in South Korea and Taiwan) led industrialization from the 1960s through the '80s. It remained strong even when the reforms demanded by the Washington Consensus—liberalization, privatization, deregulation—were adopted in the majority of Latin American countries in the '90s and delivered no growth but chronic external crisis. It did not flicker even when China, the most spectacularly successful case of development, had built its trajectory through "five-year plans" and state-owned enterprises (SOEs) led by a communist party.

In the views of the Economic Commission for Latin America and the Caribbean (ECLAC), the United Nations Conference on Trade and Development (UNCTAD), and heterodox economists, departing from a wide theoretical perspective (classical political economy, Marxian, Keynesian, and Schumpeterian), high rates of investment and exports, structural change, and technological innovation were the common features of high-growth economies. Strategic trade, capital controls, and developmental macroeconomics were present in all successful stories; development failures differed from each other. These heterodox perspectives provided substantial criticisms of mainstream development economics and useful insights on national development trajectories, but owing to their diversified theoretical approaches, their interpretations of the dynamics of economic growth, the role of exports, technological progress, and macroeconomic policies were not alike.

In the past decade, when the terms of trade strongly changed to favor primary exports, many heterodox authors and organizations such as ECLAC resumed the "new developmentalism," a perspective led in Brazil by Bresser-Pereira (2010), considering the competitiveness of the manufacturing sector the main divide that distinguished the successful (East Asian countries and modern China) from the not-so-successful (most developing primary exporter countries). Nevertheless, unlike the "classical developmentalism" of Latin American structuralist or institutionalist and Schumpeterian perspectives that have highlighted the role of industrial policy, from this perspective the main reason was the macroeconomic policy adopted and its effects on the real exchange rate (RER), considered the main lever of manufacture exports, manufacturing production, and economic growth.

This chapter draws on developmental narratives and heterodox literature on development economics to argue a different perspective based on four propositions:

1. The process of industrialization that distinguished the successful development trajectories is not synonymous with manufacturing production.

2. Capital accumulation depends on the growth of domestic and external demand. Exports play a different role in economic growth, the export rate ultimately depends on income elasticity, and the value of the exchange rate is a very limited source of competitiveness.

3. Structural change entails a multitude of instruments; industrial policies evolve but never cease to be the main lever for technological upgrading.

4. A balance-of-payments (BOP) crisis is a capital account crisis ultimately related to the composition of capital inflows and exchange rate regime.

The following five sections explore these propositions. The first discusses the connections between industrialization, technical progress, and development. The second examines different perspectives on capital accumulation, BOP constraints, and the different role that export growth plays within countries. The third argues that industrialization and export diversification demand multiple instruments. The fourth examines and contrasts different evolutions and patterns in Asian and Latin American countries. The fifth makes some final points to conclude the discussion.

INDUSTRIALIZATION AND ECONOMIC DEVELOPMENT

Developed or industrialized economies are terms indistinctly used to identify rich economies. The identification of economic development with industrialization expresses the great world divide (Findlay and O'Rourke, 2007) since the first industrial revolution in the eighteenth century, when the manufacturing industry became geographically concentrated in a few countries (the center of the world economy) surrounded by a vast area of nonindustrialized and poor agricultural or mining economies (the periphery). More than the mere existence of manufacturing production, industrialization, the growing mechanization of labor, is the material form of a vast structural change characterized by the continuous introduction of new goods and new productive processes as the main driver of productivity.

From this perspective, the classical division of labor into aggregates such as manufacturing sector (measured by its contribution to gross domestic product [GDP] or employment), agriculture, and services explains little. Friedrich List ([1837] 1983) observed that the national power was not based on material objects but "upon the creative power which makes possible the production of material goods" (List, [1837] 1983, 180). As argued by Karl Marx ([1889] 1991), the production of machines and the capital goods sector became the "core" of modern technical progress and the material form of capital accumulation. Walther Hoffmann (1958) considered the process of industrialization as an evolution from consumer goods as the key industry to capital goods. Moshe Syrquin (1988) considered development as the "increase in the overall density of the input-output matrix." In a similar analysis, Albert Hirschman (1958) described development as an increased complexity of inter- and intra-industry transactions and an increase in the variety of goods, with emphasis on capital and intermediary goods (Toner, 1999).

As Raúl Prebisch (1964) observed, the importance of industrialization was its inner connection with technical progress and its interdependence with several economic activities. As observed by P. Sai-wing Ho (2010), for Prebisch industrialization meant not only machines but also the development of "technological density," a concept very similar to "technological capabilities" explored more recently by Sanjaya Lall (1996). Alice Amsden (2001) considered economic development as a "process of moving from a set of assets based on primary products, exploited by unskilled labor, to a set of assets based on knowledge, exploited by skilled labor" (p. 2).

Ricardo Hausmann and César Hidalgo (2010), in a line of argument similar to Hirschman's, considered that the economic complexity and export diversification that distinguish developed economies result from the accumulation of non-tradable productive inputs, or what they call capabilities. Because of their complementarities, export diversification, they argue, depends on the number of capabilities the country has.

Nicholas Kaldor, in his 1966 Cambridge inaugural lecture, described a "four-stage pattern of growth" formed by a sequence of import substitution and exports of consumer and capital goods, arguing that the distinctive structure of a developed country was an integrated industrial system with the establishment of a capital goods sector. This sector "makes for a built-in element of acceleration in the rate of growth of manufacturing," and import substitution and domestic demand can generate enough demand for manufacturing production (Kaldor, 1966; Toner, 1999).

Nevertheless, in Kaldor's works, based on the "two-stage growth model" and "two-sector model" in which agriculture and exports became successively the main source of manufacturing demand (Kaldor, 1985), this qualitative distinction of industrialization as the production of machines from a generic manufacturing production became blurred or subdued. Departing from this wide division of labor, he considered manufacturing production in general as the "engine of growth." Three main arguments undergirded this proposition (Toner, 1999): that manufacturing is the unique sector that is subject to increased returns, that manufacturing of products includes continuing technical progress that is used in other sectors, and that manufacturing employment in land-based surplus-labor economies increases overall productivity.[1] This thesis had a strong influence on modern development economics, and manufacturing production became synonymous with industrialization.[2]

Prebisch (1950) and Hans Singer (1949) argued that the contrast of poor and rich countries was associated with what they produced and exported. The tendency of barter terms of trade was in favor of manufacturing increasing the polarization of rich and primary producers' poor countries. The evolution of the terms of trade was a strong argument for peripheral industrialization. Later, Singer and Ansari (1977), in a perspective similar to that of Arthur Lewis (1954), observed that this division of labor and the deterioration of terms of trade was not the problem but was rather a symptom of the crucial difference between rich and poor countries. No matter what a poor country produces, Lewis pointed out, the deterioration of terms of trade with rich countries will occur unless its productivity (and wages) in agriculture increases—or, as Singer and Ansari observed, unless technological progress increases overall productivity. Rich countries, they observe, are rich not because of what they produce but because they are the source of modern technology and the headquarters of multinationals.

In fact, after World War II, the time span between invention and profitable technological innovation dramatically decreased and technical progress became routinized and concentrated in public institutions and private labs of transnational companies working through government procurement or public finance. This opened a great gap between the innovator countries (and companies with their headquarters located in these countries) and the others; industrial production was progressively diffused to many countries, but technical progress became strongly concentrated.

The polarization of manufacturing production and agricultural and mining production ceased to be the unique divide between developed and underdeveloped countries. Manufacturing production was the main feature of the "rise of the rest" considered by Amsden (2001) in regard to the group formed by China, India, Indonesia, South Korea, Malaysia, Taiwan, and Thailand in Asia; Argentina, Brazil, Chile, and Mexico in Latin America; and Turkey in the Middle East; nevertheless, only a few of these countries became fully industrialized. As the past two decades have shown, only South Korea, Taiwan, and China have increased their capacity to produce capital goods and dislocate their production to high-tech sectors, thereby changing the hierarchy of the division of labor.

In fact, not the mere presence of manufacturing but the "the capability to use new technologies in some industries and to produce a part of the wide range of new products and services appropriate to local conditions" (Freeman, 2005, 93) is the essential meaning of industrialization. This capacity is particularly important when one considers the diffusion, since the '80s, of manufacturing production based on unskilled labor led by transnational companies in the "global value chain" (Milberg and Winkler, 2013). In this new geography of production and trade created by unbundling productive processes in supply chains, many low-labor-cost developing countries such as China, Mexico, Malaysia, Thailand, and the Philippines started producing and exporting high-tech products using imported components. This brought about a huge decline in manufacturing prices. Nevertheless, the "technological gap" became more acute as technological progress became more concentrated in a few countries and a few companies.

For those countries, the great challenge is to create "endogenous technology" and, as observed by Amsden (2001), to build "knowledge-based assets" allowing production "at or above prevailing market prices (or below market costs)" (p. 3), as happened historically in Japan and South Korea and as the Chinese modern industrial policy eloquently recognizes. In order to master current technologies and originate new ones, diffused technological capabilities and modern infrastructure have been the main assets that yesterday and today distinguished successful national development strategies.

When industrialization is considered to be synonymous with manufacturing production, the emphasis on "national innovation systems" as a key lever for technical change decreases and the emphasis on price (labor cost) competitiveness increases. The second consequence is to consider industrialization (and deindustrialization) as measured by a simple increase (or reduction) in the aggregate share of manufacturing in GDP or in employment as synonymous with development. In this shallow perspective, South Korea, Taiwan, and China seem not very different from Malaysia, Thailand, or Mexico.

INVESTMENT, EFFECTIVE DEMAND, AND PATTERNS OF GROWTH

Investment in machinery and equipment is the main driver of technical progress (De Long and Summers, 1992), and the factors that push it are the main sources of economic growth. Considering that the main logic of capitalism is not to produce goods but to sell them at a profit, private investment will grow according to the increase in final demand composed of domestic demand for consumer goods, exports, and technological innovation. Private investment follows the autonomous components of demand where government spending, credit finance consumption, and exports constitute the major sources.

Following the Marglin-Bhaduri interpretation of the crisis of the "golden age" (Marglin and Bhaduri, 1990), it was common within post-Kaleckian macroeconomics to assume an accumulation theory positively related to the profit share.[3] This original formulation of profit-led growth considered only private investment and induced consumption as sources of effective demand, with no consideration of other sources of autonomous demand (Pariboni, 2015). However, if one considers these autonomous sources, expectation of growing demand will push the investment rate, independent of the evolution of profit share. As Pierangelo Garegnani (2015) observed, "The rate of profit on new investments appears not to be a factor that influences investment independently of the two (the growth of final demand

and technological innovations); it seems rather, to be how the influence of those two factors manifests itself" (p. 11).

In his two-sector economic growth model, Kaldor (1985) blended the dynamic of capital accumulation with patterns of growth. In his demand-led growth, he follows an analysis convergent with the supermultiplier model whereby investment adjusts to exogenous demand. Nevertheless, he considered, as well, that manufacturing growth requires an external source. In a closed and less advanced economy,[4] agriculture plays this role; in an open and advanced economy, exports lead.[5] Accordingly, manufacture exports become the main source of demand for every country. One contested consequence is to consider growth strategies such as export promotion—as generically associated with the postwar Asian countries—intrinsically superior to import substitution, normally associated with Latin America.[6]

Nevertheless, independent of the level of GDP per capita, structural and institutional factors explain large national differences in the share of each source in final demand. As most historical analyses of national economic trajectories show, structural factors, relatively independent of their stage of growth, explain the different roles played by internal and external markets. Simon Kuznets (1958) showed that the importance of foreign trade was (inversely) associated with the size of a country (measured by population); Bert Hoselitz (1959) included resources and the man-to-land ratio to identify structural patterns of growth.[7] Amsden (2001) observed as well that the size of the country (measured by population) and population density affect the roles of internal and external demand.[8] The development of internal markets for manufacturing production was historically associated with agriculture and mining modernization, real wage evolution, government consumption, and infrastructure investment.

The role of agriculture and the mining sector as a source of demand for manufactured goods was essential for England and principally for the U.S. take-off in the seventeenth century, but modernization and mechanization of primary goods were an essential factor in real wage rate growth and, thus, domestic demand. As argued by David Ricardo, John Stuart Mill, and Karl Marx, the cost of production of food (the main wage good at that time) and the real wage (the quantity of food afforded by labor) determined the labor cost for the industrial sector. Thus, the rate of profit for industrial goods will depend on the evolution of technical progress, on the supply of these goods, and on the comforts paid to labor, which evolves according to political and institutional factors. Productivity increases in wage goods mean low labor costs for manufacturing, allowing higher real wages. In England and particularly in the United States, the high productivity in agriculture and in wage goods were crucial for their competitiveness and high wages.[9] In countries where agriculture was poor (as historically in Eastern Europe, or in tropical agriculture in underdeveloped countries), the wages were high for industry and low for the workers.[10] The productivity of agriculture is one essential structural dimension for income distribution.

In East Asia after World War II and in modern China, development narratives have stressed price competitiveness of manufacture exports but have frequently underrated the high productivity achieved in the agriculture sector and in the production of food. Nevertheless, this was also a crucial factor for the sustainable real wage evolution in those countries. In India, Indonesia, and the Philippines in Asia and in Brazil and Mexico in Latin America, agriculture exerted a lower demand for manufacturing production, and the conflict between real wages and labor costs was much higher (Studwell, 2012).

Besides food, the other decisive land-based good for industrialization and patterns of growth is fuel. The availability and low price of coal was an essential source of competiveness in Britain's early manufacturing might. In the United States, the access to cheap oil through domestic production or imports was central for its fast and competitive industrialization. Machines need energy and raw material supplies; without cheap sources of these goods within the country, the struggle for competitiveness in industrial goods demands great investment in transports, infrastructure finance, and diplomacy.[11] Japan, South Korea, and Taiwan are natural-resource-poor countries, and they could not achieve high competiveness in manufacturing production without cheap oil and cheap raw material. Given the geopolitics of the Cold War period, the United States provided the main access to these resources. In Latin America, by contrast, Argentina, Brazil, and Mexico—thanks to their abundant natural resources and domestic supplies of mineral ores, oil, and electricity—could implant heavy industry during the years of development after World War II.

The development of internal and external markets is quite dependent on infrastructure investment. The availability and quality of economic infrastructure, such as roads, ports, and telecommunications, directly affects and influences the extension and connectedness of markets and overall productivity. Given its externality and high social return, public investment in infrastructure, particularly in late industrialized countries, was an important driver of industrialization and the development of markets. Different from private investment that follows economic growth, public investment in infrastructure is largely autonomous and depends directly on developmental state decisions.

In his argument on the role of exports in modern economic growth, Kaldor (1978) considered the autonomous role of exports as a source not only of demand but also of the currency necessary for imports. Indeed, exports play two different roles in economic growth. In some countries, exports may constitute the predominant source of final demand, and industrial production grows according to the growth of their external markets. That was the case for nineteenth-century England, but it has not been the case for the United States (just to consider the hegemonic countries in the past three centuries). Among peripheral countries, the exports of primary goods—as occurred in Latin American countries during the nineteenth century and as is still the case in many Latin American and African mineral- or energy-rich countries—engendered a pattern of *"desarrollo hacia fuera"* (as termed by ECLAC), or export-led growth. After World War II, the exports of manufactured goods in many Asian economies—particularly in city-states, such as Hong Kong and Singapore, and in countries with large investments of multinational companies in the export sector, such as Malaysia or Thailand—became the main source of demand as well. In other countries, exports are necessary to finance their import needs and other currency expenses and, hence, to allow a higher rate of growth. This, of course, is not true for hegemonic countries that issue the world currency.

For the first group of countries, where exports are a high share of GDP, the multiplier and accelerator effect induced by export growth led GDP growth. In countries where domestic demand is a higher share of GDP, the rate of GDP growth depends on its evolution as formed by government and household consumption. For both "export-led" and "domestic-led" countries, the same BOP constraint applies. Countries that do not issue world currency cannot finance chronic BOP disequilibrium and, thus, as considered by Antony Thirwall (1979), cannot grow at a sustainable rate higher than the rate given by the ratio of rate of exports and the elasticity to import.[12]

Exports, foreign investment, and capital inflows played different roles in BOP constraints. The rate of growth of exports was important during the years when there was no abundant currency provision, as well as during the later decades when capital outflows from developed economies were abundant—though it is not enough to have high growth in exports to avoid a financially vulnerable position.

Unregulated flows are an independent source of BOP crises (Medeiros, 2008a, 2008b). Most analyses based on BOP constraints and on the "external gap" have considered financial fragility a necessary consequence of exchange rate appreciation (Bresser-Pereira, 2010) or "overexpansion" (Amsden, 2001) and of consequent current account imbalances. Nevertheless, in all BOP crises that hit developing countries (since the nineteenth century), financial overborrowing and bankers overlending played an autonomous role in the rapid deterioration in external solvency. It is important to consider that in order to keep the solvency rate (current account deficit/exports) and the liquidity rate (short-term capital inflows/reserves) manageable, the control of capital account and the flexibility of exchange regime are of utmost importance. After World War II, the world economy had three strong financial cycles, which occurred respectively in the 1970s, the '90s, and the first decade of the twenty-first century. In the '70s, capital controls ("financial repression" in orthodox jargon) were present all over, but this did not prevent high external debt in the majority of the "rest" countries, particularly in Argentina, Brazil, and Mexico and in South Korea, independently of how they deployed foreign money (import substitution, export diversification, or consumption). During the '90s, financial liberalization removed capital controls in a majority of the "rest" countries but not in China, India, and Taiwan. This generated strong enlargement of external debt and other short-term liabilities and a deep BOP crisis in Asia (except in China, India, and Taiwan) and in Latin American countries. In the last financial cycle, capital controls were back through taxation and prudent measures, but this did not prevent large amounts of capital inflows. Nevertheless, different from the previous financial cycles in this last cycle, no comparable financial crisis occurred in developing countries.

In these financial cycles, the RER followed a boom-bust pattern, appreciating during the boom and falling abruptly in the crisis. Although the solvency ratio was deteriorating along the cycle, the BOP crisis occurred after a great decrease in the liquidity ratio. This happened in the '70s; in the '90s, the elasticities of exports and imports did not affect this behavior very much. The combination during the '90s of an open financial system and a fixed peg system brought about strong short-term speculative investment. In the last cycle, independent of what happened to RER—strong valorization in Brazil, moderate valorization in China and Korea—no deterioration occurred in the liquidity ratio among developing countries, and no BOP crisis occurred. The exchange regime (the control of capital inflows and the freedom to fluctuate the nominal exchange rate) and the main composition of capital inflows (credit or other financial inflows) seem to be more significant in BOP crises than the behavior of the RER.

INDUSTRIALIZATION AND EXPORT DIVERSIFICATION DEMAND A MULTITUDE OF INSTRUMENTS

The cumulative causation of technical, financial, and trade progress might generate crucial advantages for a hegemonic country.[13] Consequently, for latecomers, the diffusion of modern industries requires new strategies. Their success depends on their adequacy to the level of the country's economic backwardness and political or geopolitical possibilities. Lower wages have not been a strategic asset sufficient to compensate for much lower productivity in all successful national catch-up experiences.

In the nineteenth century, when England exerted its hegemony through the imposition of free trade, industrialization required trade protection and many other industrial policies to compensate for the technological, trade, and financial superiority of England. John Stuart Mill's ([1848] 1968) argument on infant-industry tariff protection became predominant among the economists, but it was hardly the most important or sufficient industrial policy for latecomers. Alexander Hamilton ([1791] 1966) and Friedrich List ([1837] 1983) considered many other policies. According to Ho (2010), both Hamilton and List considered that although a protective tariff was necessary to reduce the huge differences of cost, they did not consider that it was a sufficient condition for a latecomer country to unleash the nation's productive power to compete with the technological leader, nor was it the most important policy. Besides tariffs and subsidies, effective governmental efforts on infrastructure and finance, and on science and technology, were central for late industrialization. If there are strong externalities within the economic system, the low level of productivity in a particular new branch of production in a latecomer country does not come exclusively from its particular immaturity but is based on the low level of overall efficiency of the whole economy.

Tariffs, subsidies, and exchange rate can protect and stimulate manufacturing investment for internal or export markets, but they are not a sufficient tool for industrialization or for economic growth. Tariffs and subsidies change prices in particular branches of the economy, altering their profitability. Exchange rate changes the profitability and labor cost of all tradable goods. Their effects on economic growth depend on what happens with final demand, productivity, and competitiveness. Arguably, the most controversial is the role played by exchange rate in economic growth, due to its direct effect on income distribution and its blunt nature, subsidizing all exports, irrespective of their importance for technological evolution.

Considering price competitiveness in a fixed exchange regime, increases in nominal wages higher than productivity (higher labor cost) negatively affect price competitiveness in manufacturing production. This is particularly relevant for light industries in which labor costs are important. This can happen as a result of real wage increases or higher consumption prices than industrial prices. In a flex exchange regime, exchange rate devaluation can restore price competitiveness through lower labor costs.[14] Nevertheless, unless subsidies or investments in wage goods keep their prices constant, this increase in competitiveness always occurs through a lower real wage.

Developing countries face two different roads if they seek to increase their export performance in manufacturing production: cut wages (directly or through exchange rate depreciation)—let's call it the "low road"—or, alternatively, try to raise productivity in wage goods, preserving real wages and changing specialization for new goods and activities of higher demand— a "high road." As Amsden (2001) argued, the advantage of the first method is that it is automatic, but "nevertheless, wage cuts are no guarantee that either skills will rise or total cost will fall sufficiently" (p. 6). Nor, necessarily, does a higher export rate compensate for a lower rate of consumption of domestic goods. The low road, typically represented by export processing zones, was present in all Asian countries at the beginning of their take-off; however, in most successful export countries, this road did not last and was replaced by a high road through multiple instruments.

Among classical institutionalists and in the Keynesian literature on development, the roles played by price competitiveness and by the value of exchange rate for economic growth and technical change were subsidiary. Investment in infrastructure, tariffs, subsidies, and capital controls achieved greater importance. They were quite skeptical about price elasticity of exports and imports and, thus, about the effects of exchange rate on growth. Prebisch, particularly, was concerned with the inflation and distributive effect of exchange rate devaluations. The classical developmentalism or Keynesian skepticism regarding price competitiveness includes the argument that even if the price elasticities satisfy the Marshall-Lerner conditions, the exchange rate is

> an instrument of limited effectiveness, since to sustain a rapid rate of output growth in the medium and long term, a one-off increase in competiveness is not enough: it must rise persistently. This also means that to maintain external equilibrium under conditions of rapid growth solely via exchange rate management, real wages would have to fall, not just once but repeatedly. (López Gallardo, 2008, 24)

In addition, one must consider that if external demand is not increasing, a depreciation of exchange rate only increases a country's competiveness if the exchange rates of competing countries remain constant; otherwise, a kind of "beggar-thy-neighbor" effect occurs.[15] This undermines the efforts to gain competitiveness through exchange rate, initiating an "immiserizing growth" or a "race to the bottom" strategy.

If the rate of change in the exchange rate has a limited role for export growth, the level of exchange rate only achieves a higher importance for economic growth if one follows the Marglin-Bhaduri "profit-led" growth and considers the effect of exchange rate on income distribution. This hypothesis, followed by new developmentalism, holds that a lower exchange rate or unit labor cost would bring, in an open economy, a higher investment in tradable goods (Frenkel, 2008; Bresser-Pereira, 2010). If this hypothesis does not hold, and there is no evidence that higher investment will follow (López Gallardo, 2008; Fiorito et al., 2014), the value of the exchange rate plays no predictable role in the overall rate of GDP growth.

Karshenas (2007) and Barbosa et al. (2013) connected the level of exchange rate with higher growth through the hypothesis that a devaluated exchange rate could encourage new manufacture exports, thereby increasing the rate of growth in compatibility with the external constraint.[16] This enlargement of the country's export basis has a "once and for all" effect, but its positive influence on the rate of export growth depends on its effect on the composition of export's structure toward goods with higher income elasticity. It is very difficult to see how this hypothesis holds when the country's challenge is not to export more labor-intensive manufactured goods but to export goods and services with higher value-added and technological content.

Despite these difficulties, the connections between the level of exchange rate and economic structure play a crucial role for the "Dutch disease" theories considered by Marcelo Diamand (1988) and Bresser-Pereira (2010). Diamand (1988) examined the dynamics of economies such as Argentina and other Latin American countries during the import substitution period. In these countries, an "unbalanced economic structure"[17] occurred in which the primary export sector is internationally competitive whereas the industrial sector has a higher cost. The level of the exchange rate reflected the higher productivity of primary exports. This structure did not prevent an import-substitution stage under protectionist tariffs, but it was a drawback for light manufacture exports. Devaluations of the exchange rate immediately pass through consumer prices, increasing distributive conflict and resulting in higher inflation and overvaluation. This unbalanced economic structure, as considered in early structuralist literature in Latin America, demanded many types of industrial policies.[18] Diamand considered that a comprehensive development policy, including taxes on commodity prices and policies to increase the productivity of wage goods, was necessary to correct the structural imbalance. Investment in infrastructure and many industrial policies must be in place to increase productivity and for structural diversification.

Bresser-Pereira (2010) generalizes this analysis, considering the existence in these countries of a chronic tendency for overvaluation, conceptualized as a market failure.[19] He argues that the introduction of tax on commodities can eliminate this imbalance but, different from early structuralist analysis, he considers that the neutralization of this tendency explains the successful experiences of industrialization and growth; all the failure results from the non-neutralization of this tendency. This analysis considers not the industrial policy but the level of RER as the main lever for investment and structural change.[20]

Development efforts change as the economy evolves. From the 1960s through the '80s, successful export diversification occurred in all developing countries through industrial policies, and exports' performance was normally required in exchange for subsidies and public loans. As briefly described in the next section, liberal reforms that followed in the '90s dismantled this strategy in many countries but not in China, Korea, and Taiwan, which resisted or adapted, creating new instruments through strong efforts on domestic technology, investment in modern infrastructure, and internationalization of domestic firms.

The diffusion of new information and telecommunication technologies, and the formation of global and regional production chains, placed new demands and changed national industrial policies. A "second phase of catching-up" (Chang, 2006), based on innovation and the construction of proprietary national technologies, affirmed in South Korea and China the basic challenge of industrial upgrading. Different from the period of the 1950s through '80s, this "neo-developmental" strategy has centered less on the internal market as the prevailing scale of accumulation, and the processes of productive regionalization and internationalization of "national champions" strongly expanded the horizons of firms' investments. China followed the new strategy that strongly combined public investment in infrastructure—the main inducer of overall growth productivity—with a selective industrial policy in information and telecommunication technologies. Such a strategy, as briefly described in the next section (and which also occurred in Korea and Taiwan), has a focus less centered on the productive sector, as prevailed from the 1950s through the '80s, and is based on innovation processes in new technologies through several policies and instruments.

The most recent decade in South America and in many Asian countries was much better than the '90s, when the Washington Consensus reforms, higher commodity prices, and more pragmatic macroeconomics allowed higher growth. This brought about higher employment and higher wages; nevertheless, this progress did not include the reconstruction of the developmental state's capabilities or the recuperation of the level of infrastructure investment or higher efforts toward technological upgrading.

PATTERNS AND STRATEGIES OF GROWTH IN EAST ASIA AND LATIN AMERICA

In the world led by U.S. technology and by the dollar as the dominant currency, three main obstacles challenge industrialization by latecomers: scales, currency, and developmental state capabilities. All three become crucial when manufacturing incorporates capital-intensive sectors. Initially, the diffusion of light industries did not face these obstacles or they were not restrictive. Import substitution, using imported capital goods bought through primary exports, replaced foreign suppliers of consumer goods. In large primary-exporter countries (e.g., Argentina, Brazil, and Mexico), domestic demand allowed the scales necessary for efficient productive capacity; but in small and more natural-resource-poor countries (mostly in East Asia), exports of cheap manufactured goods became the predominant market for industrial production. As long as import substitution started to include capital goods and heavy industry, BOP restrictions in both groups of countries became stronger. In large countries, export of primary commodities became progressively insufficient to finance the imports of capital and intermediary goods. The same happened in countries that exported light manufactured goods. Thus, import substitution and diversification exports toward goods of higher income elasticity in the world market became crucial for developing countries. Few countries in Latin America and in Asia surpassed, from the 1960s through the '80s, the "easy stage" of light manufacturing and created productive capacities in steel, chemicals, shipbuilding, and the automotive industry.

In order to grow and industrialize, South Korea and Taiwan needed to export manufactured goods. Because they were importers of energy and natural resources, the export of manufactured goods was the only way to obtain the necessary dollars to release the BOP constraints and dependence on U.S. aid. Moreover, in countries devastated by the war, this initial necessity to export became the principal source of growth of final demand. Exports grew in those countries not only because of their competitiveness; competitiveness grew not only as a result of exchange rate or labor cost; and investment growth was not induced solely by exports.

For geopolitical reasons, the United States strongly supported these developmental policies throughout the '60s and '70s, including national discrimination against foreign capital. Moreover, exports were encouraged by the United States, the major external buyer of goods from these countries. This "development by invitation" was still strong in the '80s, though this changed in the following decades.

Initially, given the low cost of labor (i.e., low wages and low exchange rate in a regime pegged to the dollar) and a modern technology initially bought through American aid, these countries achieved high competitiveness in light manufacturing in export processing zones. However, even in this stage, governments strongly promoted and monitored export performance. Exports grew at a high rate, but this was not the only reason for the high economic growth. In these countries, investments in infrastructure were of paramount importance, particularly in agriculture, transport, and energy. High investment and land reform in agriculture allowed steady growth of rural incomes and low food prices. Thus, real wages could grow without incurring increases in domestic labor cost, and industrial and urban wages benefited, at least partially, from industrial productivity growth.

The "high road" took place during the '70s in heavy industry and became evident in what Studwell (2013) described as the "Asian model of infant industrial promotion." This included a very discretionary and selective industrial policy combining SOEs, investment by state development banks, export targets, and a central bank acting as an arm of the ministry of finance and development. During all this period, South Korea had current account deficits (Amsden, 1989). Taiwan was more dependent on cheap currency and low added value in export processing, but this changed very fast.

Korea and Taiwan benefited from their greater backwardness compared to Japan, targeting their exports toward products in which Japanese producers had lost competitiveness in the American market. This occurred during the '70s and '80s, when the yen appreciated against the dollar and Japan's Ministry of International Trade and Industry prioritized higher-value products. This quite particular regional dynamic meant that the real exchange rate of Korea or Taiwan (which followed the dollar exchange rate) depreciated against the yen, providing an increase in the price competitiveness of those countries' manufactured goods in relation to Japanese exporters, without any cost in real wages. South Korea benefited additionally from Japanese investment and finance. External debt grew strongly in the '70s (similar to what happened in Brazil and Mexico), and a sharp BOP crisis took place after the interest rate shock of 1979, but this was different from what happened in Latin America, in that South Korea could easily finance its debt through Japanese banks. Large involvement by Japanese companies in South Korea and geopolitical factors explain this.[21] In the '80s, Korea followed the same pattern of growth, in particular with higher investment in technological innovation and consumer electronics.

Throughout this period, although exports were an important source of autonomous demand, public investment in economic and social infrastructure was central for balanced high growth. Urbanization and industrialization of agriculture pushed this investment to high levels. During the '90s, South Korea opened its financial accounts and large capital inflows took place. This generated a financial and banking crisis in 1997, but a few years later, even with a much more liberal control mechanism, South Korea restructured its chaebols and resumed its growth trajectory. This finance deregulation occurred in an economy already complex and diversified. Korea built its technological capabilities in information technology, particularly in semiconductors, and the rise of China as a great importer of these goods (as intermediaries) pushed the country's exports and investment.

South Korea and Taiwan followed Japan in a road not traveled by other Asian countries. No comparable outward-oriented developmental state led by domestic producers and backed by the United States took place in the Philippines, Malaysia, Indonesia, or Thailand. High levels of surplus labor, low wages, and competitive exchange rates in those countries did not bring the export and growth performance of South Korea and Taiwan. Backward agriculture, poor infrastructure, and state capabilities explain this difference. The other Asian countries entered the world division of labor first as primary exporters and later, since the '80s, as exporters of light manufacture goods and low-value activities integrated in a value chain led by transnational corporations. However, this much more liberal strategy through processing export zones benefited from regional "flying geese" dynamics (Medeiros, 1997) led by foreign direct investment. This inner connection between foreign investment and exports, coupled with government spending in urbanization and infrastructure, generated high growth.

Following advice from the International Monetary Fund, these economies opened their financial accounts in the '90s, which resulted in a huge capital account crisis. Malaysia introduced capital controls and tried to replicate some of the development strategy followed in Korea, and the other countries followed liberal reforms. Nevertheless, independent of domestic policies (as happened in the case of Korea), they benefited from the Chinese rise. China was a great competitor in low-wage industries and activities, but after the 1997 crisis, Chinese real wages started to increase while the nominal exchange rate became constant. This gave these countries an opportunity to achieve a lower RER after strong devaluations. Despite its contractionary effect, the high share of exports and the continuous growth of the Chinese economy pushed their economies. Moreover, during the 2000s, high commodity prices allowed larger investment in infrastructure and domestic consumption.

China followed its own way, combining the institutions of the "Asian model of infant industrial promotion" with its unique structural and geopolitical features and, above all, its incomparable scale. China opened its economy gradually in the '80s and exploited the opportunities to export products of light manufacturing and low-skilled activities in electronics and other industries through imports of capital goods and intermediaries. This strategy, different from South Korea and Taiwan but not very different from that followed by smaller Asian countries, included large participation by transnational companies. This strategy occurred simultaneously with modernization in agriculture and high rates of urbanization. This brought about high demand for imports of raw material and for heavy industry led by SOEs. Additionally, the Chinese government, in a strategy inspired by Japan and South Korea, made strong efforts toward building a "national system of innovation" aimed at developing endogenous technologies and used its domestic market to attract high-tech labs from transnational companies. In contrast to the approach followed early on by Japan and Korea, China faced a different technological reality in which capabilities are based less on sectors and more on activities and focused its strategy on international technological alliances and joint ventures. China became the hub of the global and regional value chain and a large market for global and regional exporters, mainly for raw material, parts and components of electronic goods, and labor-intensive manufacturing. Since the '90s, however, as happened in Taiwan, China is making large technological efforts to master technological capacities downstream (e.g., brand-name designers, software, and semiconductor production) and upstream (distribution and marketing) in order to appropriate a larger share of value-added. Infrastructure investment became the prime mover for high investment in modern technologies. China kept strict control on capital flows and, in recent decades, accumulated large reserves. After the 2008 international crisis, in order to keep the rate of growth high, the government decided to stimulate domestic demand through higher wages, consumer credit, and infrastructure investment. The high performance of exports was achieved not only through low labor cost; scale economics and a great capacity to sell, to finance, and to transport became central. In 2000, major SOEs in oil, electrical grid, building, engineering, and capital goods went global and China became a large investor in South America, Asia, and Africa. All investment and trade contracts included Chinese exports of machines and equipment.

Latin American countries, and particularly such large countries as Argentina, Brazil, and Mexico, achieved by 1980 diversified industrial production evolving from steel to automotive to shipbuilding and, in Brazil, to a successful aircraft industry. In this regard, Brazil was not very different from South Korea, with a competitive capital goods sector and heavy industry.

Externally, no geopolitical developmental support similar to that provided by the United States to East Asia has occurred since the Cuban Revolution took place. Foreign capital was much more significant than in East Asian countries, and exports, most composed of primary goods, were the sole source of dollars. In these large countries, exports were not the principal source of demand, and government spending and domestic consumption led the investment growth. Public investment was particularly important in infrastructure and heavy industry, and the continuous expansion of internal markets pushed private investment. As in East Asia, developmental states led economic growth and structural change by multiple macro- and micro-interventions (Bértola and Ocampo, 2015), but unlike those countries, and more similar to South Asian countries, they were less cohesive and more socially fragmented. Unlike in Argentina, where modern agriculture and higher wages were structurally distinguished aspects (Canitrot, 1983), in Brazil and Mexico large populations lived in backward agricultural economies in which wages were low. The recurrent macroeconomic challenge was the BOP constraints derived from the low capacity to import and low inflows of capital. Since the '60s, manufacture exports grew very fast, particularly in Brazil, and in the '70s large capital inflows financed high growth and heavy industry. Brazilian exports grew through diversification, controlled exchange rate, and commercial and industrial policies.

As a result of external crisis, economic growth in the Brazilian economy as well as in the majority of Latin American countries became strongly constrained and different from what had happened in South Korea; no countercyclical financial support was available in the '80s. Huge nominal depreciation in the exchange rate and fiscal contraction brought about high inflation and low growth. During the '90s, Latin American countries opened their trade and financial system and dismantled the majority of developmental institutions. This enlarged the demand for imports, and, given the low level of commodity prices, the rate of export growth did not prevent sharp deterioration in BOP. Privatization, financial deregulation, and denationalization (more than deindustrialization) enlarged the demand for currency, and fiscal contraction generated a huge decline in infrastructure investment. Large amounts of capital inflows generated a boom-bust cycle. Despite the different composition of exports and the role played by manufacture exports in Brazil and Argentina in comparison with South Korea and Malaysia, BOP deterioration was very similar. At the end of the decade, a deep financial crisis occurred in Argentina, Brazil, and Mexico.

After the North American Free Trade Agreement was implemented in 1994, Mexico followed a very different dynamics from South American countries. It exchanged the previous growth model, centered on domestic demand and oil exports, for an export-led growth model based on American and transnational corporate investment in manufacturing activities that are intensive in unskilled labor. Following this "low road," not different from the model followed by South Asian countries, it dismantled all developmental institutions and kept a depreciated RER and low labor cost.[22] Despite its diversification and high growth in manufacture exports driven by the U.S. market, Mexico's overall performance in recent decades—let alone its technological capacity, employment, and income distribution—was inferior to that of Argentina (where taxation of primary exports and low levels of capital inflow prevented the exchange rate from appreciating) and Brazil (where RER sharply increased). Agriculture remained poor; investment in infrastructure was much lower than in developmental years, and wages remained stagnant.

In Brazil and Argentina after 2003 (until 2010), the combination of high commodity prices with huge international liquidity and better administration of BOP brought about much higher growth, led by domestic markets. In Argentina, financial capital played a minor role and a Keynesian policy coupled with development policies generated strong growth. In Brazil, the influx of capital was much higher, engendering exchange rate appreciation and large accumulation of external reserves. Investment, including in manufacturing, grew very fast, pushed by domestic demand led by household consumption, higher wages, and government consumption. Unlike in South Korea, which invested in information technology, or China, which enlarged its investment in domestic technologies and infrastructure, the years of higher growth in Brazil were not followed by technological or modern investment in infrastructure. After 2011, the decline of commodity prices and of external demand resulted in a lower rate of export growth, but the foreign external reserves remained very high and no external crisis challenged domestic expansion. Nevertheless, the Brazilian government decided to change from its previous, growth policy regime, with a high decline in public investment and in consumer credit and high levels of fiscal incentives toward the tradable sector. This policy shift (Serrano and Summa, 2015) brought about a strong deceleration in private investment and income growth.

CONCLUSION

In the wake of the remarkably contrasting experiences of East Asian and Latin American economies in the past several decades, several debates occurred on development economics. The first "round" reflected the "great divide" between these regions in the '80s, opposing the World Bank and free trade economists against institutionalists and social scientists. For the World Bank and its economists, a "market-friendly" state intervention had predominated in East Asia, contrary to what had distinguished Latin American economies in which state intervention was assumed to be pervasive and distortive. The alternative perspective argued that in East Asia, and particularly in Japan, South Korea, and Taiwan, the state did not follow but led the market, creating new competitive advantages in productive sectors and activities very different from their factors endowment. In this leadership, the prices were "distorted" and investments were allocated in new areas through state banks and powerful planning agencies. The bulk of the controversy in this round regarded not macroeconomics but investment allocation, with industrial policy leading structural change. Along this line, many authors explored the role of a "national system of innovation" in achieving high external manufacturing competitiveness.

The second "round" occurred in the '90s, characterized by world financial deregulation and high financial liquidity. This exerted strong pressures for liberal reforms unequally implemented in these regions. Latin American countries enthusiastically adopted the Washington Consensus reforms and had, consequently, a "stop-and-go" pattern of growth, increasing their dependency on primary exports and capital inflows with overall disappointing results in growth, income distribution, and industrial modernization. The BOP crisis also reached South Korea and Southeast Asian countries that opened their capital accounts, but China and Taiwan did not follow this pattern, and the overall performance was much better. Contrary to the first debate round, this second round emphasized macroeconomics, particularly the role of financial liberalization in economic growth. For the post-Keynesian economists, and for organizations like UNCTAD or ECLAC, financial openness was the main cause of a highly volatile pattern of economic growth and of the external crisis that hit the region.

The high growth of commodity prices, its impact on the economic growth of primary export countries from 2003 to 2010, and the deceleration of growth afterward was the main scenario of the third "round" of economic development controversies. In this round, according to many heterodox authors following a post-Keynesian perspective, including organizations such as ECLAC and proponents of new developmentalism, the divide between the successful (East Asian countries and modern China) and the other developing countries was based on productive structure, particularly on the competiveness of the manufacture export sector. Nevertheless, contrary to the heterodox thought of the first "round" that highlighted the role of industrial policy for new developmentalism, the main reason was the macroeconomic policy. In this region, financial liberalization and high prices of commodities brought about (particularly in the past decade) an appreciated real exchange rate that precluded industrialization and higher and sustainable growth. The Asiatic catch-up was the outcome of successful export-led growth made possible by a competitive real exchange rate.

I have argued an alternative interpretation here, considering both the process of structural change and the role played by demand in economic growth. The process of industrialization and structural change that distinguished the successful development trajectories is not synonymous with manufacturing production, as in Kaldorian and new developmentalist perspectives; and capital accumulation ultimately depends on the growth of domestic and external demand. Exports play different roles in economic growth according to different national structural factors, and the export growth rate depends primarily on developmental strategies. The value of the exchange rate seems to be a limited source of competitiveness. Although the composition of exports is important for a sustainable rate of growth, national experiences show that the BOP crisis that systematically interrupted high economic growth was essentially a capital account crisis, ultimately related to the composition of capital inflows and the nominal exchange rate regime and not to the composition of exports or real exchange rate. Structural change and high levels of investment as occurred in East Asia and Latin America resulted from multiple mechanisms of intervention. Since the '90s, industrial policies have ceased to be important in the latter region, but they were rebuilt in most successful Asian economies.

.   .   .

Carlos Aguiar de Medeiros is an associate professor at the Institute of Economics, Universidade Federal do Rio de Janeiro. This research received financial support from CNPq.

NOTES

1. On the basis of such propositions, Kaldor (1985) derived his three "growth laws": a causal positive relation between the rate of growth of manufacturing and GDP; a causal positive relation between the rate of growth of manufacturing and productivity; and a causal positive relation between employment in manufacturing and aggregate productivity.

2. As argued by Toner (1999), increasing returns in manufacturing generate an endogenous mechanism of productivity growth, but there is no solid argu-

ment for why agriculture, mining, or services cannot have the same dynamics, introducing new cost-reducing methods and techniques as markets expand.

3. See Pariboni (2015). In an open economy, this theory assumes a negative net correlation of exports to wage share (see the end of this section).

4. Alternatively, the world (if we disregard national borders).

5. "Within an open economy at a fully developed stage of industrialization the primary determinant of manufacturing output growth is the growth of industrial exports" (Kaldor, 1978, 142).

6. "[T]he argument against import-substitution and domestic-led growth as a sustainable model of development has been challenged by the leading Kaldorian scholar, Professor John Cornwall," whose main finding on Japanese postwar growth was that growth in exports was not much different from growth in internal markets—and the latter growth was, in most cases, a precondition for export success (Toner, 1999, 155).

7. "This means, however, that in the smaller countries investment will have a natural tendency to flow into actual or potential export industries, and in the view of capital scarcities in underdeveloped countries in general, this will impart a certain peculiar pattern of development to these countries which probably differs significantly from developmental patterns in large countries" (ibid., 149).

8. "Thus, in terms of involuntary structural characteristics (those over which a country has no control), the greater population size, the smaller the export coefficient, and the greater population density, the greater the tendency to export" (ibid., 163).

9. Considering the evolution of internal industrial goods markets, the great divide among countries—as exemplified by European countries in the nineteenth century—was agricultural modernization and, consequently, income distribution. Higher wages and higher demand for industrial goods in modern agriculture separated Western and Eastern European countries and showed different roads for industrialization. In primary exporter countries, agriculture exerted an important demand source for manufactured goods; but only in countries where crops were important wage goods (e.g., Argentina and Uruguay) were these exports simultaneously a positive source for real wages.

10. As observed by Toner (1999) in his analysis of growth, Kaldor did not incorporate the connections of income distribution.

11. From the very beginning of the nineteenth century, direct investment and loans from industrialized countries were the main driver for the "export-led growth" of peripheral countries that specialized in primary exports.

12. Even with financial inflows, this rule holds for avoiding an unsustainable foreign debt burden.

13. In the words of Mill, "It is true, inventions spread rapidly from country to country, but not so the power of bringing them into profitable use. In that respect, the advantage of having large masses of capital already accumulated is immense. There are as many inventions made on the other side of the Channel as on this; but it is to England that the inventors bring their inventions when they desire to make money by them" (quoted in Ho, 2010, 98).

14. For the manufacturing sector, as suggested by Karshenas (2005), the relevant RER can be considered an index of final product prices in relation to those of competitor countries: RER = eP/P^*, where e is the value (in U.S. dollars) of the nominal exchange rate, P is the domestic manufacturer's price, and P^* is a composite index of the foreign manufacturers' prices. The ratio P/P^* is largely influenced by the evolution of the unit labor cost (ULC), w/y (wages in relation to productivity, the wage share), normally considered a competitiveness index. It is important to note that while w is the unitary money wage, y is the productivity measured as product, expressed in industrial prices and the quantity of labor. The relevant price for wages is the consumer price index; thus, independent of relative productivity, the country's competitiveness can decrease/increase if the consumer prices increase/decrease in relation to industrial prices. ULC is indeed important for expressing the direct cost of production and, therefore, firms' competitiveness, but overall cost depends as well on direct and indirect costs such as the interest rate, management, raw material acquisition, research and development, and costs related to sales and marketing (Kaplinsky, 2005). The superior advantage of East Asian countries in manufacturing is also related to these costs.

15. If the relative unit labor cost (ULC) is higher in manufacturing in which the country is a price maker, it will lose its market share if the markup remains constant but it will not necessarily export less. The volume of exports will not decline (although there is a lower rate of profits in comparison to the competitors) if the external market is expanding. If the external market is declining and the markup in production of these goods is already too low (as is, consequently, the rate of profit), then the production is likely to be interrupted if not compensated by subsidies or other policies. If the country is a price taker, a higher ULC has a direct effect on current markup (and rate of profit), but it will result in an interruption of that production only if the rate of profit is too low at that level of labor cost.

16. "The way devaluations lead to improved export performance is not mainly through increased quantities of the same exports through price reductions but rather through a greater variety of products becoming more profitable to export" (Karshenas, 2007, 145).

17. "La característica esencial de la nueva realidad económica de los países exportadores primarios en proceso de industrialización es lo que hemos bautizado como una *estructura productiva desequilibrada*. Se trata de una estructura productiva compuesta de dos sectores de niveles de precios diferentes: el sector primario—agropecuario en nuestro caso—que trabaja a precios internacionales, y el sector industrial, que trabaja a un nivel de costos y precios considerablemente superior al internacional" (Diamand, 1988, 1).

18. Furtado ([1957] 2008) observed this same point in Venezuela (Medeiros, 2008a). He considered that in order to eliminate the contradiction of an abundant source of dollars and underdevelopment that resulted in RER appreciation, a comprehensive development strategy was necessary, including industrial

policies, agricultural modernization, autonomous public investment in infrastructure, and income distribution policies.

19. This hypothesis seems to consider, as in canonical Heckscher-Ohlin-Samuelson trade theory, that there is no technological gap; thus, only wrong prices explain noncompetitive countries, but in "Dutch disease" countries, the exchange rate—instead of expressing manufacturing labor costs—expresses the higher competitiveness of natural resource exports. Consequently, the wrong price for manufactured goods is not automatically corrected by the market.

20. It is quite arbitrary to choose the level of exchange rate as the main developmental policy. During the high years of growth in Brazil or Mexico, exchange rate was low and tariffs were high but overall economic growth and structural change included all the instruments that drove industrialization in Asia.

21. As documented by Woo (1991), the Japanese Export-Import Bank conceded large loans to Korea after the 1982 crisis, easing its balance-of-payments adjustment without hard costs as happened in Latin American countries. This policy was part of the security triangle in Asia considered by the Reagan and Suzuki agreement in which Japan was a central economic player in securing South Korean prosperity.

22. Although RER was very unstable in Mexico, it did not appreciate in the last decade, and labor costs remained low. As Dani Rodrik (2008) recognized, Mexico did not show a positive relationship between growth and undervaluation.

REFERENCES

Amsden, A. (1989), Asia's Next Giant: South Korea and Late Industrialization. New York: Oxford University Press.

——— (2001), The Rise of "the Rest." New York: Oxford University Press.

Barbosa, N., Ferrari, M., and Freitas, F. (2013), "O papel da taxa de câmbio real nos modelos de restrição externa: uma proposta de releitura," Brazilian Journal of Political Economy, 36, pp. 919–939.

Bértola, L., and Ocampo, J.A. (2015), O Desenvolvimento Econômico da América Latina. Rio de Janeiro Campus: Elsevier.

Bresser-Pereira, L.C. (2010), Globalization and Competition. Cambridge, UK: Cambridge University Press.

Canitrot, A. (1983), "El salario real y la restrición externa de la economia," Desarrollo Económico, 23, pp. 403–427.

CEPÀL (2015), "Neostructuralismo y Corrientes heterodoxas en America Latina y el Caribe a inicios del siglo XXI," Libros de la CEPAL 132, Santiago del Chile, Naciones Unidas.

Chang H.J. (2006), The East Asian Development Experience—The Miracle, the Crisis and the Future. London: Zed Books.

Cornwall, J. (1977), Modern Capitalism: Its Growth and Transformation. Oxford, UK: Martin Robertson.

De Long, B., and Summers, L. (1992), "Equipment Investment and Economic Growth: How Strong Is the Nexus?" Brooking Papers on Economic Activity 2.

Diamand, M. (1988), Hacia la Superación de las restriciones al crecimiento económico argentino. Centro de Studio de la Realidad Económica (CERE), Buenos Aires.

Findlay, R., and O'Rourke, K. (2007), Power and Plenty: Trade, War and the World Economy in the Second Millenium. Princeton, NJ: Princeton University Press.

Fiorito, A., Giata, N., and Guaita, S. (2014), " Neodesarrolismo y el tipo de cambio competitivo," Cuaderrnos de Economia, 34(64), pp. 45–88.

Freeman, C. (2005), "New Technology and Catching Up," in R. Kaplinsky and C. Cooper (eds.), Technology and Development in the Third Industrial Revolution. London: Frank Cass.

Frenkel, R. (2008), "Tipo de cambio real competitivo, inflación y política monetaria," Revista de Economía Política de Buenos Aires, 2(3–4), pp. 21–32.

———— (2010), Lecciones de política macroeconómica para el desarrollo, a la luz de la experiencia de la última década. XV Reunión de Investigadores de Bancos Centrales del Continente Americano, La Paz, 3–5 de Noviembre. http://www.itf.org.ar/documentos.asp.

Furtado, C. ([1957] 2008), "O Desenvolvimento Recente da Economia Venezuelana," em Ensaios sobre a Venezuela, Subdesenvolvimento com abundância de divisas. Rio de Janeiro: Contraponto, Centro Internacional Celso Furtado.

Garegnani, P. (2015), "The Problem of Effective Demand in Italian Economic Development: On the Factors That Determine the Volume of Investment," Review of Political Economy, 27, pp. 111–133.

Hamilton, A. ([1791] 1966), "Report on the Subject of Manufactures," in H.C. Syrett and J.E. Cooke (eds.), The Papers of Alexander Hamilton, vol. 10. New York: Columbia University Press.

Hausmann, R., and Hidalgo, C. (2010), "Country Diversification, Product Ubiquity and Economic Divergence," Harvard University, CID Working Paper 201.

Hirschman, A.O. (1958), The Strategy of Economic Development. New Haven, CT: Yale University Press.

Ho, P.S. (2010), Rethinking Trade and Commercial Policy Theories. Northampton, MA: Edward Elgar.

Hoffmann, W.G. (1958), The Growth of Industrial Economics. Manchester, UK: Manchester University Press.

Hoselitz, B.O. (1959), "On Historical Comparison in the Study of Economic Growth," in R. Goldsmith (ed.), The Comparative Study of Economic Growth and Structure. New York: NBER.

Kaldor, N. (1966), Causes of the Slow Rate of Economic Growth of the United Kingdom. Cambridge, UK: Cambridge University Press.

———— (1978), Further Essays on Applied Economics. London: Duckworth.

———— (1985), Economics without Equilibrium. New York: ME Sharp.

Kaplinsky, R. (2005), "'Technological Revolution' and the International Division of Labour in Manufacturing: A Place for the Third World," in R. Kaplinsky and C. Cooper (eds.), Technology and Development in the Third Industrial Revolution. London: Frank Cass.

Karshenas, M. (2007), "Real Exchange Rates, Labor Markets, and Manufacturing Exports in a Global Perspective," in A. Shaikh (ed.), Globalization and the Myths of Free Trade. New York: Routledge.

Kuznets, S.S. (1958), "Long Swings in the Growth of Population and in Related Economic Variables," Proceeding of the American Philosophical Society, 102, pp. 25–52.

Lall, S. (1996), Learning from the Asian Tigers: Studies in Technology and Industrial Policy. New York: St. Martin's Press.

List, F. ([1837] 1983), The Natural System of Political Economy. London: Frank Cass.

López Gallardo, J. (2008), "Una reconsideración de las perspectivas económicas de México," Economia e Sociedade, 17 (Número Especial), pp. 677–694.

Marglin, S., and Bhaduri, A. (1990), "Profit Squeeze and Keynesian Theory," in S. Marglin and J. Schor (eds.), The Golden Age of Capitalism: Reinterpreting the Postwar Experience. Oxford, UK: Clarendon. pp. 153–186.

Marx, K. ([1989] 1991), Capital: A Critique of Political Economy, vol. 3. London: Penguin Books.

McCombie, J., and Thirwall, A.P. (1994), Economic Growth and the Balance-of-Payments Constraint. London: Macmillan.

Medeiros, C.A. (1997), "Globalização e inserção internacional diferenciada da Ásia e da América Latina" em Maria da Conceição Tavares e José Luís Fiori, Poder e Dinheiro. Rio de Janeiro: Edit Vozes.

———— (2008a), "Celso Furtado na Venezuela," em Ensaios sobre a Venezuela, Subdesenvolvimento com abundância de divisas. Rio de Janeiro: Contraponto, Centro Internacional Celso Furtado.

———— (2008b), "Financial Dependency and Growth Cycles in Latin America Countries," Journal of Post Keynesian Economics, 31, pp. 79–100.

Milberg, W., and Winkler, D. (2013), Outsourcing Economics: Global Value Chains in Capitalist Development. New York: Cambridge University Press.

Mill, J.S. ([1848] 1968), Principles of Political Economy, with Some of Their Applications from Social Philosophy. Collected Works of John Stuart Mill, vol. 3. London: Routledge and Kegan Paul.

Onaran, O., and Galanis, G. (2012), "Is Aggregate Demand Wage-Led or Profit-Led? National and Global Effects," ILO Conditions of Work and Employment Series 40.

Pariboni, R. (2015), "Autonomous Demand and the Marglin-Bhaduri Model: A Critical Note," Universita di Siena, Quaderni del Dipartimento di Economia Politica e Statistica 715.

Prebisch, R. (1950), "The Economic Development of Latin America and Its Principal Problems," United Nations Department of Economic Affairs, New York.

—— (1964), "Towards a New Trade Policy for Development," Report by the Secretary-General of the UNCTAD, United Nations, New York.

Rodrik, D. (2008), "The Real Exchange Rate and Economic Growth," Brookings Papers on Economic Activity, Fall, pp. 365–439. http://www.brookings.edu/search?start = 1&q = rodri.

Serrano, F. (1995), "Long Period Effective Demand and the Supermultiplier," Contributions to Political Economy, 14, pp. 67–90.

Serrano, F., and Summa, R. (2015), "Aggregate Demand and the Slowdown of Brazilian Economic Growth from 2011–2014," Center for Economic and Policy Research, Washington, DC.

Singer, H.W. (1949), "Relative Prices of Exports and Imports of Underdeveloped Coutries: A Study of Post-war Terms of Trade between Underdeveloped and Industrialized Countries," United Nations Department of Economic Affairs, New York.

Singer, H.W., and Ansari, J.A. (1977), Rich and Poor Countries. London: Allen & Unwin.

Studwell, J. (2013), How Asia Works: Success and Failure in the World's Most Dynamic Region. New York: Grove Press.

Syrquin, M. (1988), "Patterns of Structural Change," in H. Chenery and T. Srinivasan (eds.), Handbook of Development Economics, vol. 1. London: Elsevier. pp. 202–273.

Thirwall, A.P. (1979), "The Balance of Payment Constraints as an Explanation of International Growth Rates," Banca Nazionale del Lavoro Quarterly Review, 128, pp. 45–53.

Toner, P. (1999), Main Currents in Cumulative Causation. London: Macmillan.

Woo, J. (1991), Race to the Swift: State and Finance in Korean Industrialization. New York: Columbia University Press.

World Bank (1993), The East Asian Miracle: Economic Growth and Public Policy. New York: Oxford University Press.

3. Institutions, Property Rights, and Why Nations Fail

Esteban Pérez Caldentey and Matías Vernengo

INTRODUCTION

Institutions are, without doubt, central to explaining the way in which nations grow and develop. The study of the institutional determinants of economic performance has a long tradition dating back to the work of institutionalist economists such as Thorstein Veblen, John Commons, Wesley Mitchell, and Claren Ayres. Institutional economics had a very broad range of interests and made contributions in several different areas. Its research program introduced historical analysis, the structure of power relations, the belief systems, and the social norms of conduct to account for the factors treated in neoclassical economic analysis, including the legal, political, and monetary systems.

The new institutional economics also explains the data of neoclassical economics, but by focusing on governance structures and, especially, on property rights (Rutherford, 2001). Property rights are viewed as the crucial institution that affects and enhances economic growth and development. In contrast to the old institutional economics, the new institutional economics is not a critique but an extension of mainstream theory that tries to fill some of its main shortcomings.

For the new institutionalism, the renewed interest in institutions as determinants of economic performance is traced to the inability of the mainstream research growth program, including both exogenous and endogenous theories of economic growth, to uncover the deeper determinants of economic growth. Indeed, even after accounting for both accumulation of inputs and research and development (R&D) investment (total factor productivity), substantial differences remain in income per capita across countries and regions of the world.[1] New institutional economics exemplifies how governance structures and property rights fill this vacuum by focusing mainly on specific

45

historical source cases (such as the comparative experience of colonization experiences or the industrial revolution, among others).

Acemoglu and Robinson's influential book *Why Nations Fail* (2012) constitutes one of the most comprehensive and illustrative examples of this line of thought. Its authors argue that the economic failure or success of countries depends on whether these have inclusive or extractive political institutions. Inclusive political institutions are those that distribute power broadly, constrain arbitrary exercise, and make it harder to usurp power or set the basis for rent-seeking behavior. Inclusive political institutions require well-defined and secure property rights. Extractive institutions have the opposite characteristics.

We argue that within the logical construct of neoclassical economic theory, the contribution of the new institutional economics is a necessity, basically because exchangeability requires appropriability. Because neoclassical theory is ahistorical, the same framework derived from a priori reasoning must have universal validity and be applicable to any particular historical episode— underscoring, in this way, the invariance of human behavior in space and over time. This dictates the new institutionalists' approach to history, which materializes in providing examples of hand-picked empirical evidence across different centuries, regions, and countries and interpreting these as coherent with the deductive universal framework of neoclassical theory.

In this chapter, using two source cases (the comparative colonization experience in the Americas and the Industrial Revolution), we show that when history is understood on its own terms, the analysis does not corroborate the hypotheses of the new institutional economics. Furthermore, we present evidence from developed and developing economies in the nineteenth and twentieth centuries showing that institutions, and in particular public institutions, are central to development through active intervention and by interfering with the functioning of free markets through the creation and expansion of domestic markets, funding of R&D, innovation, and high technology, and by reducing the external and internal constraints, rather than by securing private property rights. Finally, we relate the poor performance of Latin American economies to the absence of a continuous and coherent industrial policy.

PROPERTY RIGHTS AS A CORE COMPONENT OF THE NEOCLASSICAL THEORY OF VALUE AND DISTRIBUTION

Property rights are part of the core foundation of the neoclassical theory of value and distribution. Neoclassical theory considers three sets of data that are sufficient to determine market-clearing relative prices and quantities: preferences, technology, endowments, and their distribution. The third set of data presumes that the specification of ownership of goods is required for exchange and production to take place and, thus, for the existence and determination of market-clearing relative prices and quantities and, hence, of equilibrium positions.

Generally, the importance of property rights for the theory of value and distribution is implicitly recognized in the definition of the economy under study as a "private ownership economy" and/or by defining the economy in terms of known preferences and endowments for each of the agents considered. Nonetheless, the analysis of property rights was made more explicit by earlier economists writing within the neoclassical tradition, such as Leon Walras in his *Elements of Pure Economics*. In that book, Walras ([1896] 2014) approached the issue of property rights by distinguishing between appropriability and property. According to Walras, things have value if they are useful and limited in quantity. In turn, things that have value are appropriable:

> Contrariwise, useful things that exist only in limited quantity are appropriable and appropriated. . . . Let us limit ourselves to remarking, for the moment, that appropriation (and consequently property, that is appropriation that is legitimate or in conformity with justice) is applicable only to social wealth and applicable to all social wealth. (ibid., 22)

Appropriability, or more precisely the *appropriability problem*, refers to the ability of an owner (i.e., an appropriator) of a good, service, or asset to reap whatever benefits these produce without their being taken by others (Even, 2009). And, thus, property rights constitute the institution that is meant to legitimize appropriation. In other words, appropriability is the rationale that underlies property rights and legal protection, and property rights justify appropriability. In modern neoclassical analysis, since agents are endowed with goods, services, and assets and exercise their right, given their preferences, to exchange these for other goods, services, and assets, it is necessarily presupposed that appropriability is exercised through the existence of property rights.

Insofar as the outcome of an exchange economy within a free market environment produces a Pareto optimum, property rights are a necessary condition for the efficient use and allocation of resources. More to the point, property rights are a key incentive to use and allocate resources efficiently. They align the decisions of agents to exchange and produce with the net benefits that are derived. As explained by Even (2009, 1421):

Property rights are generally thought of (in economic terms) as legal instruments that are used to incentivize efficient use of scarce resources. Their incentivizing mechanism worked by aligning usage of resources with its resulting costs and benefits; property rights ensure that users of resources will both enjoy (i.e., appropriate) as large a share as possible of the benefits that flow from such use, and bear as much as possible of the costs that are associated with such use.

In the absence of well-defined and established property rights, avoiding underuse or overuse of resources would require agents to engage in additional use of resources in order to reap the benefits of use and allocation of goods, services, and assets, while at the same time avoiding excessive and undue costs. These could include the search and information costs (obtaining and evaluating information); bargaining costs (establishing a bargaining position and locating a bargaining partner); costs of contract enforcement (negotiating a contract and monitoring the contract). These are known as transaction costs. In addition to transaction costs, the mainstream literature also considers transformation costs, which are the physical costs of combining inputs into outputs—that is, the costs of internal production (Alston, 2008).

In this sense, the existence of transaction and transformation costs reduces welfare. The welfare loss is reflected in the resources allocated to transactions and in the suppression of exchanges that would have taken place and been mutually beneficial (Niehans, 1987). By a similar reasoning, transaction and transformation costs also impinge on the incentives to secure and shape the accumulation of capital, knowledge, and innovation, which are the main driving forces of growth and development in mainstream theory. As Helpman (2007, 112) put it: "Without the protection of property rights, capital formation, land development, and investment in R&D cannot take place. For this reason institutions that promote the rule of law, enforce contracts, and limit the power of rulers are important for economic development." Obviously, institutions are not conceived as static but as adaptive to changing circumstances.[2]

One of the most recent statements of the view that institutions (and private property rights) are essential for development and growth is found in Acemoglu and Robinson's *Why Nations Fail*. These authors use the new institutionalism to provide an explanation of differences in income, standards of living, and inequality between industrialized and developing countries. The gist of their argument is that institutions explain why some economies fail and others succeed. More precisely, Acemoglu and Robinson (2012, 68) argue that economic institutions are essential in determining the prosperity of a country, but that political institutions determine economic institutions. In other words, political choices in establishing and shaping institutions and their influence on domestic institutions ultimately determine the economic fate of nations.

Acemoglu and Robinson make a distinction between two types of institutions: the inclusive and the extractive (i.e., the good and the bad). Inclusive political institutions give way to inclusive economic institutions, and extractive political institutions give rise to extractive political institutions. Inclusive political institutions are institutions that distribute power broadly, constrain arbitrary exercise, and make it harder to usurp power or set the basis for rent-seeking behavior (ibid., 82). In turn, inclusive economic institutions include "secure private rights, an unbiased system of law, and a provision of public services that provides a level playing field in which people can exchange and contract . . . [and they] permit the entry of new businesses and allow people to choose their careers" (ibid., 75). The functions of the state include the enforcement of law and order, private property, and contracts and the provision of public services (ibid., 76). Extractive political and economic institutions have the opposite attributes and are simply not a sustainable basis for promoting growth and development (ibid., 430).

INSTITUTIONS AND PROPERTY RIGHTS: READING HISTORY ON ITS OWN TERMS

The studies that have linked institutions (as understood in the new institutionalist literature), in particular private property rights, to growth, development, and the reduction of inequality are based mainly on comparative historical analyses and performance. As such, the proponents of this view claim the existence of a strong correlation between early and present-day institutions. To the extent that current institutions determine current economic performance, early institutions are also highly correlated with current economic performance (Acemoglu, 2003; Acemoglu and Robinson, 2012; Acemoglu et al., 2001, 2005). For example, the comparative performance of the United States and other industrialized countries in relation to Latin American ones is explained by the type of institutions set up during the respective colonization periods in Latin America and the United States. In the view of Acemoglu and Robinson (2012, 114), the

> extractive political and economic institutions of the Spanish
> conquistadores in Latin America have endured, condemning much of
> the region to poverty. Argentina and Chile have fared better than most
> other countries in the region. They had few indigenous people or

mineral riches and were 'neglected' while the Spanish focused on the lands occupied by the Aztec, Maya and Inca civilizations.

In many instances, fitting all different historical experiences into a single, overarching explanation forces a reading of the past that is not interpreted on its own terms but rather on the basis of the preconceptions and preoccupations of neoclassical theory. This involves making stringent assumptions regarding the choice of material that is presented or concealed, the weight attached to monocausal explanations, and the degree to which the performance of societies responds to the same type of determinism, regardless of their specificity, context, and historical evolution.

Precisely the same comparative historical episodes—the Spanish and British colonizations of the Americas and the extent to which these can be related to the current conditions in Latin America—illustrate some of the difficulties and limitations of the new institutionalist approach. The Spanish conquest and colonization is a story of subjugation, domination, and plunder of riches, but at the same time it is a story about partial conquest, cooperation, and inclusion. An early institution of the *conquistadores*, the *encomienda*,[3] which according to Acemoglu and Robinson (2012) epitomizes the extractive nature of the Spanish domination, provides a useful example of the complexity of the conquest, the colonization, and their legacy.

The conquest and colonization process produced a society that was highly complex ethnically, socially, and institutionally. It provided, within the beliefs and norms of the time, a context for the amalgamation, mixture, and coexistence of different races, identities, and cultures. In this sense, the whole process was inclusive rather than exclusive. As aptly put by Elliott (2006, 401),

> the indigenous people of Spanish America were given at least limited space of their own in the new political and social order. By seizing such religious, legal and institutional opportunities as were afforded them, individuals and communities succeeded in establishing rights, affirming identities, and fashioning for themselves a new cultural universe on the ruins of the universe that had been shattered beyond recall in the trauma of European conquest and occupation.

The early British colonizers adopted an exclusionary approach, inspired by the Irish experience and the Spanish example, which provided a role model.[4] The "expulsion" and marginalization of indigenous populations by the British settlers was not markedly different from the Iberian experience. British colonists later changed their approach and emphasized— based on the Dutch experience and the need to foster commerce, industry, and enterprise—promoting the development of Britain. This objective, which required, as a counterpart, an open immigration policy, religious tolerance, and the absence of arbitrary power (Elliott, 2006, 2007), was not present during the Spanish imperial period, simply because this concept did not exist prior to the eighteenth century (Paine, 2008). In that respect, the settlement colonies in the Northeast of the current United States provide a contrast to the exploitation colonies in the South, which were closer in their experience to Latin American colonies. In particular, the need to find alternative forms of survival to the exploitation model adopted elsewhere—based on monoculture plantations (tobacco in the American South, sugar in South America and the Caribbean) or mining activities—created the conditions for a more self-reliant domestic economy, which would not suffer from the persistent balance-of-payments problems of commodity producers.[5]

Similarly, the new institutionalist argument on the relevance of property rights to the Industrial Revolution must be taken with a dose of skepticism. The Industrial Revolution is generally portrayed by the proponents of this approach as an example of the success of securing property rights. In the words of Acemoglu and Robinson (2012, 197):

> This dynamic process was unleashed by the institutional changes that flowed from the Glorious Revolution. This was not just about the abolition of domestic monopolies. . . . It was about a fundamental reorganization of economic institutions in favor of innovators and entrepreneurs, based on the emergence of more secure and efficient property rights.

Yet the available empirical evidence starkly contradicts this hypothesis. Using data on the exhibition of technologies at nineteenth-century world fairs, Moser (2013) finds that a small share of innovations were patented. Using a broader definition of inventions for the eighteenth century, Griffiths et al. (1992) find that a small percentage of British textile inventions were patented. Further, the same set of evidence for the 1851 and 1876 world fairs indicates that the promotion of innovation does not require patenting. The number of innovations per population and the number of prizes per exhibit in countries without patent laws, such as Denmark, Switzerland, and the Netherlands, far exceeded the mean for all countries that participated in these events.[6]

Thus, not only did the system of property rights impose extra and unnecessary costs, acting as a disincentive to innovation, but it also set the stage for the creation of a perverse system of rewards and for precisely the type of extractive behavior that Acemoglu and Robinson (2012) portray as conducive to economic and social stagnation.

THE ROLE OF PUBLIC INSTITUTIONS IN PROMOTING GROWTH: SOME EVIDENCE FROM DEVELOPED COUNTRIES

If innovation is at the core of economic growth and development, the available empirical evidence from case studies of different countries underscores the centrality of active government intervention rather than property rights. The history of innovation shows that government involvement was crucial in promoting the dissemination and adoption of R&D through interventionist industrial, trade, and technology policies to foster the development of their own incipient industries, using a diverse set of instruments such as tax credits, breaks, subsidies, import controls, export promotion, and targeted and direct financial and credit policies. This intervention strategy also contemplated the development of national capacities through R&D, education, training, stimulus to foreign technology acquisition, and public-private cooperation practices. This did not involve making heavy use of public ownership (Chang, 2003; Pérez Caldentey, 2008).

The governments of Japan and South Korea, two of the more recent success stories, both followed similar policy prescriptions. Central to the development efforts in these two cases were the creation of Japan's Ministry of Industry and Trade (MITI) in 1949 and Economic Planning Board in 1961, which guided the economic policies of both nations. The MITI negotiated prices and conditions for the import of technology through the approval of the Foreign Capital Law, took effective control of the rights to import merchandise and of the foreign exchange budget, and widened and cheapened access to credit facilities through the establishment of the Japan Development Bank in order to develop key domestic industries (energy and metal production).

In the case of Korea, the government actively managed the exchange rate and interest rates and controlled credit and financial resources to promote the development of its nascent industries. These development policies and objectives proved flexible enough to change and adapt to varying circumstances. In the case of Japan, the MITI shifted its focus to export industries, production of consumer durables, creation of technologically sophisticated consumer products, and, eventually, development of high-growth technology industries. A similar evolution of objective characterizes the different "five-year economic development plans" from the 1960s to the '90s.

The evidence shows that government involvement was not limited to catch-up strategies in the earlier stages of industrialization in currently industrialized economies but was also used to consolidate the technological supremacy of the great industrial powers. As an illustrative example, between 1950 and 1978, the federal government of the United States provided 50 percent of the funding for the nation's R&D. More specifically, the government directed the technological development and the desire to innovate in new areas, such as information technology, biotechnology, nuclear energy, and nanotechnology. At a more general level, most of the great technological achievements of the twentieth and twenty-first centuries would hardly have seen the light of day without decisive government support, including innovations in computers and magnetoresistance, new molecular entities, and the birth of Silicon Valley in California (Janeway, 2012; Mazzucato, 2013). In the same line of thinking, Ruttan (2006) argues, on the basis of three high-tech innovations spurred by government initiative (and, in these particular cases, for military purposes)—jet aviation, computers, and the Internet—that innovation and R&D do not guarantee, by themselves, commercial success. Rather, commercial success requires that the government create a guaranteed market for these innovations.

Historical evidence shows that this approach to development is not unique to the developed world or to the more successful experiences of Japan and East Asia but is also a recurrent characteristic in the history of Latin America. Since at least the nineteenth century and until the 1980s debt crisis, the governments of the region—and in particular those of the larger economies of the region—actively intervened in an effort to consolidate their territories and promote the long-term development of their economies. The main areas of government intervention included the building of infrastructure such as transport roads, including the construction of railways as a way to integrate the domestic market; the protection of export sectors, including specific products and industries; the spread of colonization; and the promotion of skilled-labor immigration. The main instruments of government developmental policies included, among others, import and export taxes, tariff exemptions, subsidies, public concessions, granting of monopoly privileges, guaranteed earnings, subsidized immigration, cheap credit, and government expenditures for public works, education, and health.

These policies are very similar to those applied by European nations and the United States in their early stages of development. However, for the most part, the Latin American developmental policies were not as long-lasting, comprehensive, and effective, and in no case were these able to transform substantially the state of their economies. Latin American economies witnessed a second stage of active government intervention, lasting roughly from the 1940s to the '70s, termed "state-led industrialization" and characterized by the promotion of growth through domestic industrialization. This alternative theoretical framework implied, on one hand, that development could not be attained unless a significant effort was made to accumulate capital. On the other hand, this framework presupposed that the existing "automatic market forces" would keep the economic system entrenched at a low level of development. Industrialization was not to be left to the market, but was rather to be the product of government intervention. In fact, the state was called on to take a leading role in the inward industrialization process.

As in the nineteenth century, in implementing this development strategy the state required a variety of instruments to promote industrialization, including its legal authority to control the major natural-resource-based industries (i.e., the "crown jewels"). Governments promoted the development of new industries through fiscal, monetary, and commercial means. Such instruments included a variety of subsidies, ranging from fiscal transfers to tax exemptions, and also the use of selective tariff policy, which aimed to increase effective protection. Most importantly, the state established national or development banks to channel credit under favorable circumstances—including below-market and/or fixed nominal rates of interest—to targeted sectors. In a later stage, as the concerns for domestic industrialization gave way, in part, to those related to the promotion of exports, and in particular of manufacture exports, this strategy accommodated the instruments thus far used to that end.

This change in orientation was due, in part, to the perception that the strategy of inward industrialization did not provide the required foreign exchange, and that developing countries faced an impending foreign exchange gap. At the more general level, this change in orientation responded to the limitations of the inward industrialization process. The strategy gradually reached a point where it was unable to significantly develop the manufacturing industry and thus improve the growth prospects of Latin American economies. The contribution of the inward industrialization process to growth and development during this period was hampered by several factors. Tax and investment incentives were provided to foreign firms, but these firms contributed little in the way of value-adding and employment to the economies in which they operated and had rather regressive effects on the distribution of income. In addition, the strategy failed to create a robust domestic capital goods industry. As such, developing economies never really broke their dependence on imports of foreign machinery, equipment, and intermediate goods. Finally, the repatriation of profits by foreign firms and the substantial import requirements

TABLE 3.1 Rate of Growth of GDP per Capita by Selected Regions of the World, 1961–2014

Region	1961–70	1971–80	1981–90	1991–2000	2001–14
Latin America and Caribbean	3.3	4.4	−0.3	1.3	1.8
East Asia and Pacific	2.4	4.6	5.8	7.0	7.8
East Asia and Pacific (without China)	2.3	4.5	3.4	3.2	3.8
South Asia	2.0	0.7	3.1	3.2	5.2
South Asia (without India)	2.4	0.6	2.6	1.9	3.2
Europe and Central Asia	–	–	2.3	−0.5	3.9
High-Income: OECD	4.2	2.6	2.6	2.0	1.0
Middle East and North Africa	5.0	3.0	0.1	1.5	1.7
Sub-Saharan Africa	2.4	0.9	−1.3	−0.7	2.1

SOURCE: World Bank Development Indicators (World Bank, 2015).

of domestically produced consumer goods compounded the balance-of-payments constraint, thus weakening their trade-balance positions.

The recognition of the limits of the inward industrialization strategy opened the way for a shift toward a new "growth through trade" strategy. From this new perspective, exports of primary commodities were seen as necessary to finance imports. It also stressed the need for developing countries to export manufactured products. Moreover, it argued that nonreciprocal treatment should be granted by developed to developing countries to "promote specialization in industrial and primary commodities." Such treatment was justified on the basis of the infant industry argument. Trade—and more specifically managed trade—was considered a "primary instrument for growth." Within this strategy, the government had a key role to play in the management of trade, by implementing selected measures to monitor the evolution of imports and by promoting exports. In comparative terms, state-led industrialization produced the best economic growth performance of Latin America and the Caribbean in over half a century, with respect to the region's own history and to that of other regions of the world (Table 3.1).

The debt crisis of the 1980s and its effects on the region's economies produced a break in, and significant overhaul of, the strategy of development followed until then and the role of institutions. The debt crisis was used as an excuse to characterize state-led industrialization and its institutional framework as an autarkic strategy guided by a plethora of price-distorting incentives that had only detrimental consequences for growth (Dunn and Mutti, 2000, 264–265). State-led industrialization was portrayed as being at the root of many of the ills of Latin American countries: the decline of primary-sector output and exports; the excessive promotion of capital-intensive techniques, coupled with low-capacity utilization and high levels of unemployment and informality; and unequal distribution of incomes and high poverty rates.[7]

Central to this new approach, termed the Washington Consensus, were stabilization, trade openness, and financial liberalization. Both types of policies, which are complementary, were undertaken with the promise that they would lead to stable and sustainable growth and a reduction of financial instability (Camara Neto and Vernengo, 2002/2003). The underlying rationale for trade liberalization was provided by the main free-trade theorems arguing that "free trade" is best. The arguments for financial liberalization are an extension of those of the gains to international trade in goods to international trade in assets. Free trade and financial liberalization would lead to an increase in the rate of growth through their positive effect on investment. This new development strategy also entailed a complete overhaul of the current institutional framework. There was a shift in the focus of institutions from the public to the private sphere and from growth to the allocation of resources, with the proviso that this was the road to ensuring development.

This implied the privatization of a significant number of state-owned firms across different sectors of economic activity, including the productive sectors, infrastructure, health, and education. The scope and importance of privatization in Latin America can be gauged by the decline in the share of public firms' activity as a percentage of the gross domestic product (GDP)— roughly 10 percent and 5 percent in 1980 and 1997, respectively—and by the region's contribution to the total proceeds from privatization of the developing world. Available evidence for the period 1990–99 shows that privatization proceeds in Latin America totaled roughly U.S. $177 billion, or 56 percent of the total (Table 3.2). As a part of this trend, some institutions that had played a key role in the state-led industrialization disappeared.

As an illustration, the 1990s witnessed the privatization or suppression of a number of development banks. According to the Inter-American Development Bank (2013):

> On a global level, some 250 PDBs (Public Development Banks) were privatized between 1987 and 2003. Other banks were restructured or liquidated, based on the premise that a high degree of political interference in financial decision making invariably led to an inefficient

TABLE 3.2 Proceeds from Privatization in Developing Countries, 1990–1999

Region	Billions of U.S. dollars	Share of the total (%)
East Asia and the Pacific	44,100	14.0
Latin America	177,839	56.3
Eastern Europe and Central Asia	65,466	20.7
Middle East	8,197	2.6
South Asia	11,854	3.8
Sub-Saharan Africa	8,264	2.6
Total	315,720	100

SOURCE: Inter-American Development Bank (2005).

distribution of scarce available resources. In the Latin American and Caribbean (LAC) region, this process was reflected in the fact that membership of the Latin American Association of Development Financial Institutions (ALIDE) decreased from 171 institutions in 1988 to just 73 in 2003.

Similarly, other key institutions, such as planning ministries and labor ministries, saw their sphere of influence and resources significantly curtailed. In fact, the functions of planning ministries were taken over largely by central banks, and planning became associated with monetary stability.

The change in the focus of the role of institutions from spurring growth to ensuring the most adequate allocation of resources meant that the great majority of instruments used to foster development (i.e., those that were not used to "get the prices right") were relegated to the category of price-distortive instruments. More importantly, institutions were dissociated from the accumulation of knowledge, new technologies, and innovation or productivity—that is, from the very concepts that, according to the new institutionalism, are at the very foundation of growth and development. The vast majority of Latin American economies view industrial policy as an instrument to correct for market failures (rather than as an engine of development as in the case studies examined in the previous section), which significantly narrows the scope of action of the government. Moreover, industrial policy efforts have few resources, a low priority on the political agenda, weak institutional capacity, and very low rates of implementation.

TABLE 3.3 Rate of Growth of Labor Productivity for Selected Regions/Countries of the World, 1990–2015

Region/country	1990–95	1996–2000	2001–06	2007–09	2010–15
	Developed economies				
United States	1.4	2.6	1.7	0.6	1.2
Eurozone	2	1.2	0.9	−0.7	0.8
Other industrialized economies	3	2.8	1.9	0.6	1.7
	Developing economies				
All developing economies	0.6	1.6	4.2	4.4	3.7
China	7.8	3.5	11	10.3	7.9
India	2.3	3.6	3.2	9.3	4.6
Developing Asia (without China and India)	4.7	0.3	3.1	1.6	3.5
Latin America	0.8	0.9	0.5	1.1	0.7
Middle East and North Africa	−0.9	1	1.3	0.8	0.3
Sub-Saharan Africa	−1.7	0.8	3.7	3.2	2.4
Russia, Central Asia, and Southeast Europe	−5.6	1.7	5.6	1.4	1.7

SOURCE: Conference Board (2015).

Traditionally, interventions to correct for market failure have been mainly of the horizontal type. Governments implemented horizontal policies through an array of instruments, including debt equity swaps, tax credits, export drawbacks, credit and finance lines, and guarantee funds. The main purpose of the horizontal policies was to expand and diversify exports and attract foreign direct investment. Horizontal policies have been complemented with vertical policies that have taken on an increasingly important role in the formulation and implementation of policies to foster upgrading and structural change. However, their effects are very limited. In many cases, horizontal as well as vertical policies are numerous but manage small amounts of resources and are of limited scope to be effective in promoting development.

In fact, the available evidence shows that Latin America has experienced, since the 1990s, one of the worst performances in labor productivity growth.

TABLE 3.4 Selected Indicators of the Technological Gap between Developing and Developed Countries

Region	R&D expenditure as percentage of GDP, 2010	Number of researchers in R&D per million people, 2010	Middle- and high-tech exports as percentage of total exports, 2014
East Asia and Pacific	1.70	915	40
Eastern Europe and Central Asia	0.67	997	37
High-income: OECD	2.46	3,860	53
Latin America and Caribbean	0.84	492	28
Middle East and North Africa	0.36	626	–
South Asia	0.77	156	–

SOURCE: World Bank Development Indicators (World Bank, 2015).

NOTE: In the case of middle- and high-tech exports as a percentage of total exports, the data for East Asia and the Pacific exclude China, the data for Eastern Europe and Central Asia are limited to Eastern Europe only, and data for OECD high-income economies include only Eurozone countries.

On average, since the '90s, the growth of labor productivity has been below 1 percent for Latin America; and in comparative terms, the region has posted the worst performance of all developing regions, including developing Asia with or without China, the Middle East and North Africa, and Sub-Saharan Africa (Table 3.3).

The lack of productivity is the result of a slow rate of output growth and an impending technological gap with other regions of the world.[8] This is reflected in the comparative performance in indicators such as the share of R&D expenditures in GDP, the number of researchers in R&D (per million people), and high-tech exports as a percentage of total exports. As shown in Table 3.4, the share of R&D in GDP and the number of researchers in R&D (per million people) for Latin America and the Caribbean are 0.84 percent and 492, respectively, versus 1.7 percent and 915 for East Asia and the Pacific, and 2.5 percent and 3,860 for developed countries.

In spite of rapid growth in the period of the commodity boom (2003–07), the region remains essentially an exporter of commodities (South America) and of people (Mexico and Central America) to developed countries, and increasingly to the Asian periphery, that is, China (Pérez Caldentey and Vernengo, 2010).[9] This pattern of specialization remains problematic and indicates that the region will remain prone to recurrent crises in the near future.

CONCLUSION

New institutional economics has emphasized the role of property rights in the process of economic development. This chapter has suggested that the role of property rights in new institutional economics derives from its close relation with mainstream neoclassical economics, and the need to enshrine the role of market allocation as an efficient process central to economic development. In addition, new institutionalist authors suggest that the predatory institutions developed during colonial times have precluded the development of strong property rights in Latin America and, as a result, explain the region's relative backwardness.

While it is true that institutions matter, it is unclear that colonization was more exploitative in Latin America than in what eventually became the United States. It is clear, however, that Latin American colonies were exploitation colonies dependent on the export of commodities to the metropolis for their economic survival, something that is also true of the American South. While the effects of settlement colonies, and their different patterns of trade with the metropolis, may have played a role in the process of development in certain parts of North America, it is less clear that property rights were central to that experience or, more generally, to the Industrial Revolution.

The new institutionalist view overplays the role of the market and downplays the role of the state in the process of economic development. Several institutions of the developmental state that promoted industrialization—including the bureaucracies that managed macroeconomic and commercial and industrial policies, development banks, and publicly funded or directly public universities and research institutes—were central in many experiences of development and were also part of the Latin American experience until the debt crisis of the early 1980s. The reversal of many of these policies after the crisis, and the predominance of the Washington Consensus, has not led to vigorous growth as new institutionalist views would have indicated. In spite of the recurrent changes in development strategies, the region remains essentially connected to the world by exporting commodities and people. The types of institutions needed for a successful catching up with advanced economies would require institutions capable of promoting a change in the patterns of specialization and in the way the region is integrated into the global economy.

. . .

Esteban Pérez Caldentey is senior economic affairs officer at the Economic Commission for Latin America and the Caribbean in Santiago, Chile. Matías Vernengo is a professor at Bucknell University. The opinions expressed are the authors' own and may not coincide with those of the institutions with which they are affiliated.

NOTES

1. See Helpman (2007, 111–112).

2. The new institutionalist literature identifies several channels through which the definition of property rights provides the adequate incentives to spur growth and development (Besley and Ghatak, 2009; Locke, 2013).

3. The Crown established the *encomienda* in 1503 granting Spanish colonists a tract of land or a village jointly with its Indian inhabitants. The evidence available shows that the *encomenderos* only occupied a fragment of the native lands and that the Spaniards controlled only a small part of the continent (Kamen, 2004).

4. As pointed out by Gould (2007, 772), the Spanish and British conquests and colonizations are entangled histories that make it difficult to claim that "Britain's Atlantic Empire of the early United States . . . [is] a history of politically self-sufficient nations with full mastery over their own destiny."

5. It is important to note that while it is true that New England merchants participated in and benefited from the slave trade—that is, the exploitative part of colonization—it is also true, as many authors have noted, that the shipbuilding and rum industries that were part of the infamous "triangular trade" created the conditions, the infrastructure, and the capital for the development of the cotton industry later on (see, e.g., Bailey, 1990).

6. Several authors, including Mokyr (2009, 350–351), suggest that excessive bureaucracy and the high costs of patenting would reduce patenting's efficiency. Other authors, like Hoppit (2011) in his discussion of the British case after the Glorious Revolution, suggest that patents were actually detrimental to growth. For him: "The scale of that expropriation was such, and the consequences so profound, as to undermine an important thesis that property rights became more secure after the Glorious Revolution, developed in a notable essay by Douglass North and Barry Weingast and now conventional amongst some 'new institutional economists.'"

7. See, for example, Griffin (1989, 109–111) and Todaro (1989, 438–444). See Díaz-Alejandro (1984) for a contrary view.

8. The positive relation between output growth and labor productivity is often referred to as the Kaldor-Verdoorn law. For evidence regarding Latin America, see Bowman and Felipe (2001).

9. By "exporting people," Pérez Caldentey and Vernengo (2010) mean manufactured goods with little value added that are dependent on low wages in dollars, associated with *maquila* exports and immigration.

REFERENCES

Acemoglu, D. (2003), The Form of Property Rights: Oligarchic vs. Democratic Societies. NBER Working Paper 10037. Cambridge MA: National Bureau of Economic Research.

Acemoglu, D., Johnson, S., and Robinson, J. (2001), "The Colonial Origins of Comparative Development: An Empirical Investigation," American Economic Review, 91, pp. 1369–1401.

——— (2005), "Institutions as a Fundamental Cause of Long-Run Growth," in P. Aghion and S.N. Durlauf (eds.), Handbook of Economic Growth. London: Elsevier.

Acemoglu, D., and Robinson, J.A. (2012), Why Nations Fail. London: Profile Books.

Alston, L.J. (2008), "New Institutional Economics," in S. Durlauf and L. Blume (eds.), The New Palgrave Dictionary of Economics. New York: Palgrave Macmillan.

Bailey, R. (1990), "The Slave(ry) Trade and the Development of Capitalism in the United States: The Textile Industry in New England," Social Science History, 14, pp. 373–414.

Besley, T., and Ghatak, M. (2009), "Property Rights and Economic Development," in D. Rodrik and M. Rosenzweig (eds.), Handbook of Development Economics, vol. 5. New York: Elsevier. pp. 4526–4595.

Bowman, K., and Felipe, J. (2001), "Catch up, Convergence and Growth in Latin America." Georgia Institute of Technology, Working Paper Series 00/01–11.

Camara Neto, A.F., and Vernengo, M. (2002/2003), "Globalization, a Dangerous Obsession: Latin America in the Post-Washington Consensus Era," International Journal of Political Economy, 32(4), pp. 4–21.

Chang, H.-J. (2003), Kicking Away the Ladder: Development Strategy in Historical Perspective. London: Anthem Press.

Conference Board (2015), https://www.conferenceboard.org/data/productivity.cfm.

Díaz Alejandro, C. (1984), "Latin American Debt: I Don't Think We Are in Kansas Anymore," Brookings Papers on Economic Activity, 15, pp. 335–403.

Dunn, R.M., and Mutti, J.H. (2000), International Economics. New York: Routledge.

Elliott, J.H. (2006), Empires of the Atlantic World. New Haven, CT: Yale University Press.

——— (2007), "Dacre Lecture: Learning from the Enemy: Early Modern Britain and Spain." http://www.history.ox.ac.uk/fileadmin/ohf/images /John-Elliott-Lecture.pdf.

Even, Y. (2009), "Appropriability and Property," American University Law Review, 58, pp. 1417–1476.

Gould, E.H. (2007), "Entangled Histories, Entangled Worlds: The English-Speaking Atlantic as a Spanish Periphery," American Historical Review, 112, pp. 764–786.

Griffin, K. (1989), Alternative Strategies for Economic Development. New York: St. Martin's Press.

Griffiths, T., Hunt, P.A., and O'Brien, P.K. (1992), "Inventive Activity in the British Textile Industry, 1700–1800," Journal of Economic History, 52, pp. 881–906.

Helpman, L. (2007), The Mystery of Economic Growth. Cambridge, MA: MIT Press.

Hoppit, J. (2011), "Compulsion, Compensation and Property Rights in Britain, 1688–1833," Past and Present, 210, pp. 93–128.

Inter-American Development Bank (2005), Privatization in Latin America: Myths and Reality. Washington, DC: Inter-American Development Bank.

———— (2013), Public Development Banks: Towards a New Paradigm? Washington, DC: Inter-American Development Bank.

Janeway, W.H. (2012), Doing Capitalism in the Innovation Economy: Markets, Speculation and the State. New York: Cambridge University Press.

Kamen, H. (2004), Empire: How Spain Became a World Power, 1492–1763. New York: Perennial/HarperCollins.

Locke, A. (2013), "Property Rights and Development Briefing: Property Rights and Economic Growth." August. http://www.odi.org.

Mazzucato, M. (2013), The Entrepreneurial State. New York: Anthem Press.

Mokyr, J. (2009), "Intellectual Rights, the Industrial Revolution, and the Beginning of Modern Economic Growth," American Economic Review: Papers and Proceedings, 99, pp. 349–355.

Moser, P. (2013), "Patents and Innovation: Evidence from Economic History," Journal of Economic Perspectives, 27, pp. 23–44.

Niehans, J. (1987), "Transaction Costs," in J. Eatwell, M. Milgate, and P. Newman (eds.), The New Palgrave: A Dictionary of Economics. New York: Palgrave Macmillan.

Paine, S. (2008), España: una historia unica. Temas de Hoy: Madrid.

Pérez Caldentey, E. (2008), "The Concept and Evolution of the Developmental State," International Journal of Political Economy, 37(3), pp. 27–53.

Pérez Caldentey, E., and Vernengo, M. (2010), "Back to the Future: Latin America's Current Development Strategy," Journal of Post Keynesian Economics, 32, pp. 623–644.

Rutherford, M. (2001), "Institutional Economics: Then and Now," Journal of Economic Perspectives, 15, pp. 173–194.

Ruttan, V. (2006), Is War Necessary for Economic Growth? Military Procurement and Technology Development. New York: Oxford University Press.

Todaro, M.P. (1989), Economic Development in the Third World. New York: Longman.

Walras, L. ([1896] 2014), Elements of Theoretical Economics. Cambridge, UK: Cambridge University Press.

World Bank (2015), World Bank Development Indicators. Washington, DC: World Bank. http://databank.worldbank.org/data/reports.aspx?source = world-development-indicators.

World Trade Organization (1999), The Legal Texts. Cambridge, UK: Cambridge University Press.

4. With the Best of Intentions

Types of Development Failure in Latin America

Miguel A. Centeno and Agustín E. Ferraro

INTRODUCTION

Several Latin American countries attempted to carry out national development strategies during the twentieth century. As early as 1939, a central development corporation was established in Chile, and many other development agencies were created during the following decades in the region. However, the best economic results during the era of state-led development were achieved not in Latin America, but in East Asia. With average growth rates exceeding 3 percent from 1950 to 1980, developmental states were reasonably effective in promoting economic growth in Latin America, at least compared to the unsuccessful economic models adopted after the region's neoliberal reforms of the '90s (Trubek, 2013, 7). Nevertheless, when all is said and done, no Latin American nation reached the group of developed economies during those crucial three decades of the twentieth century.

Because of the relatively disappointing results in international comparisons, studies on Latin American cases often have to consider the failure of developmental institutions. Studies on cases such as Japan or South Korea instead analyze developmental institutions and policies that were very successful, turning these countries from poor agrarian societies into industrial and technological powerhouses in a few decades. By contrast, scholars working on Latin America confront the divergence between ambitious developmental goals and not completely successful outcomes.

In this chapter, we discuss the issue of institutional failure in relation to specific Latin American development experiences. To begin with, we would like to call attention to a very general trend or assumption regarding the issue of institutional failure in the literature on economic development.

According to a widespread perspective, development failure is caused by personal deficiencies among politicians or state servants. Politicians or state servants, instead of promoting the well-being of citizens, employ power for their own benefit, and development strategies fail as a result. In some countries, politicians or state servants are predominantly corrupt, so that instead of planning for development, they enable rent-seeking elites.

Following this general assumption, development failure is blamed on the groups that benefit from backwardness, the rent-seeking elites in collusion with corrupt politicians. As described, for example, by Acemoglu and Robinson (2012, 86):

> [P]owerful groups often stand against economic progress. . . . Growth thus moves forward only if not blocked by the economic losers who anticipate that their economic privileges will be lost and by the political losers who fear that their political power will be eroded.

Furthermore, according to the same authors (ibid., 65), mere ignorance has to be excluded as a significant cause for bad institutional performance; instead, self-interest is to blame:

> Neither Ghana's disappointing performance after independence nor the countless other cases of apparent economic mismanagement can simply be blamed on ignorance. After all, if ignorance were the problem, well-meaning leaders would quickly learn what types of policies increased their citizens' incomes and welfare, and would gravitate toward those policies.

Thus, according to Acemoglu and Robinson, flawed leaders result in bad institutional performance. From this perspective, discussions of defective institutional design focus on institutional features that allow or enable rent-seeking activities, such as institutions tolerating excessive discretion by public servants. As Shivakumar (2005, 17) summarizes the literature of the past three decades:

> By the 1980s, development failure was linked increasingly to government failure. Scholarship in Public Choice pointed out that rent-seeking and rent-avoidance activities, occasioned by excessive discretion on the part of the agents of the state, foster waste and retard growth.

In sum, defective institutional design is not a problem by itself, according to this point of view, but only insofar as institutions are not able to restrain the self-interest of public officers. Among other scholars, Schneider (2013, 140) has applied such a point of view to Latin America:

> [T]his chapter shows how distinctive features of the political system favor business interests. . . . The interests pursued are not generic but

can be traced back directly to the distinctive corporate structures and strategies analyzed. . . . Asking counterfactual questions such as why did countries of Latin America not follow development strategies like those in East Asia requires close consideration of business preferences.

As Schneider states, business groups pursue their own particular interests. And certain institutional features are defective precisely because they unfairly benefit those particular interests, instead of promoting the public good, with the result that developmental institutions fail.

We acknowledge that rent-seeking behavior can cause the failure of development strategies all by itself. However, we think that the literature's exclusive focus on rent-seeking behavior has resulted in a lack of attention to a completely different set of factors. These other factors are patterns of defective institutional design that cause institutions to underperform, but not only, or not mainly, as the result of rent-seeking behavior. Some types of institutions simply perform better than others, with or without taking predatory behavior into account.

Therefore, we propose a distinction between two *ideal types* of development failure. The first type of development failure, described above, can be defined as predatory; it is caused by rent-seeking behavior or outright corruption. The second type of development failure, which will be the focus of our discussion here, is not predatory at all. To the contrary, it is an "honest" failure, caused by specific trends of defective institutional design. We will define this second type of development failure as *institutional*. Politicians and state servants are not, as their main motivation, trying to line their own pockets in the institutional type of development failure; they are honestly trying to implement public policy programs. But certain institutions, created and run with the intention to promote economic development, fail because their design is defective. The institutional type of development failure is caused with the best of intentions.

In the first section of this chapter, we examine the configuration of developmental institutions that have shown consistently positive results, so that their design can be considered as a model or benchmark in the field. We will analyze, in the second section, two specific Latin American development experiences that showed initial success and promise but ended in failure and disappointment. However, the decisions that resulted in the failure of those experiences were not based on predatory or self-interested motivations. They were "honest" failures, the result instead of flawed institutional design. Our contention will be that there is a pattern to such institutional failures in Latin America. Countries in the region share certain similarities of defective institutional design, which can be traced back to very basic assumptions about how public organizations should be designed and managed.

BUREAUCRATIC AUTONOMY AS A KEY FOR DEVELOPMENT

In his classic study on economic development, Evans (1995) introduced the concept of "embedded autonomy" in order to capture the features of institutional design that explain the developmental achievements of the most successful East Asian cases. The concept is based on two specific institutions: Japan's Ministry of International Trade and Industry (MITI) and Korea's Ministry of Communications (MOC). The concept has two dimensions: (1) internal bureaucratic coherence, or autonomy proper; and (2) participation in external networks, or embeddedness. Evans described bureaucratic coherence as an "essential precondition" for the strong informal connections to major industrialists and other businesspeople, which constituted embeddedness in both cases (ibid., 3).

Evans based his analysis of MITI on Johnson's (1982) celebrated study of this institution. According to Johnson, the bureaucratic autonomy of MITI in postwar Japan was based on two rules, one of them formal and the other informal. The formal rule established that all the staff of the ministry consisted of career civil servants in the Weberian sense; that is to say, all staff members entered the civil service through competitive examinations, and their promotions were based on merit (ibid., 52). The minister was the only exception to this rule, and only a partial exception, since most ministers were former senior career civil servants, as were all important postwar politicians in Japan (Johnson, 1982, 38).

The informal rule, as Johnson (1982, 322) describes it, prescribed that "effective functioning of the development system requires a separation between reigning and ruling." Based on his study of the Japanese model, Johnson concluded that for a developmental institution to be successful, career civil servants must have substantial power over public policy. Elected politicians should "reign," but career civil servants should effectively "rule." At MITI, top career civil servants made all major public policy decisions without political interference.

Bureaucratic autonomy was already very strong in Japan during the postwar period. Key elements of institutional design in the country, such as the dominance of career civil servants over public policy decisions, went back to the Meiji era (1868–1912). In order to build a modern state, Japan deliberately adopted the German design of professional state governance. In this model, state institutions are run by career professionals, without interference from politicians. The case of Japan shows the extraordinary impact of this institutional design on economic development.

The case of Korea was different: it did not have a history of bureaucratic autonomy, but during the 1960s it created developmental institutions with a "Japanese" design. Once such institutions were established, the government's development strategies showed remarkable results. The Korean case thus displays the potential of deliberate institutional change. As a result of adopting Japanese-style developmental institutions, Korea went from being a poor agrarian society to becoming an advanced industrial economy in about twenty years. The overarching principle of institutional design applied in Korea was the same as in Japan: the dominance of career civil servants over public policy decisions.

After World War II, under the presidency of Syngman Rhee (1948–60), the higher ranks of the Korean ministries had been filled by political appointees, who were in charge of public policy decisions (Evans, 1995, 52). Although the Rhee administration attempted to implement development policies, these mostly failed, and the government was plagued by corruption. Evans simply concludes that "Rhee's regime was more predatory than developmental" (ibid.). A National Civil Service Act was passed in 1963, under the first presidency of Park Chung-hee, as part of a wide process of state reforms. The act established a civil service career for the national bureaucracy, with appointments to be based on competitive examinations, promotions awarded on merit, and protection from arbitrary dismissal (Kim and Leipziger, 1993, 30).

At the MOC, the reforms of 1963 created a staff of permanent career civil servants to run the operations of the ministry. Since the early 1980s, moreover, all public policy decisions in information technology began to be made by experts in the area, without political interference. In 1981, the individual who is widely acknowledged as the architect of Korea's spectacular success in information technology, Oh Myung, was appointed vice-minister of communications. With a PhD in electrical engineering from the State University of New York, Oh Myung had a solid career profile. His appointment followed the unwritten rule of filling the position of vice-minister with career professionals, as was customary in Japan. However, Korea went beyond the Japanese practice. Oh Myung was promoted to minister in 1987, and the pattern of career professionals serving as ministers continued afterward at the MOC (Larson, 1995, 118). During the presidency of Kim Dae-jung (1998–2003), the same practice of appointing career civil servants as ministers was adopted for all other government departments (Kim, 2000, 67–68).

In sum, the cases of Japan and Korea show the positive impact on economic development of a relatively straightforward institutional design, the bureaucratic autonomy of developmental institutions. The autonomy of bureaucratic institutions consists of the fact that they are run by career civil servants—that is to say, career civil servants make all major public policy decisions without political interference. Under this institutional design, public policies are much better formulated and more efficiently implemented.

But bureaucratic autonomy adds a second positive dimension to public governance that is crucial for development strategies. State institutions run by career civil servants are much more willing and able to consolidate their own "embeddedness"—that is, to engage and build networks with private-sector organizations, civil society actors, and citizens in general. In other words, bureaucratic autonomy is not only a necessary condition for embeddedness, as Evans emphasized, but also encourages and supports embeddedness.

Since the publication of Evans's (1995) study, the willingness and capacity of autonomous bureaucratic agencies to promote their own embeddedness have been explored by new research. The main contribution in this area is the *theory of agency reputation*. Originally developed by Daniel Carpenter (2001, 2010), the theory of agency reputation has been further elaborated by scholars working in empirical areas such as public policy, regulation, agency capture, and special-interest influence (Carpenter and Moss, 2013). The theory of agency reputation has been developed on the basis of case studies of autonomous bureaucratic institutions in the United States, known as "independent agencies" in U.S. legal language. The studies go from the first creation of federal independent agencies, in the late nineteenth century, to present times.

The theory of agency reputation has shown that successful independent agencies deliberately pursue strategies to consolidate and protect their reputations within the private sector, civil society organizations, professional associations, and the public at large. A strong positive reputation has many advantages for a bureaucratic agency. It is an essential tool for successful public policy implementation, in terms of ensuring cooperation from social actors and the public. Furthermore, a strong positive reputation preserves the independence of autonomous bureaucracies, by making politicians reluctant to interfere with their decisions. Given a positive reputation of the agency, political interference will be perceived negatively by citizens.

The theory of agency reputation is a fundamental resource for identifying the characteristics of autonomous bureaucratic institutions that make them so effective at promoting their own embeddedness. Reputation and embeddedness provide autonomous bureaucratic institutions with their main source of political legitimacy as organizations that wield state power. In case studies going back to the nineteenth century, it can be seen how American public managers recognized, early on, the need to cultivate the skills associated with reputation and embeddedness, such as network building, communication, participatory public policy deliberation, and other similar procedures and techniques (Carpenter and Moss, 2013).

THE REJECTION OF BUREAUCRATIC AUTONOMY IN LATIN AMERICA

During the developmental era, Latin American institutions were designed very differently from the model prevailing in the East Asian cases discussed above. Simply put, the kind of bureaucratic autonomy that was crucial for the success of development policies in East Asia never existed in Latin America. Contrary to typical assumptions among the development literature, however, the lack of bureaucratic autonomy in Latin American public institutions did not result from the predatory or self-interested behavior of politicians. The rejection of bureaucratic autonomy is mandated by constitutional principles in Latin American public law, and such principles are far from a mere legal abstraction; they are firmly anchored in constitutional practices and widely accepted as political values in public life.

In this section, we will analyze two of the most promising development projects in Latin America during the twentieth century: the creation of a computer industry in Brazil during the 1970s and the successful policy of industrial growth in Chile during the '40s and '50s. We will discuss the ultimate failure of both development strategies, which was caused by similar factors: defective institutional design leading to disruptive political interference. After discussing these cases, we will examine the constitutional norms and values that exclude bureaucratic autonomy from Latin American public life.

Brazil and the Politics of Presidential Administration

The development of a computer industry in Brazil was a model of "far reaching policy innovation" in Latin America (Evans, 1995, 117). The project closely resembled successful development initiatives in Japan and South Korea, not least because of its quite spectacular (initial) success. The institution in charge of the project was CAPRE (Comissão de Coordenação das Atividades de Processamento Eletrônico), established in 1972 as a division inside the structure of the planning ministry. The institution's original mandate was to rationalize the government's use of electronic resources. For this purpose, CAPRE received substantial regulatory powers in 1974, such that imports of computers and electronic components were subject to its previous approval. However, instead of just trying to restrain the import of superfluous hardware, as its mandate was intended, CAPRE used its regulatory power to put in practice a long-term "greenhouse" industrial strategy, aimed at the development of a Brazilian electronics industry.

The project was remarkably successful in the first eight to ten years. During that relatively short period, CAPRE's policies encouraged the creation of a domestic computer industry that could compete for a substantial share of the local market with international corporations such as IBM, Burroughs, and Hewlett-Packard. With support and guidance from CAPRE, several medium-sized firms and many small producers were able, by 1982, to manufacture 67 percent of installed computers in the country. There were about a hundred Brazilian domestic firms in the electronics industry in 1983, providing close to 18,000 jobs, with gross sales of $687 million, or approximately 46 percent of total gross sales of computers in Brazil (Adler, 1986, 680–681). Moreover, the new Brazilian electronics industry was not just replicating technology; a minicomputer designed in Brazil with original architecture, and its own indigenous operating software, was a huge commercial success, outselling all minicomputers produced with licensed foreign technology (Evans, 1995, 136).

From 1964 to 1985, Brazil was ruled by a military dictatorship, but presidential terms and other pseudo-constitutional forms were maintained. Therefore, presidential transitions could involve political changes. However, in a turn of events that still puzzles scholars, the 1979 change of administration from President Geisel to President Figueiredo resulted in a surprisingly self-destructive governmental decision. CAPRE was dissolved by Figueiredo shortly after his inauguration. A whole new institution was put in charge of informatics policies, with the acronym SEI (Secretaria Especial de Informática). The dissolution of CAPRE was followed by an extensive purge of its top and middle managers, most of whom were immediately dismissed (Luzio, 1996, 8).

CAPRE had been created in 1972 under the initiative of Minister João Velloso, an economist with a strong expert profile, not a politician or army officer. Velloso was minister for planning for ten years, under presidents Medici (1969–74), and Geisel (1974–79). His profile had similarities to those of the career experts in charge of development policies in Japan and South Korea, and he has been described as one of the architects of the

Brazilian "economic miracle" in the late '60s and early '70s (Gordon, 2004, 79). But bureaucratic autonomy was far from assured in Brazil, in contrast to the East Asian cases described above. Velloso was not reappointed as minister for planning by President Figueiredo, effectively ending his career as an expert in charge of public policy. According to Velloso's own memoirs, his dismissal was the result of not having a cordial relationship with Figueiredo (D'Araujo and Castro, 2004, 218).

Even as a division inside the planning ministry, the autonomy of CAPRE was assured under Minister Velloso. An expert himself, Velloso supported the authority of experts to take all major public policy decisions without political interference. By contrast, the new institutional structure created to replace CAPRE was fatally exposed to political interference from above. The SEI was created as a branch of the presidential office, directly subordinated to the president. The dissolution of CAPRE, and the resulting loss of bureaucratic autonomy in this area, created many complications and setbacks. Before considering those problems, however, we will try to answer the foremost question related to this issue. Why would the Figueiredo administration dissolve CAPRE? In a few years, CAPRE had implemented a very successful strategy to create a Brazilian informatics industry. Simply from a military perspective, without considering economic development, the national informatics industry was a crucial asset. Why risk destroying everything?

Of course, the first impulse in the search for explanations for the dissolution of CAPRE has been to blame self-interest or capture. Interestingly, however, authors disagree on who is to blame for the predatory self-interest—CAPRE itself or the executive power. Both perspectives have been advanced. Some authors suggest that CAPRE showed signs of weakness toward multinational corporations, thereby forcing the government to take over (see Luzio, 1996, 41). Other authors believe that the Figueiredo administration was eager to have policies that were more beneficial to multinational corporations, as a reaction to pressures by the U.S. government (see Adler, 1986, 696).

Ideological differences have also been suggested as an explanation, since some experts of the CAPRE commission were left-leaning, up to a point, and President Figueiredo was the head of a military dictatorship (Adler, 1987, 266). However, CAPRE had been created under the same military dictatorship now presided over by Figueiredo, and previous military dictators were never suspected of any sympathy toward the left. According to the available evidence, neither self-interest nor ideology or personal inclinations—the fact that Figueiredo did not like Velloso—appear to be decisive reasons for the dissolution of CAPRE. Neither was a change of policy the goal behind the dissolution of CAPRE, even if we take into account the purge of its top and middle management levels. The new organization in charge of electronics policy, SEI, continued to implement the same green-house development strategy carried out by CAPRE (Luzio, 1996, 8). There was no sudden "liberalization" of the market in order to accommodate mul-tinationals or placate the U.S. government; the informatics policy continued its protectionist orientation.

Our own explanation for this puzzle is based on the idea that CAPRE was a victim of its own success, in the context of Latin American assump-tions about the most effective institutional design for public organizations. The new military government under Figueiredo was not irrational; they knew very well that a national computer industry was a fundamental resource for economic development, and for military purposes as well. Precisely because of this, they thought that putting informatics policy under the direct aegis of the president was the best way to consolidate and promote this area of government. Direct presidential authority is regarded in Latin America as a necessary condition for effective public administra-tion, and the principle is proclaimed as such in many constitutions in the region, as we demonstrate below. The principle states that the president must have direct control and authority over every area of the public bureaucracy, even if the president chooses to leave specific divisions to work more or less independently for a period of time. The principle is usually designated as "supreme" or sometimes as "superior" administrative author-ity of the president. It was written as law in several Latin American consti-tutions during the nineteenth century, with the explicit purpose of ensur-ing the effectiveness of state institutions.

The principle of supreme administrative authority corresponds to the relatively commonsense belief that organizations are most effective, as a whole, if there is a clear and final authority for all important decisions. It follows logically from this belief that ultimately a single person has to be in charge, with oversight and authority over all significant issues. The princi-ple is based on commonsense, certainly, but it does not seem to apply to the operations of modern governments. In the specific case of developmental institutions, as shown in the first section above, bureaucratic autonomy is a precondition for their effectiveness, and this has been amply demonstrated by successful development models. But the principle of supreme presiden-tial authority makes consistent bureaucratic autonomy impossible to main-tain in Latin America. The idea of allowing an area of government to be run by experts, without outside interference, goes straight against the principle of supreme presidential authority, and it arouses fears of chaos and mismanagement. President Figueiredo and his advisors did not for a second want to risk the destruction of all that had been achieved by CAPRE. To the contrary, they wanted to make sure that the informatics policy of CAPRE was further implemented, but now with sponsorship, guidance, and encouragement from the highest political level. What could possibly go wrong?

The concept of embeddedness in general terms, and the theory of agency reputation in more specific detail, allow one to anticipate and explain what was probably going to happen with the dissolution of CAPRE. As Evans made clear, the key to CAPRE's success had been its bureaucratic autonomy and its effective embeddedness (Evans, 1995, 124). The top- and middle-level management of CAPRE had built a strong network of connections with the most significant actors in this policy field. Such actors included the scientific and academic community in the area of informatics, associations of professionals and technicians, leaders of the growing number of local small and medium-sized businesses related to computers and electronics, members of the press covering these topics, and diverse other organizations such as associations of computer users. Together with the creation of such networks, CAPRE had been very effective at consolidating its own reputation and, most decisively, promoting the conviction among the public that the field of computer technology was flourishing, prestigious, and rewarding. As a result, for example, there were about eighteen candidates for each place in courses related to computer sciences at the entrance examinations to the universities of Rio de Janeiro in those years (Schwartzman, 1985, 8).

The dissolution of CAPRE devastated all those carefully built networks. To make things worse, SEI, the new institution in charge of electronics policy, had a tendency to make inconsistent decisions from the beginning, with chaotic results. In March 1980, SEI promulgated a set of guidelines for imports of computer technology, supporting and strengthening the greenhouse strategy, with measures such as preferences given to "national alternatives" and domestically developed software (Adler, 1986, 697). A few months later, however, SEI gave permission to the multinational IBM to manufacture medium-sized computers in Brazil with proprietary technology and software, causing an uproar among computer and professional associations, scientists, and domestic producers. Several of those groups formed a new organization, the Alliance for the Defense of National Technology, with the explicit purpose of publicly confronting SEI (Baaklini and Rego, 1991, 139). Under instructions from President Figueiredo, that policy decision was reversed, and the strong opposition to SEI diminished to a certain degree; but this disaster was the initial misstep leading to the later resignation of SEI's first general secretary, Octávio Gennari (Vigevani, 1995, 96).

A year after its creation, as an obvious exercise in damage control, SEI was restructured and an "advisory council" was formed, with private- and public-sector representatives (Adler, 1987, 269). This attempt at reconstructing embeddedness showed only modest success. The situation was made worse by the apparent incompetence of SEI at basic bureaucratic or technical tasks, as a result of the purge of expert managers in charge of informatics policy under CAPRE and their replacement with amateur political appointees. The head of one of the most successful national producers of technology in Brazil, Jairo Cupertino, declared in an interview that for the development of computer terminals and electronics applications, it was crucial to import specific components if these could not be produced locally. In such cases, speed was of enormous importance. But the new top managers at SEI, while assuring in meetings that the import of those components was going to be approved immediately, took seven or eight months to make the decision official (Vigevani, 1995, 97).

Confronted with the mismanagement and erratic policy decisions of SEI, the biggest national investors in the area of electronics began to show less and less disposition to develop new projects. Even worse, the civil society associations and the public, which had enthusiastically backed the initial development of a national computer industry, began to lose enthusiasm. Without the active support of scientists and intellectuals, the informatics policy could not find the same resonance in public opinion (ibid., 98). In 1990, President Collor assumed office with a neoliberal policy orientation, strongly opposed to greenhouse strategies for the development of national industries. The new administration dissolved SEI, and the national informatics policy was terminated at once. However, this drastic change of course did not cause much reaction among the public or among social actors. Computer associations did not even try to mount a public campaign against the liberalization of the informatics market, choosing instead to try to negotiate—unsuccessfully—with senior officials of the administration in order to retain some level of protection for national producers (Erber, 1995, 183). In the meantime, the press had also turned against greenhouse policies in the field of computer electronics. The electronics market was hastily deregulated by the Collor administration, and the industry went into a deep crisis (ibid.). Ironically, although the U.S. government had for some years been pressuring Brazil to open its informatics market, the big winners in the market's deregulation were Japanese computer producers (Schoonmaker, 2002, 124).

The Fatal Weakness of Autonomy in Chile

The second case of an initially successful development strategy, implemented by an autonomous bureaucratic institution, occurred in Chile. In a pioneer initiative for Latin America, Chile was the first country in the region to create a national developmental institution, during the administration of President Aguirre Cerda. In 1939, with the ambitious mandate to carry out a series of policies to develop the different sectors of the national economy, the institution was created by an act of Congress under the name CORFO (Corporación de Fomento de la Producción).

The original proposal for the creation of CORFO came from a group of high-ranking career civil servants, most of them engineers, not associated with the political coalition in government, the Popular Front (Pinto, 1963, 653). Nevertheless, as Silva (2008, 92) points out, the government was very receptive to the proposal. Well-known international experiences had created a favorable climate for state-led development in Chile. Among these was the Tennessee Valley Authority (TVA), a federal agency created in 1933 with the mission to provide economic development for a vast geographic area in the United States (ibid., 93). The institutional design of CORFO showed similarities to the design of TVA. Both institutions were defined as "corporations," with boards of directors that included representatives from civil society, businesses, the legislature, and labor organizations. In both cases, the board of directors appointed a chief executive officer or executive vice-president with similar roles (TVA, 1933; CORFO, 1939).

However, there was a crucial difference in the institutional designs of TVA and CORFO. The first was created as an independent agency of government, and the members of its board were appointed by the president of the United States, with advice and consent of the Senate, for fixed terms of nine years (TVA, 1933). The president could not fire members of the board or the chief executive officer of TVA. Having been designed as independent, TVA was not subordinated to the president at all (we will return to the design of independent agencies in the United States below). The flaw in CORFO's design, which was to prove fatal, was that the president of Chile appointed several members of the board at will, without advice and consent from the Senate or any other restriction. Moreover, the board members and the executive vice-president were not protected by fixed terms; several of them could be fired at any time, at the president's discretion (CORFO, 1939). In sum, CORFO was not really autonomous, except on paper. If it came to any kind of conflict, the institution was to be critically unprotected from the executive power.

After its creation in 1939, CORFO began to implement wide-ranging development programs based on the strategy of import substitution industrialization. Most of the projects included already existent, or newly created, private firms. The plural composition of the board of directors facilitated the embeddedness with businesses and other social actors. At the same time, CORFO consistently preserved its bureaucratic autonomy—that is to say, decisions on investments and industrial projects were based on expert criteria. A series of interviews with business representatives in Chile, carried out during the '60s, confirmed this point, respondents stating that projects at CORFO were strictly adjudicated on technical grounds (Cavarozzi, 1975, 124). Successive administrations were respectful of CORFO's autonomy, and policy decisions were free from political interference (ibid., 130; Muñoz Gomá and Arriagada, 1977, 28).

The theory of agency reputation, as previously explained, maintains that autonomous bureaucratic agencies have powerful incentives to develop and strengthen their own embeddedness among social actors, in order to increase and consolidate support for their autonomy. This was the case with CORFO. The agency's top management developed crucial skills in networking and conciliation among opposing interests. The agency became the facilitator for a new basis of agreement on public policy between the political parties in government, the right-wing opposition, and private-sector representatives. One particular issue of contention was public initiative in creating new businesses, which the private sector regarded with suspicion. Nevertheless, "this and other latent conflicts between the executive and business organizations were defused by the state technocrats" (Silva, 2008, 100). CORFO's influence among social actors was based on its reputation for professionalism (Cavarozzi, 1975, 127).

The results achieved by CORFO were impressive. From 1940 to 1955, industrial production in Chile grew at an average of 8.4 percent every year, going from a share of 13.06 percent of GDP to a share of 23.40 during that period (Braun et al., 2000, 28, 32). National industrial production increased by 340 percent from 1939 to 1955 (ibid., 26). Taking inspiration from TVA's policies, CORFO set itself the goal of rapidly increasing the production of energy. A subsidiary of CORFO was created in 1943 under the name ENDESA. From 1943 to 1960, ENDESA constructed twelve thermal and seven hydroelectric power stations (CORFO, 1962, 16). The production of electricity was thus able to keep pace with the fast growth of industrial production. In the years between 1940 and 1960, production of electricity increased by 235 percent (Braun et al., 2000, 48).

From the beginning, the development strategies of CORFO involved the participation of the private sector. Particularly in the areas of manufacturing and mining industries, many private firms were created, or strengthened, with financial and technical support from CORFO. After twenty years of successful growth, the new business groups began to acquire a sense of their own power and significance (Silva, 2008, 104). The new political awareness of industrial groups was a decisive factor in the victory of Jorge Alessandri in the presidential election of 1958. An independent candidate, Alessandri was a successful businessman and a former president of the central association of business owners. His main goal as president was to focus the development process much more on private business, and to reduce as far as possible the participation of the public sector in the economy. He presented himself as the leader of a "managerial" transformation of Chile (Cavarozzi, 1975, 340).

Nevertheless, the ruthlessness of the changes that Alessandri carried out, soon after assuming office, caused astonishment and alarm. A few weeks after his inauguration, Alessandri ordered extensive purges of the leading career experts at several public organizations (Silva, 2008, 106). First of all, the president of the Central Bank of Chile, a civil servant with three decades of experience in public banking, was summarily dismissed. He was replaced with a close political associate of Alessandri, who had been a successful manager in the steel industry but had no banking experience (Cavarozzi, 1975, 355). The executive vice-president of CORFO was fired next and replaced with another confidant of Alessandri whose professional background was also in private business. Immediately after that, CORFO was purged of all its top and middle management, including engineers and other experts who had been in charge of policy decisions since the creation of the corporation (ibid., 357). With the support of Alessandri, the new executive vice-president dismissed the general manager of CORFO, the heads of each one of CORFO's ten departments, and all the career engineers who had worked directly under the former general manager as a team preparing public policy decisions. Similar brutal purges of permanent public officers were carried out at the ministries, and also in decentralized public agencies. Not only were the top management levels summarily dismissed, but middle managers and advisors were as well (Silva, 2008, 107). As Cavarozzi (1975, 395) describes it, with a certain understatement, the result of all these brutal and extensive bureaucratic purges was a "relative de-autonomization of the state." Alessandri put all key areas of the Chilean state under his direct political control.

The operational capacity of CORFO was shattered by the purges. The first significant project negatively affected was the creation of a large new subsidiary of the Italian automobile manufacturer FIAT. The project had been negotiated since 1956, and it involved the creation of Chile's first tractor manufacturing plant, with 54.5 percent of the capital provided by CORFO and the rest by FIAT. The project would have been "one of the most important ventures undertaken by the institution during its lifetime" (ibid., 358), but it was never implemented. As a matter of fact, for two years after the purge, CORFO was simply inoperative and not a single new project was launched (ibid.; CEDEM, 1968, 45).

During the first two years of Alessandri's term, 1959 and 1960, the administration deregulated international trade, reduced tariffs, and lifted import restrictions (CEDEM, 1968, cuadro II-44). In addition to rendering CORFO inoperative, the deregulation of international trade had a very negative impact on industrial growth. For the first time in fifteen years, the index of industrial production failed to increase from 1959 to 1960, going down by almost three points (ibid., cuadro II-12).

Industrial growth in Chile had a weakness that tends to affect developing economies. Most of the new industrial firms produced consumer or intermediate goods, while capital goods, such as equipment and machinery, were not manufactured in the country. CORFO had plans to produce equipment and machinery by creating public-private partnerships, such as the agreement with FIAT mentioned above. However, those plans were undone by the massive bureaucratic purges at CORFO, which rendered the institution inoperative. In any case, the new administration favored private initiative as the mechanism to solve economic problems. Accordingly, a new regime of tax exemptions and financial assistance for the import of machinery and equipment for industrial plants was created, targeting private firms (Cavarozzi, 1975, 373). However, even with the deregulation of international trade ordered by the Alessandri administration, the import of capital goods grew only slightly, increasing by 16.5 percent from 1958 to 1961. By contrast, the import of consumer goods grew by 79.1 percent during the same period (CEDEM, 1968, cuadro II-52).

At the beginning of his term, Alessandri was strongly supported by business associations. Prominent business representatives assumed high-level positions in the administration. However, after barely two years, business representatives began to express their frustration at the administration's incompetence in key technical areas, such as the operation of the new credit system to support private investment in the production of capital goods (Cavarozzi, 1975, 383). According to the Chamber of Commerce, by 1961 the Central Bank had made accessing the new credit system so difficult that private businesses were simply forced to rely instead on foreign loans. The influential business association SOFOFA went public with a similar complaint, namely that access to low-interest credits for capital investment was almost impossible because of the many conditions imposed on the granting of loans (business representatives quoted in Cavarozzi, 1975, 383). Similarly telling was the perplexity expressed by business representatives at not being consulted by the Central Bank before it issued new dispositions on this line of credit, considering that SOFOFA had promoted the initiative in the first place (ibid.). Of course, bureaucratic and technical incompetence was only to be expected as a consequence of the massive purge of professional managers at the Central Bank, CORFO, and other public agencies. The new, amateur, politically appointed managers failed utterly at their complex bureaucratic and technical tasks. Worse still, the new managers showed an embarrassing lack of consultation and networking skills, causing mounting anger among their own political allies in the business sector.

The political parties supporting Alessandri, Liberal and Conservative, suffered a crushing defeat in the midterm elections of 1961, losing many congressional seats. The opposition Radical Party won the elections by a wide margin. Forced to acknowledge defeat, Alessandri offered several ministerial portfolios to the Radical Party, including the crucial Ministry of Economy. During its previous era in government (1932–52), the Radical Party had been very respectful of the autonomy of experts working at CORFO, the Central Bank, and other key state institutions. However, most of those career experts had been summarily dismissed in Alessandri's bureaucratic purges, and reconstructing a career civil service can take years. In the short term, the only viable solution was a political deal. Top and middle management positions all across the public administration were distributed among political appointees of the three political parties now supporting the administration, in proportion to their electoral results (Cavarozzi, 1975, 386).

The political deal of 1961 sanctioned the politicization of the Chilean public administration. Reserved for career civil servants until 1958, top and middle management positions were now part of the spoils, to be negotiated by political parties and filled with political appointees. Such de-autonomization of the state, in the words of Cavarozzi, certainly had a very negative impact on the quality of public governance. And it produced an even more ominous result. Another consequence of the politicization of the state bureaucracy, again in the words of Cavarozzi, was that "Chile's political scene experienced a process of accelerated polarization which peaked in the 1964 elections when the voters aligned themselves in two sharply separated political coalitions" (ibid., 395).

The nonpartisan public bureaucracy used to have a moderating effect on political confrontation in Chile. After 1961, winning elections implied taking control over the whole public administrative apparatus, including a much increased capacity for patronage, extending to key management positions. The stakes in winning or losing elections became suddenly very much higher. It was only logical for the polarization of the political scene to become more intense, even brutal, in the next years. This polarization weakened the democratic system, and it had a tragic conclusion in 1973.

Supreme Administrative Authority

The two cases of development failure in Latin America discussed in this chapter show the very negative impact of presidential interference on public policy programs, which career experts had run successfully until the presidents intervened. In order to reaffirm their authority, presidents dissolved bureaucratic institutions (such as CAPRE in Brazil) or purged top and middle career management levels (as again with CAPRE, and with CORFO in Chile). It must be observed that presidential interventions in those cases have not been regarded as predatory in the literature; presidents Alessandri and Figueiredo have gone into history as relatively honest administrators. Figueiredo must be considered a criminal, of course, but for presiding over a military dictatorship that committed human rights violations.

If we contrast the design of developmental institutions in East Asian and Latin American cases, one lesson is quite clear: Latin American developmental institutions would have greatly benefited from less interference from politicians. And it is not the case that the two Latin American presidents we discussed were particularly "intrusive" in their management styles. The constitutions of Brazil and Chile, and of other Latin American nations, establish the administrative authority of presidents as "supreme" or "superior" in very imposing terms. In assuming office, presidents are not only tempted to use their strong commanding powers to reassert their authority over the public bureaucracy, but Latin American constitutions actually prescribe such acts of affirmation. Taking control of bureaucratic institutions by firing top managers, appointing political loyalists to replace them, even dissolving bureaucratic agencies created under their predecessors—all these seem to be required acts of presidential authority.

Indeed, the principle of supreme administrative authority of the president is solemnly declared in Latin American constitutions. The most literal formulation is contained in the Constitution of Colombia, which states in article 115 that the "president of the Republic is chief of State, head of government, and supreme administrative authority." Legal scholars and the courts in Colombia understand that "supreme administrative authority" means that the president can give orders and instructions to all agencies and departments of the national public administration, including those that the constitution itself defines—rather confusingly—as "autonomous" (Perdomo et al., 2006, 99). The Constitution of Brazil is slightly less emphatic, declaring in article 84 that the president has "exclusive competence" to exercise the "superior direction" of the federal public administration. Nevertheless, this clause is also understood by legal scholars, and the courts in Brazil, as giving the president direct authority over all areas of the federal public administration, including the "decentralized" agencies (Gomes and Morgado, 2012).

Another strong formulation is found in the Constitution of Mexico: article 80 states that the president holds the "supreme executive power." Legal scholars and the courts understand this clause in the same way that similar dispositions in the constitutions of Brazil and Colombia are understood. The president of Mexico is considered the "top of the administrative pyramid" (Carpizo, 2004, 45), and the president can be defined as the highest "leader" *(conductor)* of the federal public administration (Pagaza, 2002, 83). The Constitution of Argentina, in force from 1853 to 1994, declared in article 86 that the president was the "supreme chief of the Nation" and, further, that the president was "in charge of the general administration of the country." This clause was understood in the usual terms, meaning that the president had command authority over all departments and agencies of the federal public administration, including the "autarchic entities" (Gordillo, 2010). The constitutional reform of 1994 in Argentina changed the formulation of article 86, which states now that the president is "politically responsible" for the public administration. The power to "exercise the general administration of the country" has been assigned instead to the "cabinet chief." However, the cabinet chief is subordinated to the president, so that the president retains as much supreme administrative authority as before (Sabsay, 2014, 43).

Among Latin American countries, bureaucratic autonomy as an institutional design has only been consolidated in present-day Chile. Four public organizations have been declared autonomous by adding specific clauses to the constitution, and thus they are protected from political interference by the executive power. They are very significant exceptions to the principle of presidential supremacy. We have described above how CORFO, which the constitution never declared autonomous, was the target of a devastating bureaucratic purge by President Alessandri. By contrast, since 1943, the Contraloría General de la República, a national audit office, has been declared autonomous by a clause added to the Constitution of Chile. The constitutional reform of 1980 added two further autonomous public institutions, the Central Bank and the National Television Council. A further constitutional reform in 2015 declared the autonomy of the national electoral commission

(Servicio Electoral). These four institutions are emphatically not under the authority of the president or any other member of the administration. The Contraloría is considered the main factor that contributes to the very low level of corruption in Chile (Franko, 2007, 161). Considering that corruption is endemic in Latin America, it is certainly remarkable that the Chilean design of a politically independent national audit office, declared autonomous by the constitution, has not been adopted as a model by other countries in the region. Once again, this is a testimony to the influence of presidential supremacy, the principle that the president must have command authority over all departments and agencies of the public administration.

Another partial exception to the principle of presidential supremacy has been introduced relatively recently in Mexico. For several decades, the country's political regime of one-party dominance under control of the PRI (Partido de la Revolución Institucional) had been based on the manipulation of elections by national governments. As the result of negotiations between all main political forces, including the PRI, the opening of the political system was agreed upon during the 1990s. The key institutional tool for ensuring fair competitive elections was a new national electoral commission (Instituto Federal Electoral), declared autonomous by special amendment to the constitution in 1996. Since the new electoral commission is not under the authority of the president, the governing party has lost the power to overturn adverse electoral results—as happened often in the past (Farah Gebara, 2015, 677–678). On the basis of the success of this institutional reform for the democratic transition, further autonomous or independent public bodies were created in the following years by means of specific amendments to the constitution, such as a federal communications commission, a commission for openess of public information, and others. However, the creation and functioning of independent public bodies remains highly controversial in Mexico, precisely because it goes against traditional, deeply held constitutional values and principles (Dussauge Laguna, 2015). Independent public bodies do in fact undermine the president's supreme authority over all departments and agencies of the federal public administration. This is actually a good thing from our point of view, but it has not been widely accepted in Mexico yet, and in other Latin American countries it has barely been tried—again, Chile remains the clear exception. The autonomous bureaucratic institutions in Chile are important exceptions to the pattern of presidential supremacy in Latin America. However, even in Chile, as regards all other areas of the public administration, article 24 of the constitution still declares that "government and administration of the State correspond to the president, who is the chief of State." This clause is understood by legal scholarship and the courts in the usual terms. The president of Chile can be described as the "supreme administrator of the State," and the president's administrative authority also extends to the "decentralized" public organizations (Cimma, 1995, 89); the exception remains the bureaucratic institutions declared autonomous by the constitution, however, over which the president has no power whatsoever (ibid., 170).

In any case, the fact that the principle of presidential supremacy is declared solemnly by many constitutions in the region does not make it eternal or unchangeable, as shown by the experience of Chile, and in part by Mexico. The Chilean model of good governance, amply acknowledged in the region, proves that it is perfectly possible to change or make exceptions to the principle of presidential supremacy. However, any kind of institutional reform in this area would require, as a first step, widespread awareness and public discussion. And yet such a necessary debate is hampered by two widespread assumptions about these issues. In the first place, the general approach in developmental studies, already discussed in the introduction above, explains development failure as the result of predatory self-interest, thus neglecting institutional deficiencies. Secondly, there is a trend of ignoring presidential supremacy in political science literature, which results from the general belief that Latin American political institutions are very similar to the political institutions of the United States. Diverse "Americanist" assumptions, which are often imported into the study of Latin American politics, have been discussed by Weyland (2002). One of those assumptions represents precisely the failure to consider the dominance of the executive power over public policy formulation and implementation in Latin America, as well as a general lack of interest in the study of state institutions and public bureaucracies (ibid., 64). The Americanist perspective leads to an assumption that Latin American presidents and U.S. presidents have similar powers, and that the differences between them are not substantial. Because presidential supremacy, as we will show below, does not exist in U.S. constitutional law and political practices, it is often simply ignored in the study of Latin American political institutions.

The presidents of the United States do not have supreme authority over the public bureaucracy—that is to say, American presidents do not have the power to give commands or instructions to all departments and agencies of the federal administration. For legal scholars and the courts, the matter has been decided since the pronouncement of the U.S. Supreme Court in 1935 regarding the case *Humphrey's Executor v. United States*. In this ruling, the Supreme Court declared that, according to the U.S. Constitution, the president of the United States has no authority whatsoever over those departments or offices of the public administration that Congress declares independent (*U.S. Supreme Court Reports,* vol. 295, pp. 602, 627).

The text of the "appointments clause" in the U.S. Constitution (art. 2, § 2) indeed makes it quite clear that Congress can establish limits to the presidential power to appoint federal officers and, thus, to the authority of the president over the departments and agencies of the federal administration run by such officers. This clause supports the institutional design of independent agencies of government, which the Supreme Court confirmed were outside of the president's authority in 1935. Such agencies are not under the authority of the president because Congress has established their independent character by law. In short, the president has no administrative supremacy in the U.S. constitutional system. This is a very marked and substantial contrast to the administrative supremacy of the presidents in Latin America.

CONCLUSION

Presidential supremacy is regarded in Latin America as a necessary condition for effective democratic government, and the principle is proclaimed as such in many constitutions in the region. The principle states that the president must have direct control and authority over all government departments and agencies. The principle was written as law in several Latin American constitutions during the nineteenth century, with the explicit purpose of ensuring the effectiveness of state institutions. The idea of allowing an area of government to be run by experts, without outside interference, goes straight against the principle of supreme presidential authority, and it arouses fears of chaos and mismanagement.

As mentioned above, the principle of presidential supremacy corresponds to the relatively commonsense belief that organizations are most effective, as a whole, if there is a clear and final authority for all important decisions. A single person has to be ultimately in charge, with oversight and authority over all significant issues. The principle is based on common sense, but it does not apply to the operations of modern governments. In the specific case of developmental institutions, bureaucratic autonomy is a precondition for their effectiveness, as has been amply demonstrated by successful development models in Japan and South Korea. The advantages of bureaucratic autonomy have been experienced in Latin America as well. The most successful development strategies in the region were formulated and implemented by experts without political interference, such as the creation of a computer industry in Brazil by CAPRE and the industrial policies implemented by CORFO between 1940 and 1958 in Chile. In the end, however, the initial success of those development experiences was wrecked by presidential interference. Presidential supremacy has often resulted in the defective design, and the operational failure, of Latin American developmental institutions—even with the best of intentions.

. . .

Miguel A. Centeno is a professor of sociology and international affairs at Princeton University. Agustín E. Ferraro is a professor of political science and public administration at the Universidad de Salamanca.

REFERENCES

Acemoglu, Daron, and James Robinson. 2012. Why Nations Fail: The Origins of Power, Prosperity, and Poverty. New York: Random House.

Adler, Emanuel. 1986. "Ideological 'Guerrillas' and the Quest for Technological Autonomy: Brazil's Domestic Computer Industry." International Organization 40: 673–705.

———. 1987. The Power of Ideology: The Quest for Technological Autonomy in Argentina and Brazil. Berkeley: University of California Press.

Baaklini, Aldo, and Carlos Pojo do Rego. 1991. "Congress and the Development of a Computer Industry Policy in Brazil." In Legislatures in the Policy Process: The Dilemmas of Economic Policy, ed. David M. Olson and Michael L. Mezey, 130–159. Cambridge, UK: Cambridge University Press.

Braun, Juan, Matias Braun, Ignacio Briones, Jose Diaz, Rolf Lüders, and Gert Wagner. 2000. "Economia Chilena 1810–1995: Estadisticas Historicas. Documento de Trabajo Nr. 187." Santiago: Pontificia Universidad Catolica de Chile—Instituto de Economía. Accessed August 19, 2015, http://www.memoriachilena.cl/archivos2/pdfs/mc0023154.pdf.

Carpenter, Daniel P. 2001. The Forging of Bureaucratic Autonomy: Reputations, Networks, and Policy Innovation in Executive Agencies, 1862–1928. Princeton, NJ: Princeton University Press.

———. 2010. Reputation and Power: Organizational Image and Pharmaceutical Regulation at the FDA. Princeton, NJ: Princeton University Press.

Carpenter, Daniel P., and Daniel Moss. 2013. Preventing Regulatory Capture: Special Interest Influence in Regulation and How to Limit It. New York: Cambridge University Press.

Carpizo, Jorge. 2004. El presidencialismo mexicano (18th edition). Cuidad de México: Siglo XXI Editores.

Cavarozzi, Marcelo. 1975. The Government and the Industrial Bourgeoisie in Chile: 1938–1964. PhD dissertation, University of California, Berkeley.

CEDEM (Centro de Estudios Estadístico-Matemáticos de la Universidad de Chile). 1968. "Elementos para un análisis de la intervención del Estado en la economía chilena." Paper presented at the "Seminario sobre Estudios de

Integración," Santiago de Chile, July 15–19, 1968. Accessed August 19, 2015, http://repositorio.cepal.org/handle/11362/19411.

Cimma, Enrique Silva. 1995. Derecho administrativo chileno y comparado: el servicio público. Santiago: Editorial Jurídica de Chile.

CORFO (Corporación de Fomento de la Producción). 1939. Ley 6334. "Crea la corporación de reconstrucción y auxilio a los damnificados del terremoto, y establece, además, la corporación de fomento a la producción." Accessed August 8, 2015, http://www.leychile.cl/Navegar?idNorma = 25337&id Version = 1939–04–29.

———. 1962. Veinte años de labor: 1939–1959. Santiago: Editorial Zig-Zag. Accessed August 12, 2015, http://www.memoriachilena.cl/archivos2/pdfs /MC0023066.pdf.

D'Araujo, Maria Celina, and Celso Castro. 2004. Tempos Modernos. João Paulo do Reis Velloso, memórias do desenvolvimento. Rio de Janeiro: Editora FGV.

Dussauge Laguna, Mauricio I. 2015. "Mitos y realidades de los Organismos Constitucionales Autónomos mexicanos." Revista de Administración Pública 50: 225–245.

Erber, Fabio Stefano. 1995. "The Political Economy of Technology Development: The Case of the Brazilian Informatics Policy." In Politics of Technology in Latin America, ed. Maria Ines Bastos and Charles Cooper. London: Routledge. pp. 173–199.

Evans, Peter. 1995. Embedded Autonomy: States and Industrial Transformation. Princeton, NJ: Princeton University Press.

Farah Gebara, Mauricio. 2015. "Jorge Carpizo. Inspirador de la creación de los órganos constitucionales autónomos." In Estado constitucional, derechos humanos y vida universitaria. Estudios en homenaje a Jorge Carpizo, vol. 1, book 4: Estado constitucional, ed. Miguel Carbonell, Héctor Fix-Fierro, Luis Raúl González Pérez, and Diego Valadés. Mexico City: UNAM. pp. 669–682.

Franko, Patrice. 2007. The Puzzle of Latin American Economic Development. Lanham, MD: Rowman and Littlefield.

Gomes, Eugenio Maria, and Almir Morgado. 2012. Compendio de adminis-traçao. Administraçao publica e privada de A a Z. Rio de Janeiro: Elsevier.

Gordillo, Agustín. 2010. Tratado de derecho administrativo y obras selectas. Tomo 4: el procedimiento administrativo (10th edition). Buenos Aires: F.D.A.

Gordon, Lincoln. 2004. Brazil's Second Chance: En Route toward the First World. Washington, DC: Brookings Institution.

Johnson, Chalmers. 1982. MITI and the Japanese Miracle: The Growth of Industrial Policy, 1925–1975. Stanford, CA: Stanford University Press.

Kim, Byung-Kook. 2000. "The Politics of Crisis and a Crisis of Politics: The Presidency of Kim Dae-Jung." In Korea Briefing: 1997–1999: Challenges and Change at the Turn of the Century, ed. Kongdan Oh. Armonk and London: M.E. Sharpe. pp. 35–74.

Kim, Kihwan, and Danny Leipziger. 1993. Korea: A Case of Government-Led Development. Washington, DC: World Bank.

Larson, James F. 1995. The Telecommunications Revolution in Korea. Oxford, UK: Oxford University Press.

Luzio, Eduardo. 1996. The Microcomputer Industry in Brazil: The Case of a Protected High-Technology Industry. Westport, CT: Praeger.

Muñoz Gomá, Oscar, and Ana María Arriagada. 1977. "Orígenes políticos y económicos del Estado empresarial en Chile." Estudios CIEPLAN Nr. 16. Santiago: CIEPLAN. Accessed August 8, 2015, http://www.cieplan.org /media/publicaciones/archivos/275/Origenes_politicos_y_economicos_del_ Estado_empresarial_en_Chile.pdf.

Pagaza, Ignacio Pichardo. 2002. Introducción a la nueva administración pública de México, vol. 1 (2nd edition). Cuidad de México: Instituto Nacional de Administración Pública.

Perdomo, Jaime Vidal, Catalina Atehortúa García, Fernando Brito Ruíz, Viviana Díaz Perilla, and Miguel Malagón Pinzón. 2006. Teoría de la organización administrativa colombiana. Una visión jurídico-administrativa. Bogotá: Editorial Universidad Nacional del Rosario.

Pinto, Aníbal. 1963. "Desarrollo económico y relaciones sociales en Chile." El Trimestre Económico 30: 641–658.

Sabsay, Daniel. 2014. "A 20 años de la reforma constitucional ¿se han cumplido sus objetivos?" Pensar en Derecho 5: 35–66.

Schneider, Ben Ross. 2013. Hierarchical Capitalism in Latin America: Business, Labor and the Challenges of Equitable Development. Cambridge, UK: Cambridge University Press.

Schoonmaker, Sarah. 2002. High-Tech Trade Wars: U.S.–Brazilian Conflicts in the Global Economy. Pittsburgh, PA: University of Pittsburgh Press.

Schwartzman, Simon. 1985. "High Technology vs. Self Reliance: Brazil Enters the Computer age." Paper presented at the MIT Symposium on "The Computer Question in Brazil," Cambridge, MA, April 16, 1985. Accessed June 23, 2015, https://ia802708.us.archive.org/8/items/HighTechnologyVsSelf-relianceBrazi lEntersTheComputerAge/TheComputerQuestion.pdf.

Shivakumar, Sujai. 2005. The Constitution of Development: Crafting Capabilities for Self-Governance. London: Palgrave Macmillan.

Silva, Patricio. 2008. In the Name of Reason: Technocrats and Politics in Chile. University Park: Pennsylvania State University Press.

Trubek, David M. 2013. "Law, State, and the New Developmentalism: An Introduction." In Law and the New Developmental State: The Brazilian Experience in Latin American Context, ed. David M. Trubek et al. Cambridge, UK: Cambridge University Press. pp. 3–27.

TVA. 1933. Tennessee Valley Authority Act of 1933. Accessed June 23, 2015, http://www.tva.com/abouttva/pdf/TVA_Act.pdf.

Weyland, Kurt. 2002. "Limitations of Rational-Choice Institutionalism for the Study of Latin American Politics." Studies in Comparative International Development 37: 57–85.

Vigevani, Tullo. 1995. O contencioso Brasil × Estados Unidos da informática: uma análise sobre formulação da política exterior. São Paulo, Brazil: Alfa Omega–Editora da Universidade de São Paulo.

5. What Makes an Institution "Developmental"?

A Comparative Analysis

Alejandro Portes and Jean C. Nava

INTRODUCTION[1]

The advent of the institutional perspective in the study of national development not only revolutionized the field, but it brought together the views of economists, political scientists, and sociologists. Henceforth, a common understanding of the role of social mechanisms in sustained economic growth would be common to these disciplines, moving the search to those factors that "make a difference" in bringing about this outcome (Kohli, 1987, 2004; Roland, 2004). A necessary, logical step in this search is a rigorous identification of what institutions are, and on this point a curious definitional vacuum has emerged. It is not the case that definitions of the concept have not been advanced, but they have been both too numerous and too vague (Jutting, 2003).

Attempting to fill the gap, Portes (2006; 2010, ch. 4) examined classical sociological theory to separate the conceptual domain of "institutions" from related but different concepts such as values, norms, and roles. This search led to a definition of institutions as "blueprints specifying relations among role occupants in social organizations" (Portes and Smith, 2012, 4). The distinction between "institutions" as normative blueprints and the organizations that they underlie was actually anticipated by North (1990). It can be compared with definitions advanced by other authors (e.g., Greif, 1993) that bring together, under the same conceptual umbrella, a number of disparate social elements.

Aside from its greater rigor, the definition advanced by North and then by Portes has the advantage of rendering problematic the relationship between institutions and the organizations that they underlie. For it is not the case that, once set in place, institutional blueprints are followed blindly. Granovetter (1985, 1995) referred to this permanent tension between ideal

90

rules and real practices as the problem of "embeddedness"—that is, the extent to which actual social interactions modify or even derail original institutional goals and rules. In his exchange with economist Oliver Williamson, Granovetter (1985, 1990) demonstrated that the problem is present not only in arm's-length market exchange, but also within the established hierarchies of complex organizations.

A second problem with the institutional approach to development is the tendency to use nation-states as units of analysis, to the detriment of subnational variations. While, for the sake of methodological expediency, it may be acceptable to deal with samples of nation-states, the resulting analyses risk tautology. This happens because scores in "institutional quality" assigned to individual nations are often reputational, being based on the opinions of experts. Such opinions are influenced, in turn, by the level of development already achieved by a country, which can lead to interesting conclusions, such that Sub-Saharan African countries are less developed than Scandinavian ones because the "quality" of African institutions is poorer (Nee and Opper, 2009).

In the end, the empirical literature on institutional economics arrived at three elements deemed to be necessary conditions for long-term economic development: (a) protection of property rights; (b) constraints on the power of the executive; and (c) absence of vast disparities in income per capita. When these conditions are present, sustained economic growth can be expected to follow. Thus, Helpman concludes his review of this literature on the following note:

> Countries that start with similar endowments can follow different developmental paths as a result of differences in institutional structures, because institutions affect the incentive to innovate and to develop new technology, the incentives to reorganize production and distribution in order to exploit new opportunities, and the incentives to accumulate physical and human capital. (Helpman, 2004, 39)

Some sociologists have taken our understanding of the role of institutions in national development to a higher plane by arguing that it does not suffice for public agencies to protect property rights or constrain the executive if they do not engage actively with strategic actors in order to promote the outcomes that Helpman describes. Following the lead of economic historian Alexander Gerschenkron (1962), this line of thinking asserts that institutions that just stand aside and let private markets work their "magic" will not lead to developmental "take-offs." For such a take-off to happen, it is necessary for the state to promote, finance, and otherwise incentivize investments and technological innovation. This thesis is also grounded in the work of the German economic historian Friedrich List ([1984] 2011), who also argued in favor of an interventionist role for the state, at least in the early stages of development. This argument culminated in Evans's study of economic take-offs and unexpected crash-landings in his now classic *Embedded Autonomy* (Evans, 1995).

Accepting a rigorous, limited definition of institutions; acknowledging that institutions within countries may not be uniform, but can vary in their internal structure and performance; and singling out their capacity to engage with actors in the private economy as a key element in their developmental potential provides us with a suitable theoretical springboard for the study of events in reality. This means examining in detail how different types of institutions emerge and what consequences they have for economic growth and social equity. This is the framework for the present study.

DETERMINANTS OF INSTITUTIONAL QUALITY

The first problem noted above—absence of nuance concerning intraregional and intranational differences in institutional development—can be addressed directly with empirical studies that define institutions, not countries, as units of analysis. The second limitation—lack of attention to the inner workings of organizations and determinants of their effectiveness—is also addressable by empirical studies of real organizations. As just seen, the bulk of the institutional literature converges on the idea that "effectiveness" lies in the existence of legal protection for property rights, their proper enforcement, and limitations on the power of the executive. Logically, such institutions must approach the ideal type of "bureaucracy," as defined by Max Weber: they must be meritocratic, immune to corruption, and devoid of internal cliques or "islands of power" (North, 1990; La Porta et al., 1999; Nee and Opper, 2009).

As also noted, other authors have taken this literature one step further by arguing that "Weberian" institutions do not suffice. They assert that developmental institutions must engage with strategic players in society in order to stimulate innovation, protect nascent industries, and guide them toward international competitiveness. Evans has labeled this criterion "embeddedness," although it could be more properly called "proactivity" in that it requires organizations to go beyond their institutional remit (i.e., their original blueprints) and to interact with key actors in their fields of competence, investing in promising initiatives and even creating them when absent (Evans, 1995; Prebisch, 1964, 1986; Sunkel, 2005).

In order to implement such an approach, institutions must possess two additional features. First, they must be technologically advanced and open to innovation. Otherwise, they can neither be alert to the existence of new economic opportunities nor lead the way in their "incubator" function toward new entrepreneurial ventures. Technological prowess requires the recruit-ment of personnel of high human capital and their proper remuneration to avoid their being captured by private interests (Gereffi, 1989; Evans, 1989). Second, an organization, no matter how well designed and proactive, that lacks backers and sponsors among top officialdom or influential elites is likely to fall prey to powerful interest or confront a class "wall" frustrating its mis-sion. The experiences of numerous failed agrarian reforms in Latin America and elsewhere in the developing world, as well as the demise of privatization programs confronted by entrenched interests, attest to the significance of top-down institutional protection (MacLeod, 2004; O'Donnell, 1994).

Synthesizing this theoretical literature, it is hence possible to identify six factors as potential criteria of, first, institutional adequacy and, second, significant contribution to development. Three of these factors are internal to organizations, corresponding to the Weberian ideal type, and three are external to them:

INTERNAL

Meritocracy

Immunity to corruption

Absence of entrenched cliques or "islands of power" (Nee and Opper, 2009; Helpman, 2004)

EXTERNAL

Proactivity toward relevant actors

Technological openness to innovation and flexibility

External allies in top officialdom and/or dominant classes (Evans, 1995; Prebisch, 1986; Portes and Smith, 2008)

The relative importance of these factors and their interplay are empirical questions not examined systematically in the existing literature. It is pos-sible, for example, that internal determinants are not necessary to bring about a developmental institution, while external ones prove sufficient to produce that outcome. This and related issues will be examined in detail in the following sections.

RESEARCH DESIGN
Selection of Countries and Cases

To accomplish the above goals, our study sought to examine a sample of institutions of national relevance in a group of less developed to moderately developed countries. This sample includes institutions in six nations, five in Latin America and one in Southern Europe: Argentina, Chile, Colombia, the Dominican Republic, Mexico, and Portugal. These nations span the length of the South American continent and include both large and relatively developed countries and those commonly classified as part of the Third World. Chile and Mexico, for example, are members of the Organization for Economic Cooperation and Development, generally considered a rich country club. Despite many political and economic ups and downs, Argentina still maintains the highest income per capita among large countries in the region. On the other hand, the Dominican Republic is emblematic of the smaller and poorer countries of the Caribbean subregion. Brazil was not included in this sample because its size and complexity would have required separate study. Instead, we included Portugal, its former colonial power, a nation whose size and compactness renders it amenable to comparison with countries like Chile and which also provides an upper end to the sample in terms of current level of development.

We selected institutions of national scope that differed in their functions along an axis ranging from "primarily economic" to "primarily technical" to "primarily social." Most of these are state agencies, although they include important private entities, such as the stock exchange and the national energy company. We endeavored to include the same institutions in as many countries as possible, although this was not always feasible (for example, there is no stock exchange in the Dominican Republic). While the universe of organizations amenable to study is quite large, we believe that those selected are emblematic of economic, technical, and social functions fundamental to the proper organization and progress of nations. In total, we obtained data on twenty-nine institutions in the following categories.

Stock Exchanges   Stock exchanges have been studied in the past as ideal types of unfettered capitalism, evolving in time from closed clubs to regulated entities open to public investment (Weber, [1904] 1949, [1905] 2009; Abolafia, 1996). Even small nations currently possess stock exchanges, though they vary greatly in scope and modes of operation. Although private entities, stock exchanges play a potentially strategic role in economic development as vehicles for capitalizing a wide range of enterprises, both public and private. The extent to which they do so depends, however, on the transparency of their operations and on the trust that companies and investors have in the inviolability of property rules (Sabel, 1994; Hollingsworth, 2002).

Tax Authorities   Tax authorities underwrite the capacity of states to support themselves and implement policy in the most diverse fields. As Velasco (2008) noted, citing Schumpeter, the budget is the core skeleton of the state, devoid of any pretenses. Tax receipts are the fundamental precondition for budget planning and its implementation. In the past, many less developed countries financed themselves through a combination of import-export tariffs, external indebtedness, and inflation. A series of global crises have progressively constrained these sources, compelling states to increasingly finance themselves by extracting resources from a reluctant domestic population. The capacities of tax authorities to do so and to promote a culture of tax payment among the public represent key criteria reflecting their institutional quality.

Public Health Services   Public health services are redistributive institutions that seek to make the right to health a reality by attending to the needs of the citizenry. In all countries studied, health is enshrined as a constitutionally guaranteed right, and a system of publicly financed clinics and hospitals has been created to implement it. However, the capacity of the system to deliver is limited by two fundamental constraints. The first is budgetary limitations, given the restricted financial means of many states (linked, in part, to their low tax receipts) to underwrite redistributive policies. The second is the intrinsic paradox that the more a public health service succeeds in its mission, for example by reducing infant mortality, the greater the demands that are placed on it by a growing and aging population. How the system copes with these dilemmas is the fundamental criterion of its equality.

Postal Systems   The postal system is a traditional state public service that has played a fundamental role in national integration in many countries by bringing the presence of the state to the country's most remote corners. From its original function of mail delivery, postal systems have diversified, following the pace of technology by incorporating the telegraph, money wiring, parcel post deliveries, and even bank services. Postal systems commonly operate at a loss, and in recent years their finances have been further compromised by competition from private operators. A number of countries, both advanced and less developed, have opted to privatize the post, with very mixed results. One of the most common limitations of privatized mail service is that it focuses on the most profitable segments of the market, neglecting poorer clients and isolated regions (Cereceda, 2009; Gomes Bezerra, 2015). In one form or another, the postal system continues to be a fundamental public service, and its degree of efficiency and honesty is a direct indicator of its role in development.

Civil Aviation   Airports are the face of a nation, and ensuring safe air traffic is a technical function of the utmost importance. Governments can scarcely afford accidents to occur, given the incapacity of their air control-lers or the obsolescence of their equipment. This suggests, a priori, that civil aeronautics should be an "island of excellence" (Evans, 1989) within the state apparatus, insulated from political pressures and private interests. The extent to which this is true is an empirical question. As we shall see, there is significant variation in the extent to which real civil aviation authorities fulfill this technocratic ideal.

Food Security   In all countries, ensuring the safety of the food supply for the general population is also a vital state function. Lapses in vigilance can result in tragic consequences, as attested by the bovine encephalitis (i.e., "mad cow") epidemic that affected the United States, Great Britain, and other countries a decade ago and by regular outbreaks of bacterial infec-tions due to poor handling of fresh products or poor preservation of canned items. Countries dependent on tourism to buttress their economies are par-ticularly vulnerable to outbreaks of *E. coli*, salmonella, and similar bacterial pathogens that can easily scare away foreign visitors. In the United States, the Food and Drug Administration is entrusted with the safety of the food supply and is generally considered a reliable supervisor. Other countries vary significantly in the quality of their food security apparatus and even the extent to which one exists at all.

Energy   Access to a reliable energy supply is another major requirement of any modern country. In the past, the provision of electricity was a state monopoly, but it has been gradually privatized. In most countries, the pro-duction and distribution of electricity are still considered "natural monopo-lies" and entrusted to a single operator, whether public or private. Advanced countries have increasingly opened the provision of electricity to competi-tion, as well as allowed decentralization of the production of electricity, its distribution via high-tension networks, and its retailing. Nevertheless, in most less developed countries, a single operator dominates the field. The quality of the energy supply in terms of its capacity to meet demand, its reliability, and its costs are major criteria for long-term capital investments. Global industrial and commercial corporations commonly base their invest-ment decisions precisely on these criteria (Vaz da Silva, 2015).

Data Collection

Not all the organizations described above could be studied in every country, either because they did not exist or because it was otherwise unfeasible to access them. In the end, the sample of agencies included in this study numbered twenty-nine; no country had fewer than four institutions studied, and five of those described above were studied in at least three countries, permitting multiple cross-national comparisons. In each country, teams of experienced investigators were assembled and entrusted with intensive analysis of selected cases.

Each institutional study lasted one year and encompassed the following steps: (a) compilation of the legal rules defining the mission and governing the activities of the organization; (b) compilation of internal reports and evaluations; (c) compilation of external academic and journalistic reports; (d) interviews with institutional personnel at the levels of top management, mid-level management, and technical personnel; (e) interviews with expert informants; and (f) interviews with strategic users of institutional services (e.g., commercial airlines, pension funds investing in the stock market, mass-mail marketers). For each organization and each country, fifteen to thirty detailed interviews were conducted, divided about equally between internal personnel at different levels and external informants.

By combining these different forms of data collection, investigators were able to arrive at authoritative assessments of all dimensions of interest. These were presented in detailed reports and were scored on a list of pre-specified characteristics. Scores were assigned for each internal or external determinant described previously and for the two outcomes of interest—institutional adequacy and contribution to development. Scores were assigned on two scales: (1) a dichotomous scale indicating "presence" or "absence" of the specific dimension; and (2) a five-point scale, with higher scores indicating greater membership in the set-theoretic space defined by it. Table 5.1 presents the total sample, including the names of institutions, the country, and the dates of completion of the respective studies.

The data produced by the study thus include detailed qualitative reports on the twenty-nine institutions plus two sets of quantitative scores. The latter can be arranged in truth tables and subjected to systematic analysis employing qualitative comparative analysis (QCA). Through this combination, it is possible to carry out a meso-level investigation that takes into account subnational and interinstitutional variations that are generally omitted from the existing research literature on institutions and national development.

RESULTS

General Observations

It is worth examining first the general tendencies evident in the pattern of scores assigned to this sample of institutions.[2] Table 5.2 is a truth table based on the binary scores, and Table 5.3 is a second truth table based on

TABLE 5.1 Institutions Included in the Comparative Study, 2006–2008

Institution	Name	Website	Year report completed
	Argentina		
Postal service	Correo Oficial de la República Argentina (CORASA)	www.correoargentino.com.ar	2010
Civil aviation	Comando de Regiones Aéreas (disbanded); Administración Nacional de Aviación Civil (ANAC)	www.anac.gov.ar	2010
Stock exchange	Bolsa de Comercio de Buenos Aires (BCBA)	www.bcba.sba.com.ar	2010
Tax agency	Dirección General Impositiva (DGI)	www.afip.gob.ar	2010
	Chile		
Postal service	Empresa de Correos de Chile (CorreosChile)	www.correoschile.cl	2006
Civil aviation	Dirección General de Aeronáutica Civil (DGAC)	www.dgac.cl	2006
Stock exchange	Bolsa de Comercio de Santiago de Chile (BCSC)	www.bolsadesantiago.com	2006
Health system	Complejo Asistencial Barros Luco/Ministerio de Salud	redsalud.gov.cl	2010
Tax agency	Servicio de Impuestos Internos (SII)	www.sii.cl	2010
	Colombia		
Postal service	La Administración Postal Nacional (Adpostal)	www.adpostal.gov.co (disbanded)	2006
Civil aviation	Unidad Administrativa Especial de la Aeronáutica Civil (Aerocivil)	www.aerocivil.gov.co	2006
Stock exchange	Bolsa de Valores de Colombia (BVC)	www.bvc.com.co	2006
Health care	Clínica San Pedro Claver/Empresas Promotoras de Salud (EPS)	(disbanded)	2010

Tax agency	Dirección de Impuestos y Aduanas Nacionales (DIAN)	www.dian.gov.co	2010

Dominican Republic

Postal service	Instituto Postal Dominicano (INPOSDOM)	www.inposdom.gob.do	2010
Civil aviation	Instituto Dominicano de Aviación Civil (IDAC)	www.idac-gov.do	2010
Health system	Sistema Público de Salud	www.sespas.gov.do	2010
Tax agency	Dirección General de Impuestos Internos (DGII)	www.dgii-gov.do	2010

Mexico

Postal service	Servicio Postal Mexicano (Sepomex)	www.sepomex.gob.mx	2007
Civil aviation	Dirección General de Aeronáutica Civil (DGAC)	dgac.sct.gob.mx	2010
Stock exchange	Bolsa Mexicana de Valores (BMV)	www.bmv.com.mx	2006
Health system	Hospital General Manuel Gea González (HGMGG)	www.hospitalgea.salud.gob.mx	2010
Tax agency	Servicio de Administración Tributaria (SAT)	sat.gob.mx	2010

Portugal

Postal service	CTT Correios de Portugal	www.ctt.pt	2013
Health system	Hospital de Santa Maria/Servico Nacional de Saude (SNS)	www.chln.min-saude.pt	2013
Stock exchange	NYSE Euronext, Lisbon	www.euronext.pt	2013
Tax agency	Autoridade Tributaria e Aduaneira	www.portaldasfinancas.govt.pt	2013
Energy company	Energias de Portugal (EDP)	www.edp.pt	2013
Food security authority	Autoridade de Seguranca Alimentar e Economica (ASAE)	www.ASAE.pt	2013

TABLE 5.2 Truth Table of Institutional Adequacy and Contributions to National Development

1 = presence, 0 = absence

Institution	Determinants						Results	
	A. Meritocracy	B. Immunity to corruption	C. No "islands of power"	D. Proactivity	E. Technological flexibility	F. External allies	I. Institutional adequacy	II. Contribution to development
Argentina								
Postal service	0	0	0	1	1	1	1	0
Civil aviation	0	0	0	0	0	0	0	0
Stock exchange	0	1	0	1	1	1	1	0
Tax agency	1	0	0	1	1	1	1	1
Chile								
Postal service	1	1	1	1	0	0	1	1
Civil aviation	1	1	1	1	1	0	1	1
Stock exchange	1	1	1	1	1	1	1	1
Health-care system	1	1	1	1	1	0	1	1
Tax agency	1	1	0	1	1	1	1	1
Colombia								
Postal service	0	0	0	0	0	0	0	0
Civil aviation	1	1	1	0	1	0	1	0
Stock exchange	1	1	1	0	1	1	1	0

Health-care system	0	0	0	0	1	0	0
Tax agency	0	0	1	0	1	0	0

Dominican Republic

Postal service	0	0	0	0	0	0	0
Civil aviation	1	1	1	1	1	1	1
Health-care system	0	0	0	0	0	0	0
Tax agency	0	1	1	1	1	1	1

Mexico

Postal service	0	0	0	1	0	1
Civil aviation	1	1	1	0	1	0
Stock exchange	1	1	1	1	1	1
Health-care system	1	1	1	1	1	1
Tax agency	0	1	1	1	1	1

Portugal

Postal service	0	1	1	0	0	1
Civil aviation	1	1	1	1	1	1
Health-care system	0	1	1	1	1	1
Tax agency	1	1	0	0	1	0
Energy company	1	1	1	1	1	1
Food security authority	0	1	1	0	1	1

TABLE 5.3 Truth Table of Scores Assigned to Institutions in Hypothesized Predictors and Outcomes[a]

Institution	Determinants						Results	
	A. Meritocracy	B. Immunity to corruption	C. No "islands of power"	D. Proactivity	E. Technological flexibility	F. External allies	I. Institutional adequacy	II. Contribution to development
Argentina								
Postal service	2	1	2	3	4	4	3	2
Civil aviation	2	2	2	1	2	1	2	1
Stock exchange	3	3	2	4	3	3	4	2
Tax agency	4	1	3	4	5	5	4	4
Chile								
Postal service	4	3	4	5	3	2	4	5
Civil aviation	3.5	4	3	4	5	3	5	4
Stock exchange	4	4	3.5	5	4	5	4	4
Health-care system	3.5	3.5	2.5	3.5	2	1	4	3.5
Tax agency	4	4	2.5	4	5	4	3.5	4
Colombia								
Postal service	2	2	3	2	2.5	1	1	1
Civil aviation	4	3	3.5	2	5	2.5	4	3

Stock exchange	4	3.5	3.5	2	3.5	4	2
Health-care system	2	2	3	2	4	1	1
Tax agency	2	1	2	4	4	2	2

Dominican Republic

Postal service	1	1	2	2	2	2	2
Civil aviation	3.5	3.5	3.5	5	3.5	4	4
Health-care system	1	2	1	2	2	1	2.5
Tax agency	3	3	4	4	5	4	4

Mexico

Postal service	1	2	1	3.5	1	1	3.5
Civil aviation	4	3.5	4	1.5	3.5	4	2.5
Stock exchange	4	3.5	3.5	3.5	5	4	4
Health-care system	4	3	4	4	4	3	4
Tax agency	2	4	5	4	5	3	4

Portugal

Postal service	2	3.5	4	4	4	4	3.5
Civil aviation	5	5	5	4	5	5	3.5
Health-care system	1	2	1	4	3	2.5	3
Tax agency	4.5	4	4	3.5	4.5	4	3.5
Energy company	4.5	4.5	4	5	5	5	4.5
Food security authority	1	5	5	5	4	5	5

[a] 1 = "Entirely outside the conceptual set defined by the variable." 2 = "More outside than inside." 3 = "Neither." 4 = "More inside than outside." 5 = "Entirely inside."

continuous scores, as described above. Each table is arranged by country and by institutions within countries.

The first main trend is that it is easier for an institution to be ranked as "adequate" than as "developmental." In Table 5.2, 76 percent of the organizations studied were ranked as "institutionally adequate" (i.e., as fulfilling their original blueprints), but only 59 percent were considered to contribute effectively to national development. In Table 5.3, the average score in the continuous set-theoretic scale defined by institutional adequacy is 3.41; that denoting contribution to development is only 3.22. This first tendency supports the Evans line of argument, according to which developmental institutions must do more than just fulfill their original blueprints.

Second, scores on the six hypothesized determinants are consistently lower for social organizations dedicated to providing services to the general population than for economic organizations. Zeros denoting "absence" of a given criterion in Table 5.2 are far more common for public health services and postal systems than for stock exchanges, tax authorities, or energy companies. There is also a close overlap of this difference with the private vs. public dimension, as private agencies (i.e., energy companies and stock exchanges) are more likely to garner high scores on both scales than public institutions. The exception is tax authorities, for reasons examined below.

Third, there are systematic disparities across nations. Looking at the right-most columns of both tables, we find that the two outcomes of interest—institutional adequacy and contribution to development—are most commonly present in Chile and Portugal, and most commonly absent in Colombia and the Dominican Republic, with the other countries in between. Such differences agree with expectations in the development literature that has singled out Chile as the "success story" in Latin America in recent decades and that generally classifies southern European countries, including Portugal, as less advanced than those in northern Europe but more so than those in Latin America (Wormald and Brieba, 2012). In this case, such differences are not reputational but emerge from detailed studies of a sample of existing institutions in each country. These preliminary observations serve as a framework for a systematic analysis of the two truth tables.

QCA Results

For the sake of brevity, we omit the analysis of binary scores in Table 5.2, with the observation that they generally converge with those presented next. The continuous scores in Table 5.3 can be analyzed through QCA analysis on the basis of fuzzy-set algebra (Ragin, 1987, 2008). Continuous scores are seen as generally superior because they overcome the constraints

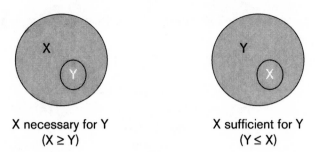

FIGURE 5.1   Necessary and sufficient conditions in fuzzy-set algebra.

of binary rankings. In addition, the method allows for identification of necessary and sufficient conditions. Necessary conditions are always present when the outcome is positive, but they may be present without the outcome materializing. Fuzzy sets translate this criterion into the expectation that scores in the predictor will be higher than or equal to the outcome. Intuitively, membership in the set defined by the effect is a subset of that defined by the cause (Ragin, 1987, ch. 8).

Sufficient conditions always lead to the effect, but the latter may also occur in their absence, as a result of other factors. The translation in fuzzy-set algebra is the expectation that scores in the cause be equal to or lower than those in the effect. Sufficient conditions thus create a "floor" for the outcome, assuming that the memberships in them are subsets of the latter. Figure 5.1 explains these relationships.[3]

A final consideration is the distinction between consistency and coverage. *Consistency* refers to the extent to which a determinant fulfills the criteria for necessity or sufficiency; *coverage* refers to the size of the sample (i.e., number of cases) covered by that determinant. The distinction is important because a causal path may be always right in terms of fulfilling the relevant criteria but may apply only to a few cases. QCA provides formulas for coverage for different solutions of necessity and sufficiency.

Table 5.4 presents fuzzy-set solutions for necessary conditions for the two effects of interest, and Table 5.5 presents the corresponding results for sufficient conditions. The analysis of scores assigned to the twenty-nine cases identifies two principal necessary conditions for institutionally adequate organizations: technological flexibility (E), with almost perfect consistency (.97/100); and proactivity (D), with a score also exceeding 90 percent consistency.

TABLE 5.4 Necessary Conditions for Institutional Adequacy (IA) and Developmental Institution (DI)

Sufficient conditions: $(X < Y) = \varepsilon \min (Xi) (Yi)/\varepsilon Xi$

Conditions	IA	DI
A. Meritocracy	82.5/95.5 = .864	74.5/93.5 = .797
B. Immunity to corruption	82/95.5 = .859	78/93.5 = .834
C. No "islands of power"	82.5/95.5 = .864	76/93.5 = .813
D. Proactivity	88/95.5 = .921	89.5/93.5 = .957
E. Technological flexibility	92.5/95.5 = .969	84.5/93.5 = .904
F. External allies	75.0/95.5 = .882	75.5/93.5 = .807

	Consistency		Coverage	
IA	D	E	D	E
	.921	.969	.876	.853
DI	D	E	D	E
	.957	.904	.891	.779

TABLE 5.5 Sufficient Conditions for Institutional Adequacy (IA) and Developmental Institution (DI)

Sufficient conditions: $(X < Y) = \varepsilon \min (Xi) (Yi)/\varepsilon Xi$

Conditions	IA	DI
A. Meritocracy	82.5/85.5 = .965	74.5/86.5 = .871
B. Immunity to corruption	82/86.5 = .948	78/86.5 = .902
C. No "islands of power"	82.5/87.5 = .943	76/87.5 = .868
D. Proactivity	88/100.5 = .876	89.5/100.5 = .891
E. Technological flexibility	92.5/108.5 = .853	84.5/108.5 = .779
F. External allies	75.0/85.0 = .882	75.5/85.0 = .888

	Consistency					Coverage		
IA	A	B	C	ABC	A	B	C	ABC
	.965	.948	.943	.943	.833	.828	.833	.828
DI	B	D	BD			B	D	BD
	.902	.891	.891			.834	.957	.834

Table 5.4 also shows that the same determinants are major prerequisites for the emergence of a developmental institution. Proactivity is the most consistent necessary condition, followed by technological flexibility. In this case, coverage drops to below 80 percent for the latter predictor; joining both with the operator "and" would produce the same result.[4] Thus, we settle for a single determinant, proactivity.

The parallel analysis of sufficient conditions in Table 5.5 yields a novel result. Fuzzy-set scores in this case revindicate the role of internal predictors, so heavily emphasized by institutional economists. Indeed, the main sufficient cause of institutional adequacy in this sample is meritocracy (A), followed closely by the other two internal criteria. The combination of the three covers 83 percent of the cases and, for this reason, is adopted as the preferred solution for institutional adequacy (IA):

$$IA = ABC \text{ (sufficient)}$$

This result, combined with the previous analysis of necessity, produces a final solution leading to an institutionally adequate organization:

$$IA = ABCE \text{ (necessary and sufficient)}$$

This equation supports expectations in the organizational and economic literatures discussed previously about the importance of "Weberianness." Without the three internal criteria, plus openness to technological innovation, it is evidently not possible for an organization to fulfill the institutional blueprints for which it was created.

Ability to make a significant contribution to development is determined differently. The principal determinants in this case are immunity to corruption (B) and proactivity (D). The latter criterion was already identified above as the necessary condition for that effect. The combination of both predictors covers over 80 percent of the cases and is thus adopted as the final solution leading to a developmental institution (DI):

$$DI = BD \text{ (necessary and sufficient)}$$

Figure 5.2 maps scores for cause and effect in two-dimensional space. This graph shows the typical concentration of cases in the upper-left triangle corresponding to a proper sufficient condition.[5] This solution implies that an institution need not be fully "Weberian" in order to make a contribution to development; it may not be very meritocratic and may even harbor internal cliques. Yet, to the extent that it has overcome the stigma of being "for sale" to external bidders and that it has adopted a proactive stance toward relevant external actors, it can play a significant developmental role. This final

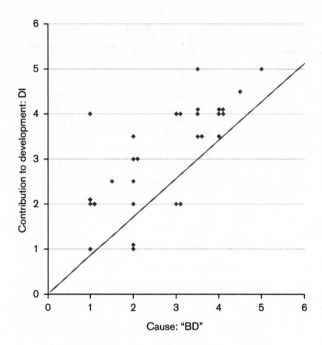

FIGURE 5.2   Institutional membership in the causal combination "BD" and contribution to development (see text).

solution supports the theory about the importance of dynamic institutions able to influence civil society and to mold the national economy.

The solution is theoretically satisfactory and is given additional weight by holding across a sample of quite diverse organizations across different countries. It is worth emphasizing that support for this outcome does not arise solely from theory or isolated case studies, but from systematic analysis across a number of institutions in six countries. Selected cases are presented next.[6]

THE FINAL SOLUTION (BD): EXAMPLES

The Mexican Tax Authority

The Mexican Tax Authority (SAT in its Spanish acronym) is ranked as an institutionally competent and developmental institution, despite its many defects, in particular the absence of meritocracy:

> Compared to other Mexican institutions, SAT's views against meritocracy may look rather trivial. But when measured by SAT's own

standards—and by the requirement of an institution that must extract resources from an uncooperative population and particularly from powerful and often hostile economic elites—those features seem far more serious. (Velasco, 2012, 148)

The most flagrant failure of SAT lies in the non-implementation of the civil service rules established since the inception of the institution. Since 2007, SAT employees have been submitted to ambitious "360-degree evaluations." But, by the time of fieldwork for our study, there was no system to sanction or reward employees according to performance. Therefore, talented functionaries tended to remain only a few years in the SAT and then move on to the business sector, where their expertise on tax matters becomes much more highly rewarded.

Despite these shortcomings, SAT was ranked as a developmental organization, mainly because of its increasing probity and productivity. SAT was the best-ranked Mexican institution in our study in terms of immunity to corruption. Opinion surveys conducted by SAT itself show that taxpayers' perception of corruption within the agency has decreased significantly in recent years. Interviews with people who interact regularly with SAT confirm that corruption has largely been stamped out. To reduce the risk of corruption, SAT has adopted a highly centralized structure: its sixty-six local offices are internally segmented, with each segment directly connected to the respective central authority; in none of these offices is there a local chief who coordinates all segments and would thereby be vulnerable to bribing.

The evaluation of SAT as proactive is grounded in a series of new strategies that include the implementation of risk management techniques (useful for deciding which taxpayers to audit); the creation of a Large Taxpayers Unit (to deal with tax avoidance strategies by the most economically powerful actors); the creation of a taxpayer assistance unit to promote voluntary compliance; and the outsourcing of selected services. Despite all these improvements, the institutional report notes that the agency still has not been able to gain access to (and tax) the informal economy or to overcome the resistance to taxation by the most powerful members of the Mexican economic elite (Velasco, 2012, 153).

The Chilean Civil Aviation Directorate

The Chilean Civil Aviation Directorate (DGAC in its Spanish acronym) has long been run by the Chilean Air Force, which appoints its principal managers. The agency's high rank in terms of fulfillment of its institutional blueprint and its contribution to development is due to its stellar performance, including repeated annual records of zero accidents per 100,000 civilian flights and the endorsement of the U.S. Federal Aviation Authority that ranks the DGAC as a "Category I" agency. Its top management speaks of making the DGAC an institutional leader and an example, not only within the Chilean state but for all of Latin America.

The organization's strengths lie in its immunity to corruption, which would seriously jeopardize safety standards, and its strong proactive stance, which includes close relationships with commercial airlines and other strategic clients. Its principal shortcoming is the absence of meritocratic recruitment and promotion. This stems from the agency's inability to fire deficient or poorly qualified personnel once they become protected by the Chilean Civil Service Statute. It is also based on its role as a recruiter of retired Air Force officers, sidelining potentially better-qualified civilian personnel. As noted in the institutional study: "All departmental directors of the DGAC are former or active members of the Air Force, and at the vice-director general level, all are former members" (Thumala, 2009, 184).

Nonetheless, the study concludes that these limitations do not fundamentally impair the fulfillment of the agency's mission, since it hires specialized and highly trained personnel. Hence, whether they are (allegedly cheaper) retired military officers or selected via examinations, all chosen candidates appear to possess the requisite minimum qualifications for the functions they perform. Yet the dominance of military personnel in an agency performing civilian functions does raise questions about the presence of an entrenched "island of power" (i.e., a military caste) within this institution (Thumala, 2009; Wormald and Brieba, 2012, 73).

The Food and Economic Security Authority of Portugal

The Food and Economic Security Authority of Portugal (ASAE in its Portuguese acronym) is a relatively young agency, having been established in 2006. Until 2013, it was led by the same inspector general. In addition to detailed institutional ethnographies, the Portuguese study added surveys of each organization's personnel focused on evaluations of the agency on the six criteria examined previously. To ensure truthful answers, respondents were guaranteed anonymity.[7]

There was near unanimity among the agency's personnel that ASAE is *not* a meritocratic institution. Meritocracy has been weakened by the suspension of new hiring and the freezing of merit promotions due to the severe economic crisis suffered by Portugal since 2008. In addition, according to well-placed informants, one-third of the personnel are "parachutists" *(paraquedistas)* that were not hired through regular universalistic channels. Thus, a majority of surveyed personnel (62 percent) agreed that "appointments and promotions in ASAE depend essentially on personal relations" (Contumelias, 2015, 57).

In contrast, there is near universal agreement that the agency is immune to corruption. The perfect score assigned to ASAE on this criterion in the institutional report is due to major efforts by the leadership to prevent and, when necessary, punish corrupt acts by its inspectors. The charismatic inspector-general who led ASAE since its creation has paid particular attention to this feature. Thus, not one informant, internal or external, reported a single case of corruption. According to the national director of operations, "I don't know of any case of corruption; this is the result of setting up mechanisms to prevent it since the beginnings of the agency" (Contumelias, 2015, 58). Further confirmation comes from the institutional survey: only 2 percent of respondents disagreed with the statement that "most of ASAE's personnel are immune to corruption."

ASAE is also proactive in two related ways. First, it has been an effective police agency that fulfills its mission even against opposition from powerful actors. Indeed, the agency has been publicly criticized for its excessive zeal. It has closed fashionable restaurants and, on at least one occasion, shut down the dining facilities of Parliament on the eve of a reception for a major foreign dignitary because of sanitary infractions. This resilient stance has guaranteed that the food chain and all establishments serving the general public as well as tourists are quite safe in Portugal.

The agency has also been proactive in a second way, by engaging merchant associations and consumer organizations in regular dialogue, listening to their complaints and demands, and educating the public on various safety norms. ASAE possesses its own digitized information system, "GESTASAE," and supports a website accessible to all food wholesale firms, grocery and restaurant operators, and the general public. In 2012, this site registered over 300,000 visits. Accordingly, 72 percent of respondents in the institutional survey agreed with the statement that "ASAE seeks to be updated with respect to the use of new technologies and all innovative procedures" (Contumelias, 2015, 62).

CONCLUSION

The advent of the "institutional turn" in the study of development represents a welcome shift for a field previously dominated by culturalistic explanations of underdevelopment or by an exclusive economic focus on savings rates and capital accumulation. The major contribution made by North (1990), Greif (1993), and Hoff and Stiglitz (2001) is that they succeeded in shifting attention away from such concerns and toward the character and quality of national institutions. Sociologists and other social scientists have welcomed these developments as a vindication of their own ideas but have failed, so far, to pay full attention to the shortcomings in the institutionalist literature that followed such pronouncements.

These shortcomings stem from a failure to arrive at a rigorous definition of the concept of institution and at reliable measurements of it. When institutions can be anything from cultural values to property laws to the central bank, it is impossible to cumulate empirically reliable evidence. Furthermore, a single-minded focus on nations as the units of analysis obscures attention from subnational differences in the character of organizations and in their internal structure and dynamics.

The study of Latin American and Portuguese institutions presented in this chapter demonstrates that it is possible to transcend such limits and arrive at a more nuanced assessment of institutional quality, as well as systematic comparisons within and between nations. The analysis of the inner workings of Latin American and Portuguese institutions in this study yields another important lesson, namely that it is possible to rapidly improve the quality and performance of organizations when vital interests of the state are at stake. The consistently high scores assigned to tax authorities in various countries reflect well the operation of this principle.

Tax authorities were traditionally dormant or corrupt institutions in these countries. Governments financed themselves through customs receipts, foreign indebtedness, and currency printing (i.e., inflation). It took a series of major economic crises and, in Portugal, entry into the Common Market and then the European Union to bring this system to an abrupt end, forcing governments to look for other sources of finance. The Mexican debt crisis of 1982 compelled Latin American governments to open their doors to foreign investors and trade as a precondition for assistance from international finance organizations. In Portugal, the same result was produced by the country's entry into the Common Market. This did away with customs as the key source of state finance. Neither further external indebtedness nor inflation could be relied upon, since external assistance was made conditional precisely on governments bringing their internal accounts into balance (Rodriguez-Garavito, 2012; Evans, 2015).

This situation left governments with little recourse but to extract resources from a reluctant domestic population. Tax authorities were rapidly and drastically revamped, new strong and competent administrators were appointed, and advanced monitoring technologies were introduced (Velasco, 2012; Evans, 2015). Fiscal inspectors were put on a salary scale above the rest of the government bureaucracy to discourage corruption. A Directorate of Large Contributors was created in country after country to address both the information needs and sophisticated evasion strategies of powerful economic actors (Lozano, 2012; Velasco, 2012). In a country like Chile, the tax authority (Servicio de Impuestos Internos) has achieved enough technological prowess to prepare tax returns for individuals and corporations and send them electronically. All that recipients have to do is review them, sign them, and send them back (Wormald and Cardenas, 2008; Wormald and Brieba, 2012). These collective experiences demonstrate that, when the survival of the state is in question, decisive and effective measures can be taken to improve the quality of relevant institutions. As the prior analysis showed, no such luck accompanied the evolution of agencies providing services to the general population, in particular the public health system and the postal service.

These developments are not part of any general cultural trend, but elements of the specific histories of these countries and the resulting pressures to which particular institutions within them have been subjected. Absent detailed field studies, such contrasting results would not have surfaced. While it would be impossible to investigate all relevant institutions within a single country, a judicious selection of a few strategic ones and their comparative study across countries offer promise for transforming the "institutional turn" in development studies into a reliable tool for knowledge creation and effective policy making in the future.

. . .

Alejandro Portes is a research professor at the University of Miami and a professor of sociology (emeritus) at Princeton University. Jean C. Nava is a doctoral candidate in sociology at Princeton University.

NOTES

1. This chapter is an abridged version of an article published by the authors (Portes and Nava, 2017) based on several prior publications (see Portes, 2009; Portes and Smith, 2008, 2012; Portes and Marques, 2015).

2. This analysis combines data from five Latin American countries and Portugal that have not been combined previously. The combination yields original results, discussed in the text (see Portes and Nava, 2017).

3. The formula for necessity is $Y < X = \mathcal{E} \min (Xi) (Yi)/\mathcal{E}Yi$, where X is the determinant, Y is the effect, and "min" is the smaller of the scores on either for each case i. The formula for sufficiency is the obverse: $X < Y = \mathcal{E} \min (Xi) (Yi)/\mathcal{E}Xi$.

4. According to fuzzy-set rules, coverage of a complex term is equal to the *lower* coverage of its individual components.

5. The same result is obtained when the final solution for IA (ABCE) is graphed in two-dimensional space (for explanations of this graphic solution, see Ragin, 2008).

6. The following summaries are drawn from the corresponding institutional studies (see Velasco, 2012; Thumala, 2009; Contumelias, 2015).

7. Eighty-seven percent of the agency's personnel responded to the institutional survey, yielding a sample of 256 cases. Despite the 13 percent attrition rate, the sample can be considered representative of all ASAE's personnel, as nonresponses were mostly random rather than systematic.

REFERENCES

Abolafia, M. (1996). Making Markets: Opportunities and Restraint on Wall Street. Cambridge, MA: Harvard University Press.

Cereceda, L. (2009). "Institucionalidad y Desarrollo: El Caso de Correos de Chile." In A. Portes (ed.), Las Instituciones en el Desarrollo Latinoamericano. Cuidad de México: Siglo XXI. pp. 210–237.

Contumelias, M. (2015). "A Autoridade de Seguranca Alimentar e Economica—ASAE." In A. Portes and M.M. Marques (eds.), Valores, Qualidade Institucional e Desenvolvimento em Portugal. Lisbon: Francisco Manuel dos Santos Foundation. pp. 29–79.

Evans, A.M. (2015). "A Administração Tributária em Portugal." In A. Portes and M.M. Marques (eds.), Valores, Qualidade Institucional e Desenvolvimento em Portugal. Lisbon: Francisco Manuel dos Santos Foundation. pp. 81–113.

Evans, P. (1989). "Predatory, Developmental, and Other Apparatuses: A Comparative Political Economy Perspective on the Third World State." Sociological Forum 4: 561–587.

———. (1995). Embedded Autonomy: States and Industrial Transformation. Princeton, NJ: Princeton University Press.

———. (2004). "The Challenges of the Institutional Turn: Interdisciplinary Opportunities in Developmental Theory." In V. Nee and R. Swedberg (eds.), The Economic Sociology of Capitalist Institutions. Princeton, NJ: Princeton University Press. pp. 90–116.

Gereffi, G. (1989). "Rethinking Development Theory: Insights from East Asia and Latin America." Sociological Forum 4: 505–533.

Gerschenkron, A. (1962). Economic Backwardness in Historical Perspective: A Book of Essays. Cambridge, MA: Belknap Press.

Gomes Bezerra, R. (2015). "Etnografía Institucional: Uma Analise dos Correios de Portugal." In A. Portes and M.M. Marques (eds.), Valores, Qualidade Institucional e Desenvolvimento em Portugal. Lisbon: Francisco Manuel dos Santos Foundation. pp. 155–186.

Granovetter, M. (1985). "Economic Action and Social Structure: The Problem of Embeddedness." American Journal of Sociology 91: 481–510.

———. (1990). "The Old and the New Economic Sociology: A History and an Agenda." In R. Friedland and A.F. Robertson (eds.), Beyond the Marketplace, Rethinking Economy and Society. New York: Aldine de Gruyter. pp. 89–122.

———. (1995). "The Economic Sociology of Firms and Entrepreneurs." In A. Portes (ed.), The Economic Sociology of Immigration: Essays in Networks, Ethnicity, and Entrepreneurship. New York: Russell Sage. pp. 128–165.

Greif, A. (1993). "Contract, Enforceability, and Economic Institutions in Early Trade: The Maghribi Trader's Coalition." American Economic Review 83: 525–548.

Helpman, E. (2004). The Mystery of Economic Growth. Cambridge, MA: Harvard University Press.

Hoff, K., and J. Stiglitz. (2001). "Modern Economic Theory and Development." In G. Neier and J. Stiglitz (eds.), Frontiers of Development Economics. New York: Oxford University Press. pp. 389–460.

Hollingsworth, J.R. (2002). "On Institutional Embeddedness." In J.R. Hollingsworth, K.H. Muller, and E.J. Hollingsworth (eds.), Advancing Socio-economics: An Institutionalist Perspective. Lanham, MD: Rowan and Littlefield. pp. 87–107.

Jutting, J. (2003). "Institutions and Development: A Critical Review." Working Paper 210, OECD Development Centre.

Kohli, A. (1987). The State and Poverty in India. Cambridge, UK: Cambridge University Press.

———. (2004). State-Directed Development: Political Power and Industrialization in the Global Periphery. Cambridge, UK: Cambridge University Press.

La Porta, R., F. Lopez-de-Silanes, A. Shleifer, and R. Vishny. (1999). "The Quality of Government." Journal of Law, Economics, and Organization 15: 222–279.

List, F. ([1841] 2011). The National System of Political Economy. New York: Cosimo Classics.

Lozano, W. (2012). "Development Opportunities: Politics, the State, and Institutions in the Dominican Republic." In A. Portes and L.D. Smith (eds.), Institutions Count: Their Role and Significance in Latin American Development. Berkeley: University of California Press. pp. 113–129.

Lujan, P.N. (2009). "El Tiempo se Acabo: El Servicio Postal de Mexico en la Encrucijada de su Modernización." In A. Portes (ed.), Las Instituciones en el Desarrollo Latinoamericano. Cuidad de México: Siglo XXI. pp. 117–154.

MacLeod, D. (2004). Downsizing the State: Privatization and the Limits of Neoliberal Reform in Mexico. University Park, PA: Pennsylvania State University Press.

Nee, V., and S. Opper. (2009). "Bureaucracy and Financial Markets." Kyklos 62: 293–315.

North, D.C. (1990). Institutions, Institutional Change, and Economic Performance. Cambridge, UK: Cambridge University Press.

North, D.C., W. Summerhill, and B.R. Weingast. (2000). "Order, Disorder and Economic Change: Latin America vs. North America." In B.B. de Mesquita and H.L. Root (eds.), Governing for Prosperity. New Haven, CT: Yale University Press. pp. 17–58.

O'Donnell, G. (1994). "The State, Democratization, and Some Conceptual Problems." In W.C. Smith, C.H. Acuña, and E.A. Gamarra (eds.), Latin

American Political Economy in the Age of Neoliberal Reform. New Brunswick, NJ: Transaction. pp. 157–179.

Portes, A. (2006). "Institutions and Development: A Conceptual Reanalysis." Population and Development Review 32: 233–262.

———, ed. (2009). Las Instituciones en el Desarrollo Latinoamericano: Un Estudio Comparado. Cuidad de México: Siglo XXI.

———. (2010). Economic Sociology: A Systematic Inquiry. Princeton, NJ: Princeton University Press.

Portes, A., and M.M. Marques, eds. (2015). Valores, Qualidade Institucional e Desenvolvimento em Portugal. Lisbon: Francisco Manuel dos Santos Foundation.

Portes, A., and L.D. Smith. (2008). "Institutions and Development in Latin America: A Comparative Study." Studies in Comparative and International Development 43 (Summer): 101–128.

———, eds. (2012). Institutions Count: Their Role and Significance in Latin American Development. Berkeley: University of California Press.

Portes, A. and J.C. Nava. (2017). "Institutions and National Development: A Comparative Study." Revista Española de Sociologia 26: 1–23.

Prebisch, R. (1964). The Economic Development of Latin America in the Post-War Period. New York: United Nations.

———. (1986). "Notes on Trade from the Standpoint of the Periphery." CEPAL Review 28 (April): 203–216.

Ragin, C. (1987). The Comparative Method: Moving beyond Quantitative and Qualitative Strategies. Berkeley: University of California Press.

———. (2008). Redesigning Social Inquiry: Fuzzy Sets and Beyond. Chicago: University of Chicago Press.

Rauch, J. (1995). "Bureaucracy, Infrastructure, and Economic Growth: Evidence from U.S. Citites during the Progressive Era." American Economic Review 85: 968–979.

Rodriguez-Garavito, C. (2012). "The Colombian Paradox: A Thick Institutional Analysis." In A. Portes and L.D. Smith (eds.), Institutions Count: Their Role and Significance in Latin American Development. Berkeley: University of California Press. pp. 85–112.

Roland, G. (2004). "Understanding Institutional Change: Fast-Moving and Slow-Moving Institutions." Studies in Comparative International Development 38(4): 109–131.

Sabel, C. (1994). "Learning by Monitoring: The Institutions of Economic Development." In N.J. Smelser and R. Swedberg (eds.), Handbook of Economic Sociology. Princeton, NJ: Princeton University Press. pp. 137–165.

Sunkel, O. (2005). "The Unbearable Lightness of Neoliberalism." In B.R. Roberts and C.H. Wood (eds.), Rethinking Development in Latin America. University Park, PA: Pennsylvania State University Press. pp. 55–78.

Thumala, M.A. (2009). "Cultura Militar y Demandas del Mercado: La Modernización de la Dirección General de Aeronautica Civil de Chile." In A. Portes (ed.), Las Instituciones en el Desarrollo Latinoamericano. Cuidad de México: Siglo XXI. pp. 182–209.

Vaz da Silva, N. (2015). "EDP-Energias de Portugal." In A. Portes and M.M. Marques (eds.), Valores, Qualidade Institucional e Desenvolvimento em Portugal. Lisbon: Francisco Manuel dos Santos Foundation. pp. 187–221.

Velasco, J.L. (2008). "Servicio de Administración Tributaria de Mexico." Final report to the project Institutions and Development in Latin America, Center for Migration and Development, Princeton University.

———. (2012). "The Uneven and Paradoxical Development of Mexico's Institutions." In A. Portes and L.D. Smith (eds.), Institutions Count: Their Role and Significance in Latin American Development. Berkeley: University of California Press. pp. 130–166.

Weber, M. ([1904] 1949). "Objectivity in Social Science." In The Methodology of the Social Sciences, translated by E.A. Shils and H.A. Finch. New York: Free Press. pp. 49–112.

———. ([1905] 2009). The Protestant Ethic and the Spirit of Capitalism. New York: W.W. Norton.

Wormald, G., and D. Brieba. (2012). "Institutional Change and Development in Chilean Market Society." In A. Portes and L.D. Smith (eds.), Institutions Count: Their Role and Significance in Latin American Development. Berkeley: University of California Press. pp. 60–84.

Wormald, G., and A. Cardenas. (2008). "Formación y Desarrollo del Servicio de Impuestos Internos (SII) en Chile: Un Analisis Institucional." Final report to the project Institutions and Development in Latin America, Center for Migration and Development, Princeton University.

PART II

The Post-Boom Challenges

6. Latin America's Mounting Development Challenges

José Antonio Ocampo

INTRODUCTION

The decade 2003–13 was, in many ways, an exceptional one for Latin America. Some authors have claimed that the first ten years of the twenty-first century were "golden years" for Latin America and, based on that performance, others suggested that the 2010s were going to be "Latin America's decade"—a term that was coined to contrast it to the "lost decade" of the 1980s.[1] The past decade (the term I will use to refer to the period 2003–13) was outstanding in many ways, particularly in terms of social outcomes. In economic terms, the quinquennium 2003–07, rather than the decade as a whole, was the period that was exceptional. Furthermore, economic conditions are rapidly shifting in the negative direction, as part of a process that is global in nature but has hit the emerging economies in particular in recent years; 2014–16 will mark three consecutive years of very slow regional economic growth, including a strong recession in South America in 2015–16, associated with that experienced by Brazil and Venezuela (IMF, 2015).

Here, I analyze the mounting economic challenges the region is facing. The chapter is organized in four major sections. The first reviews Latin America's social and economic performance over the past decade. The second offers an interpretation of that performance based on external factors that affected it. The third analyzes the region's short- and long-term prospects, arguing, in particular, that overcoming the conditions that have led to the current slowdown will require facing structural challenges that the region has accumulated after market reforms—challenges that were, to a large extent, sidetracked by the exceptional external conditions that facilitated good performance over the past decade. The fourth section concludes the chapter by outlining the policies necessary for restoring dynamic long-term growth in Latin America.

A BRIEF OVERVIEW OF ECONOMIC AND SOCIAL PERFORMANCE DURING THE PAST DECADE

In social terms, improvements in human development in Latin America have been a long-term trend associated with the rapid expansion of social spending since the 1990s. To a large extent, these improvements can be characterized as a "democratic dividend," in that they followed the broad-based return to democracy in most Latin American countries in the 1980s. But what was unique in 2003–13 was the coincidence of this now long-term improvement in human development with one of the most significant advances in poverty reduction in history. The latter was, in turn, associated with the reversal of adverse trends that had been experienced in labor markets and income distribution during the previous two decades.

Regional unemployment fell from 11.3 percent in 2003 to 6.2 percent in 2013, according to data from the Economic Commission for Latin America and the Caribbean (ECLAC) and the International Labor Organization (ILO).[2] An additional 4.6 percent of the population of working age found jobs, with a growing proportion of them in formal employment. However, even more remarkable, given the region's history, were improvements in income inequality, which, mixed with faster economic growth, led to a very rapid process of poverty reduction. Furthermore, this is particularly remarkable given the relatively entrenched adverse trends experienced since the 1980s.

Indeed, income distribution improved in most Latin American countries in 2003–13, giving rise to a burgeoning middle class.[3] For several countries, this was the reversal of the adverse trend they had experienced during the previous two decades, which had been, in turn, the result of the macroeconomic adjustment that took place during the lost decade, the effects of market liberalization, and the emerging countries' crisis which broke out in East Asia in 1997. For some of them—particularly Argentina, Bolivia, Brazil, El Salvador, Mexico, Nicaragua, and Panama—current levels of income distribution stand at better levels than in 1990. Perhaps in a subset of them, those levels are better than in 1980—but this is harder to judge, given the lack of comparable data for 1980.[4]

The joint effect of falling inequality and more rapid economic growth was a spectacular reduction in poverty levels. As Figure 6.1 indicates, 2002 poverty head-count ratios were still above 1980 levels, but then experienced

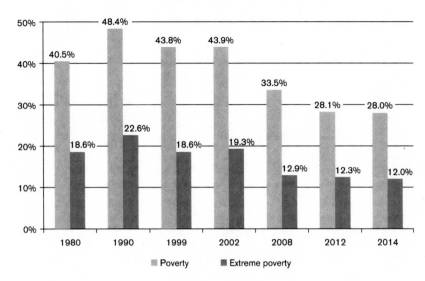

FIGURE 6.1   Poverty and extreme poverty in Latin America, 1980–2014. (Source: ECLAC.)

a reduction of 16 percentage points in 2002–12. This is unique in Latin American history. In fact, it is matched only by the reduction that took place in the 1970s.[5]

These improvements must be understood, in any case, with some caveats. The significant increase in the coverage of education and health that underlie improvements in human development has not been matched by improvements in quality, as indicated by the recent discussion of how poorly the region has scored in the OECD's Program for International Student Assessment tests. Informality fell during the past decade but still predominates in most countries' labor markets, and income inequality continues to be the highest in the world, together with that of some Sub-Saharan African countries. Furthermore, as we will see, improvements in income inequality and poverty seem to have stagnated in recent years as a result of the slowdown in economic growth.

In economic terms, there have also been long-term improvements in several areas. Most countries have now experienced over two decades of low fiscal deficits and over one decade of one-digit inflation rates. The 2003–07 boom led to a sharp reduction in debt ratios and a massive accumulation of foreign exchange reserves. The result was a reduction in the external debt net of foreign exchange reserves from an average of 28.6 percent of gross domestic product (GDP) in 1998–2002 to 5.7 percent in 2008, a level that

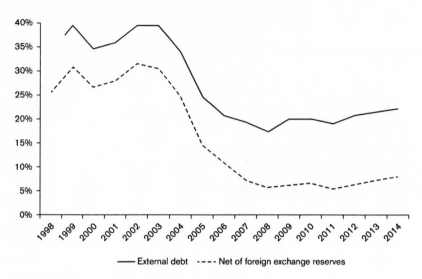

────── External debt   - - - - Net of foreign exchange reserves

FIGURE 6.2   External debt as a percentage of GDP, 1998–2014. (Source: Author estimates based on ECLAC data.)

has only moderately increased since then (Figure 6.2). This result, together with the global financial boom that was typical during these years, led to an extraordinary access to external financing at moderate interest rates, which in 2005–07 reached levels not seen since the second half of the 1980s (Bértola and Ocampo, 2012, 204–206). These exceptional conditions of external borrowing were only briefly interrupted by the collapse of Lehman Brothers in September 2008 (see below). This allowed the region to manage the 2008–09 North Atlantic financial crisis[6] with unprecedented room to maneuver; the region adopted countercyclical monetary and credit policies, which were complemented in a few countries by countercyclical fiscal policies (Ocampo, 2012).

In terms of economic growth, the period 2003–07 was also the best the region has experienced since 1967–74 (Figure 6.3). Furthermore, in contrast to the 1990–97 expansion, investment ratios also increased substantially. These have remained high since 2007, at levels that are only slightly below the peak reached in the second half of the 1970s. Indeed, investment ratios are similar to the peak in the late '70s if we exclude Brazil and Venezuela, two countries that continue to invest less than was typical at that time.

However, the North Atlantic crisis generated a broad-based slowdown and a recession in several countries, notably in Mexico. This was reflected in an overall regional recession in 2009, the worst experienced by the region

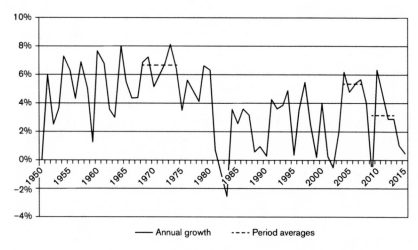

FIGURE 6.3   Growth of Latin American GDP, 1950–2015. (Source: ECLAC.)

since 1983. Recovery was very strong in 2010 but was followed by a strong slowdown, which in 2012 and 2013 led to growth rates under 3 percent a year. Overall, growth slowed from an average of 5.4 percent a year in 2003–07 to 3.2 percent in 2007–13, similar to the mediocre annual growth rate achieved since 1990 (also 3.2 percent in 1990–2014). So, in a significant sense, we can talk of a "quinquennium of Latin America" (i.e., 2003–07) rather than of a "Latin American decade." It should be said, nonetheless, that a few economies did experience an exceptional decade—notably Panama, Peru, and Uruguay, which grew at average annual rates of over 6 percent a year in 2003–13.

To take a still more nuanced approach, even in 2003–07, Latin America grew at a slower rate than the average for the emerging and developing world—which reached 7.4 percent a year according to United Nations data.[7] Indeed, the region grew during its golden quinquennium at slower rates than all of the Asian subregions, Sub-Saharan Africa, and the transition economies of Eastern Europe and Central Asia. Latin America surpassed North Africa by only a narrow margin.

AN INTERPRETATION OF RECENT ECONOMIC TRENDS

How can we interpret economic trends over the past decade? Beyond the advances in macroeconomic policies and outcomes, what characterized the period 2003–07 was the extraordinary coincidence of four positive external factors: (1) migration opportunities (regular and irregular), particularly to the United States and Spain; (2) booming international trade; (3) the upward phase of a long-term cycle (or "super-cycle") of commodity prices; and (4) broad access to external financing at terms that, as already indicated, were the best since the second half of the 1970s. Only one negative factor can be identified: the strong competition of China in the U.S. market that negatively affected Mexican manufacturing exports, which explains why Mexico was the poorest performer in the region during those years (3.9 percent vs. a Latin American average of 5.4 percent).

The first two of these positive conditions disappeared with the North Atlantic financial crisis. Non-oil prices started to weaken in 2012, and oil prices collapsed in the second half of 2014. Thus, only one element of the factors that fed the boom remained—good access to external financing—and this may be at risk now, due to the turmoil in emerging economies' capital markets (e.g., the Chinese-led turmoil of 2005 and early 2006) and the ongoing rise of interest rates in the United States.

Migration opportunities are, indeed, largely gone. There is now net migration out of Spain and, according to the Pew Hispanic Institute, the number of unauthorized migrants in the United States fell during 2008–09 and has leveled off since then (Passel et al., 2014). A major effect was the reduction in remittances during the worst years of the North Atlantic crisis, which was followed by a gradual recovery; in 2014, they finally surpassed, by a small margin, the record levels of 2007–08 (IDB–MIF, 2015).

In turn, international trade experienced a dramatic initial contraction (in fact, the worst peacetime contraction in world history) after the collapse of Lehman Brothers. Although it recovered fast, international trade has settled since 2011 at a relatively slow rate of growth. The net effect, as Figure 6.4 shows, is that the world economy has experienced in recent years the slowest rate of growth in trade since World War II. This is due not only to the slower growth of the world economy but also to the lowest elasticity of world trade volumes to GDP (i.e., the ratio of the growth rate of trade to that of GDP) of the postwar period. As major global institutions have recently recognized, this reflects not only cyclical but structural factors associated with the dynamics of world trade.[8]

Commodity prices fell rapidly after the Lehman shock but recovered relatively fast. However, non-oil commodity prices peaked in 2011 and started falling moderately since then. This was reflected in the terms of trade of Latin American countries, which experienced in 2014 their third consecutive year of deterioration (ECLAC, 2015a) and continued to fall in 2015–16. The decline was initially modest, and stronger for minerals and

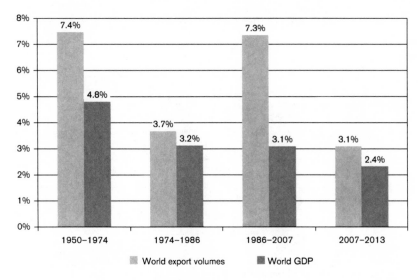

FIGURE 6.4   Growth of world GDP and world export volumes, 1950–2013. GDP is estimated at market exchange rates and prices. (Source: Author estimates based on United Nations data until 2007 and International Monetary Fund for recent years.)

tropical agriculture than for oil and temperate-zone agriculture, but it became widespread after mid-2014 (Figure 6.5). As we will see, the risks associated with the winding down of the positive phase of the commodity super-cycle are substantial.

As in the past, external financing continues to be pro-cyclical, but the associated cycles have moderated substantially. As Figure 6.6 shows, the Lehman shock generated a reversal of the very favorable external financing that prevailed prior to the crisis, as reflected in the evolution of risk spreads and total yields of Latin American bonds. But the shock was much more moderate than the one that the region experienced after the sequence of the emerging countries' crisis of the late 1990s. The region was shut out of private capital markets only for about a year,[9] compared to six years in the late '90s to early 2000s and eight years during the Latin American debt crisis of the 1980s. Furthermore, the shocks generated by the Eurozone crisis in 2011–12 had only minor effects on Latin American risk spreads. In addition, the region was only weakly affected by the U.S. Federal Reserve's gradual tapering of bond purchases, because the stronger initial shock when tapering was announced in May 2013 was partly reversed during the first half of 2014. But, as we will see in the next section, conditions have worsened since mid-2014.

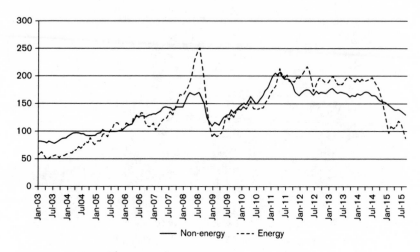

FIGURE 6.5   Monthly commodity prices, 2003–2015 (2005 = 100).
(Source: International Monetary Fund.)

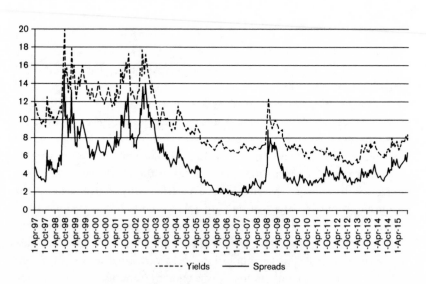

FIGURE 6.6   Risk spreads and yields of Latin American bonds,
April 1997–August 2015. (Source: J.P. Morgan.)

The strong resilience of Latin America's external financing to recent shocks has two interlinked explanations: (1) the relatively low debt ratios that the region has exhibited since the mid-2000s (Figure 6.2), which make it look like a lower-risk destination compared to the region's past record as well as to other potential destinations of capital flows; and (2) the high liquidity that characterizes global financial markets, due to the expansionary monetary policies of all major developed countries. The latter is likely to continue, although it will moderate in the United States as the Federal Reserve has already entered a phase of gradual normalization of its monetary policy.

GOING FORWARD

Short-Term Uncertainties

Overall, this means that the exceptional conditions that facilitated the 2003–07 Latin American boom were followed by more mixed external conditions since the North Atlantic financial crisis. Many added uncertainties are now at play, as reflected in the significant slowdown of emerging economies. This is associated, in turn, with a contraction of international trade, particularly in value terms, and with the turmoil in emerging countries' capital markets, which was particularly strong in August and September 2015. The latter included China's stock market collapse, its global repercussions, its effects on commodity prices, the August devaluation of the renminbi, the downgrade of Brazilian debt to junk status by Standard and Poor's on September 9, and the major uncertainties surrounding the possible increase of the Federal Reserve's funds rate. The latter was cleared for a time by the Fed's decision to keep those rates unchanged as a response to global uncertainties, though with the implicit assumption that it would be increased anyway in the near future.

Many of the added uncertainties Latin America is facing are associated with the Chinese economy. This reflects the strong slowdown of the Chinese export and industrial engines in 2015, which is not totally reflected in its GDP figures,[10] but also the stock market collapse during the summer of 2015, the high corporate debt ratios of Chinese firms, and, equally important, the sense of the reduced degrees of freedom and the hesitation that authorities have transmitted, in sharp contrast with the major decisions and certainty about their policy stance that they conveyed in the face of the 2008–09 shock. The Chinese connection is, of course, critical for Latin America, due to the fact that it has been the most dynamic trading partner for the region over the past decade (ECLAC, 2015b, ch. III), but also due to the centrality of Chinese demand in global commodity markets and the

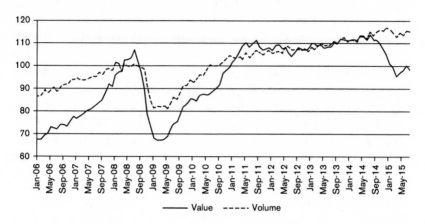

FIGURE 6.7   World exports, 2006–2015 (January–June 2008 = 100). (Source: CPB Netherlands Bureau.)

significant degree of contagion that characterizes international financial markets, which was revealed in the global repercussions of the August 2015 Chinese stock market crash.

The elements of the recent trade turmoil are shown in Figure 6.7. The monthly numbers reproduced in this figure show the very slow growth of international trade since 2011, consistent with the fact, already pointed out, that world trade has experienced in recent years the slowest growth since World War II. The recent events include the stagnation or even small contraction in the volume of world exports since late 2014 and the strong reduction of the value of world exports since mid-2014. As the background information for Figure 6.7 indicates,[11] the first of these processes has been essentially associated with Emerging Asia, which had been the most dynamic component of world trade after the Lehman collapse; the volume of exports of Emerging Asia in 2015 shows a stagnation compared to a year before. This is what the Chinese export data also indicate.

In turn, the reduction in world export values is associated with the collapse of commodity prices shown in Figure 6.5.[12] Non-oil commodity prices have fallen by about a third with respect to their 2011 peak, and energy prices by half. If real commodity prices follow the long-term "super-cycles" they have experienced since the late nineteenth century (long-term price cycles of around thirty years), we may be seeing the first phase of a prolonged period of falling and low real commodity prices (Erten and Ocampo, 2013). In other words, this may not be just a short-term cyclical phenomenon generated by the slowdown in Chinese demand.

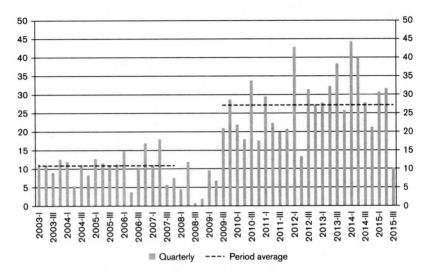

FIGURE 6.8   Quarterly issuance of Latin American bonds, in billions of U.S. dollars, 2003–2015. (Source: ECLAC, based on Latin Finance Bonds Database.)

In turn, although access to international finance has continued to be relatively positive, conditions in this regard may be changing. This is reflected in the mounting information on net capital outflows from emerging economies that have taken place for several quarters now. In terms of risk spreads, the accumulation of the negative shocks associated with the collapse of commodity prices during the second semester of 2014 and the turmoil in global markets in July–September 2015 was an increase of risk spreads of around two percentage points (200 basis points). This also had major effects on exchange rates in several countries, particularly Brazil and Colombia. Brazil's downgrade by Standard and Poor's, but also the economic and political uncertainties that surround the conjuncture of the largest Latin American economy, is reflected in the strong increase in Brazil's risk spreads, particularly since mid-September 2015, which is the major explanation for the widening of Latin America's spreads vis-à-vis the average for emerging countries. In any case, as Figure 6.6 indicates, the accumulated increases in the costs of financing are still smaller than those experienced after the September 2008 Lehman Brothers bankruptcy or during the emerging countries' crisis of the late twentieth century, which took off in East Asia in 1997.

This is, in fact, what the data on bond issues also show. The third quarter of 2015 was, in this regard, the worst since the North Atlantic crisis (Figure 6.8). However, the tendency of bond markets to temporarily dry out is not

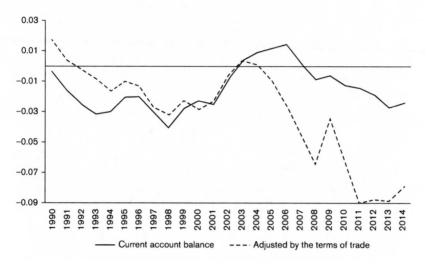

FIGURE 6.9   Current account balance as a proportion of GDP, with and without terms-of-trade adjustment, 1990–2014. The adjustment is an estimate of gains and losses of export values associated with improvements or deterioration of terms of trade in relation to 2003. (Source: author estimates based on ECLAC data.)

an uncommon phenomenon. The current turmoil is weaker than that which followed the Lehman collapse. Furthermore, it is in fact similar to the issuance of Latin American bonds in 2003–07, and thus only weak if the comparison is done with the exceptional market for Latin American bonds that characterized the years after the North Atlantic crisis, in which Latin American bond issuance almost tripled in relation to precrisis levels.

In the face of changing external conditions, the greatest strength is low external indebtedness mixed with high foreign exchange reserves (i.e., strong external balance sheets; see Figure 6.2), as well as the broader perception (a few countries aside) of stronger macroeconomic management than in the past. The greatest risk is the potential current account deficit of the balance of payments, associated with the fact that the region has spent and, in fact, *overspent* the commodity boom.[13] Indeed, despite the very favorable terms of trade, the region has been running since 2012 a growing current account deficit, which in macroeconomic terms indicates that aggregate spending has increasingly surpassed aggregate production. This is reflected in Figure 6.9, which shows a simple estimate of the current account adjusted by the evolution of the terms of trade (taking the start of the commodity boom, the year 2003, as a reference). One way to understand the estimates in this graph is that the "potential" current account deficit of Latin America (i.e., the current account deficit estimated at 2003 terms of trade) was about 9 percent of GDP in 2011–13, a situation that is much worse than the deficit estimated at current prices and, particularly, the deficit that prevailed prior to the crisis of the late 1990s according to either of the two estimates. With the fall in commodity prices, and despite the significant slowdown and the strong depreciation of several of the region's exchange rates, this will be reflected in 2015 in an even higher effective current account deficit. This, together with a similar phenomenon in the fiscal area—the much weaker fiscal balances vs. those that prevailed prior to the North Atlantic crisis—explain why Latin America lacks the degrees of freedom to adopt countercyclical policies that it enjoyed after the Lehman Brothers shock. As a result of these limited degrees of freedom, the deterioration in external conditions led in 2015–16 to the strongest recession since the debt crisis of the 1980s (Figure 6.3), which has been particularly severe in South America.

Long-Term Issues

The sharp slowdown in Latin America—and particularly in South America—led to a stagnation or reversal of the progress that took place during the past decade. The overall employment rate (the proportion of working-age population employed) has been declining since mid-2013 (ECLAC, 2015a, fig. 1.26), which was compensated by reductions in labor market participation but will lead to an increase in open unemployment in 2015. Advances in poverty have ceased (see Figure 6.1), and this is also most likely true of income distribution, though data on this issue will come later.

Furthermore, improvements in social conditions are starting to face a more difficult environment. This is true in terms of the expansion of social spending that fed improvements in human development since 1990. Going forward, this may require designing a more redistributive taxation system, an area in which Latin America lags significantly behind OECD countries.[14] Reducing informality, which continues to be very high in several countries, will also be a major challenge. This is also true of the quality of education, essential for the major long-term economic challenges that the region faces.

The central issue in this regard is the slow long-term economic growth that has prevailed since market reforms were put in place a quarter of a century ago (Bértola and Ocampo, 2012, ch. 5). There are several interpretations of such weak performance, but the most important one is that the orthodox export-led model that Latin America adopted during this period—

that is, a model that relied essentially on trade liberalization to generate the signal to specialize according to the comparative advantage of countries—has *not* proved to be a strong engine of economic growth. By the adjective "orthodox," I mean that the export-led model followed by Latin America is different from the equally export-led model pursued by rapidly growing East Asian economies, the latter exhibiting a clear focus on the technological upgrading of the export basket, as well as significant state intervention to facilitate this process. The Latin American variant was able to deliver, at best, mediocre rates of growth in the region, even in the face of the spectacular expansion of world trade that characterized the two decades prior to the North Atlantic financial crisis (Figure 6.4). As we have seen, growth only reached 3.2 percent in 2007–13 and the region entered into a strong recession in 2015–16.

This is, of course, consistent with the views long espoused by the structuralist tradition that the technological upgrading of the production structure is the key to dynamic growth (see, e.g., Ocampo et al., 2009). In export-led models, this means that the technological upgrading of the export basket is the key to success. This may not be confined to manufactured goods; it should include the technological upgrading of natural-resource production and the development of modern services. This is why I prefer the term *production-sector strategies* to the older concept of *industrial policies*.[15]

The problems generated by Latin America's patterns of specialization in inducing poor growth and productivity performance are now clear.[16] The associated problems include a premature deindustrialization and abandonment of prior production-sector policies, which were substituted at best by "competitiveness" strategies largely aimed at facilitating private business activity (i.e., at improving the "business environment"). The region specialized according to its static comparative advantages in sectors that offered fewer opportunities for diversification, dynamic technological change, and improvements in product quality (Hausmann, 2011; Palma, 2011). The technological gap widened in relation not only to the dynamic Asian economies but also to the more developed natural-resource-intensive economies. This is reflected, for example, in a lower share of engineering-intensive industries, the meager resources used for research and development, and a near absence of patenting compared to those groups of economies (ECLAC, 2012, ch. II). The massive deindustrialization that has taken place since the 1980s is shown in Figure 6.10; this graph also indicates that the 2003–07 subperiod was an exception to the trend but

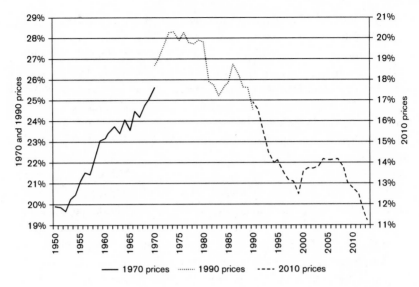

FIGURE 6.10 Share of manufacturing in GDP, 1950–2013. (Source: ECLAC.)

was followed by massive reduction in the share of manufacturing in GDP in 2007–13, which drove downward that share for the past decade as a whole.

CONCLUSION

Given these trends, there is a need to return to more active production-sector strategies if the region wants to speed up long-term economic growth. These include "horizontal" policies to improve education, increase research and development funds and capacities, encourage investment, and significantly increase infrastructure investment. But this should be accompanied by more sector-specific policies to encourage the complementary investments necessary to develop new economic activities, which will vary country by country, according to their specific national characteristics. It is true that these "vertical" policies involve risks of failure and rent seeking—problems that, in any case, are not unique to them.[17] Developing such new activities is a learning process in which "winners" are, in a sense, created rather than chosen *ex ante*. The new activities that should be promoted depend on domestic capacities, must be done in close partnership with the private sector, and should have technological upgrading as the central criterion. And they must be supported by competitive exchange rates.

Needless to say, the need for clear attention on technological upgrading is critical, given the prospect of a lack of dynamism in world trade and the evidence that Latin America is ceasing to be a region of abundant low-skilled labor—a fact that is, no doubt, one of the factors contributing to a better income distribution. Given this outlook, three additional ingredients are essential. The first is the need to continue linking to China, but in a way that overcomes the current pattern that characterizes Latin America's trade with the Asian giant, in which the region exports a handful of commodities in exchange for an increasingly diversified array of manufactured goods—a specialization pattern that has amply benefited China. The lack of dynamism in world trade and the premium it places on domestic markets create the need for a second ingredient: a new emphasis on the "expanded domestic market" fostered by the Latin American integration process. But this means stopping the political stalemate that currently characterizes integration processes in Latin America, particularly in South America. The third ingredient is overcoming the significant lag in physical infrastructure that the region has accumulated since the debt crisis. In this regard, public-sector investment has remained depressed since the "lost decade" of the 1980s, and public-private partnerships did not deliver as much in terms of infrastructure development as expected. According to existing studies, infrastructure investments should at least double in relation to the low levels that have prevailed in the region over the past several decades.[18]

Technological upgrading, high-quality education, significant diversification of trade with China, betting on strong regional integration processes, and heavy investing in physical infrastructure are, together, the structural keys to dynamic long-term growth in Latin America. The recent slowdown has made clear that advances in all these areas have been limited at best, and that market reforms actually had adverse effects on some of them. Indeed, it is this "structuralist agenda," which follows the Latin American tradition, that should prevail over the new call for "structural reforms," the term that has been coined in international debates to refer to market reforms, but which have failed to deliver rapid economic growth in Latin America over the past quarter century.

. . .

José Antonio Ocampo is a professor, co-president of the Initiative for Policy Dialogue, and a member of the Committee on Global Thought at Columbia University. He is also chair of ECOSOC's Committee for Development Policy and a nonresident fellow in the Baker Institute's Latin America Initiative at Rice University. Formerly, he was United Nations Under-Secretary General for Economic and Social Affairs, executive secretary of the Economic Commission for Latin America and the Caribbean, and served as minister of finance, of planning, and of agriculture in Colombia. This paper builds upon two briefs published by the Baker Institute (Ocampo, 2014, 2015) and reflects on regional trends up to 2015, with a few updates to reflect current events.

NOTES

1. See, for instance, Talvi and Munyo (2013) for the "golden years" idea, and Moreno (2011) for the concept of "Latin America's decade."

2. See ECLAC and ILO (2014).

3. See, for example, Gasparini and Lustig (2011), ECLAC (2013, part I), World Bank (2013), and Cornia (2014).

4. See the estimates regularly produced by the United Nations Economic Commission for Latin America and the Caribbean and regularly reported in the *Social Panorama of Latin America*, as well as those produced by the Centro de Estudios Distributivos, Laborales y Sociales of Universidad de La Plata (CEDLAS).

5. On improvements during the 1970s, see Londoño and Székely (2000), although there are reasons to think that they probably overestimated them.

6. I prefer this term to "global financial crisis" since, although the crisis had global effects, the financial meltdown was concentrated in the United States and Western Europe.

7. These data are published regularly in the UN's *World Economic Situation and Prospects*. See the latest at United Nations (2015).

8. See WTO (2015), World Bank (2015, 169–173), and the work of IMF researchers Constatinescu et al. (2015).

9. Of course, a few countries have been partly or totally shut out from global private capital markets as a result of external default and debt restructuring (Argentina) and/or the perception of political risk (Venezuela). Ecuador belonged to these categories, but in recent years it has partly joined the group of countries with access to private markets. Argentina also did so after its negotiations with the "holdout" creditors in early 2016.

10. This has raised significant questions about the quality of official GDP statistics, which may be underestimating the magnitude of the growth slowdown.

11. See the CPB World Trade Monitor, July 2015, at http://www.cpb.nl/en/number/cpb-world-trade-monitor-july-2015.

12. It has also been partly associated with the appreciation of the U.S. dollar, as the index is estimated in that currency.

13. This was already true at the end of the 2003–07 boom (see Ocampo, 2009) and worsened in later years (Ocampo, 2012). For a detailed analysis, see IMF (2013).

14. See, for example, Goñi et al. (2011) and Hanni et al. (2015).

15. Specifically, the term *industrial policies* is generally understood in Latin America as referring to manufactured goods. In English terminology it has the broader meaning I give to *production-sector strategies*.

16. See, in this regard, an analysis of productivity performance in Latin America since 1990 in ECLAC (2014, part 2, ch. 3).

17. They were indeed present in market reforms, notably in the privatization process in several countries.

18. See, in particular, CAF (2014).

REFERENCES

Bértola, Luis, and José Antonio Ocampo (2012), The Economic Development of Latin America since Independence. Oxford, UK: Oxford University Press.

CAF (Development Bank of Latin America) (2014), "Infraestructura en el desarrollo de América Latina." Caracas: CAF.

Constatinescu, Cristina, Aadita Matoo, and Michel Ruta (2015), "The Global Trade Slowdown: Cyclical or Structural?" IMF Working Paper 15/6 [see also, by the same authors, "Slow Trade," in Finance & Development, December 2014].

Cornia, Giovanni Andrea (2014), "Inequality Trends and Their Determinants: Latin America over the Period 1990–2010," in Giovanni Andrea Cornia (ed.), Falling Inequality in Latin America: Policy Changes and Lessons. Oxford, UK: Oxford University Press.

ECLAC (Economic Commission for Latin America and the Caribbean) (2012), "Cambio estructural para la igualdad: Una visión integrada del desarrollo." Santiago: ECLAC.

——— (2013), "Social Panorama of Latin America 2012." Santiago: ECLAC.

——— (2014), "Economic Survey of Latin America and the Caribbean." Santiago: ECLAC.

——— (2015a), "Economic Survey of Latin America and the Caribbean." Santiago: ECLAC.

——— (2015b), "Latin America and the Caribbean and China: Towards a New Era in Economic Cooperation." Santiago: ECLAC.

ECLAC and ILO (International Labor Organization) (2014), Coyuntura Laboral en América Latina y el Caribe, no. 10. Santiago: ECLAC.

Erten, Bilge, and José Antonio Ocampo (2013), "Super-cycles of Commodity Prices since the Mid-nineteenth Century," World Development, 44, pp. 14–30.

Gasparini, Leonardo, and Nora Lustig (2011), "The Rise and Fall of Income Inequality in Latin America," in José Antonio Ocampo and Jaime Ros (eds.), The Oxford Handbook of Latin American Economics. Oxford, UK: Oxford University Press.

Goñi, Edwin, J. Humberto López, and Luis Servén (2011), "Fiscal Redistribution and Income Inequality in Latin America," World Development, 39, pp. 1558–1569.

Hanni, Michael, Ricardo Martner, and Andrea Podestá (2015), "El potencial redistributivo de la fiscalidad en América Latina," Revista de la CEPAL, 116 (August).

Hausmann, Ricardo (2011), "Structural Transformation and Economic Growth in Latin America," in José Antonio Ocampo and Jaime Ros (eds.), The Oxford Handbook of Latin American Economics. Oxford, UK: Oxford University Press.

IDB–MIF (Inter-American Development Bank–Multilateral Investment Fund) (2015), "Remittances in Latin America and the Caribbean Set a New Record High in 2014." Washington, DC: Inter-American Development Bank.

IMF (International Monetary Fund) (2013), "World Economic and Financial Surveys, Regional Economic Outlook, Western Hemisphere: Time to Rebuild Policy Space." Washington, DC: IMF.

———— (2015), "World Economic and Financial Surveys, Regional Economic Outlook, Western Hemisphere: Adjusting under Pressure." Washington, DC: IMF.

Londoño, Juan Luis, and Miguel Székely (2000), "Persistent Poverty and Excess Inequality: Latin America, 1970–1995," Journal of Applied Economics, 3, pp. 93–134.

Moreno, Luis Alberto (2011), "La Década de América Latina y el Caribe, una oportunidad real." Washington, DC: Inter-American Development Bank.

Ocampo, José Antonio (2009), "Latin America and the Global Financial Crisis," Cambridge Journal of Economics, 33, pp. 703–724.

———— (2012), "How Well Has Latin America Fared during the Global Financial Crisis?" in Michael Cohen (ed.), The Global Economic Crisis in Latin America: Impacts and Prospects. Milton Park, UK: Routledge.

———— (2014), "Latin America's Mounting Economic Challenges," Baker Institute, Rice University, October. http://bakerinstitute.org/research/latin-americas-mounting-economic-challenges/.

———— (2015), "Latin America's Recent Economic Turmoil," Baker Institute, Rice University, October. http://bakerinstitute.org/research/economic-turmoil-latin-america/.

Ocampo, José Antonio, Codrina Rada, and Lance Taylor (2009), Growth and Policy in Developing Countries: A Structuralist Approach. New York: Columbia University Press.

Palma, José Gabriel (2011), "Why Has Productivity Growth in Latin America Practically Stagnated since 1980?" in José Antonio Ocampo and Jaime Ros (eds.), The Oxford Handbook of Latin American Economics. Oxford, UK: Oxford University Press.

Passel, Jeffrey S., D'Vera Cohn, Jens Manuel Krogstad, and Ana Gonzalez-Barrera (2014), "As Growth Stalls, Unauthorized Migrant Population Becomes More Settled." Pew Research Center, September. http://www.pewhispanic.org/files/2014/09/2014-09-03_Unauthorized-Final.pdf.

Talvi, Ernesto, and Ignacio Munyo (2013), "Are the Golden Years for Latin America Over?" in Latin America Macroeconomic Outlook: A Global Perspective. Brookings Global–CERES Economic and Social Policy in Latin America Initiative, June.

United Nations (2015), "World Economic Situation and Prospects 2015." New York: United Nations.

World Bank (2013), "Economic Mobility and the Rise of the Latin American Middle Class." Washington, DC: World Bank.

——— (2015), "Global Economic Prospects, January." Washington, DC: World Bank.

WTO (World Trade Organization) (2015), "Trade Statistics and Outlook: Modest Recovery to continue in 2015 and 2016 Following Three Years of Weak Expansion." https://www.wto.org/english/news_e/pres15_e/pr739_e.htm.

7. Economic Performance in Latin America in the 2000s

Recession, Recovery, and Resilience?

Juan Carlos Moreno-Brid and Stefanie Garry

INTRODUCTION

In this chapter, we analyze Latin America's economic performance with the objective of assessing whether it entered a new phase of high and robust long-term growth in the early 2000s. We consider, in particular, the extent to which the region has been able to alleviate or remove important restrictions that have often constrained its growth path: fiscal and balance-of-payments constraints as well as inflationary pressures. Our work is rooted in the neo-structuralist perspective and thus focuses on the composition of demand, with emphasis on the dynamics of exports and investment. One feature of this chapter is a comparison of different aspects of Latin America's economic performance in 2000–13 vis-à-vis the 1990s, when neoliberal reforms were being implemented and, in some countries, deepened.

LATIN AMERICA: NO LONGER TRAPPED IN A LOW, SLOW GROWTH PARADOX?

After its "lost decade" in the 1980s and a slow and unstable economic rebound in the '90s, Latin America emerged in the early 2000s as a dynamic economy, driven by exports and foreign direct investment, supported by prudent fiscal management and low inflation (Ocampo, 2009). Increasingly, observers perceived that the region was decoupling from the industrialized world. Although its gross domestic product (GDP) fell in 2009, the quick rebound in the following year strengthened the view that Latin America had solid macroeconomic foundations (IMF, 2014; ECLAC, 2013b). Some saw it as proof that the region was finally reaping the benefits of the neoliberal reforms put in place years before. In this regard, Dabla-Norris et al. (2013) and Rojas-Suarez

(2009) considered it as the consequence, in part, of an improved institutional context buoyed over the previous decades by market reforms. Trade openness and investment deregulation favored technology transfer and the buildup of a better business climate for private investment (Spillan et al., 2014). Other analysts, from a neo-structural perspective, considered that this phase was mainly driven by the extraordinary improvement in the region's terms of trade, coupled with a shift of its export sector in favor of primary products, all of which gave room to boost private and public consumption without putting excessive pressure on the fiscal budget and the balance of payments (Bértola and Ocampo, 2012; Moreno-Brid, 2015).

As Table 7.1 indicates, Latin America's annual average rate of expansion of real GDP was 1.8 percent in the '80s, climbed to 3.1 percent in the '90s, and increased further to 3.6 percent in 2000–08. Its collapse in 2009 (−1.2 percent) was less acute than that of the European Union (−4.2 percent) or the fall of GDP in advanced economies as a whole (−3.5 percent) (IMF, 2013b). In 2010 the region's economic activity sharply rebounded (6.3 percent), due partly to the resilience of its financial and banking system and partly to the adoption of countercyclical policies. Such policies included the depreciation of the nominal exchange rate, the reduction of interest rates, and the expansion of public expenditure, in particular on programs oriented toward social assistance and employment protection. However, since 2011 economic activity has slowed in the region. Real GDP rose 2.9 percent in 2013 and just 1.1 percent in 2014, and it was not expected to gain more momentum in 2015.

The favorable evolution of the long-term rates of expansion of GDP since the '80s, however, masks the fact that a number of Latin American economies have suffered major balance-of-payments or financial crises. Just recall the "tequila crisis" triggered by Mexico in 1994–95 and the "tango and corralito crisis" detonated by Argentina in the early 2000s, all of which had significant contagion effects in the region. Moreover, the vast majority of countries have been subject to acute cyclical fluctuations that impinge on their long-term rate of expansion. Pérez Caldentey et al. (2014) show that the business cycle in Latin America has two distinctive features that have detrimental implications for its long-term growth. First, the duration of periods of economic expansion in Latin America is shorter, and in many cases weaker, than that in other world regions. Second, periods of contraction in Latin America's business cycle tend to be similar in length and intensity to those in other regions. This has damaging impacts on the region's prospects for strengthening long-term trends in investment, productivity, and growth.

The region has also made substantial gains in the fight against inflation and fiscal indiscipline. Indeed, the annual average increase in the consumer

TABLE 7.1 Key Macroeconomic Indicators for Latin America, 1980–2014

Indicators	1980s	1990s	2000–08	2009	2010	2011	2012	2013	2014
GDP growth (%)	1.8	3.1	3.6	-1.2	6.3	4.7	2.9	2.9	1.1
GDP growth per capita (%)	-0.4	1.4	2.2	-2.3	5.1	3.6	1.8	1.8	0.1
Fiscal balance (% of GDP)	-3.6	-1.6	-1.6	-2.8	-1.8	-1.6	-2.1	-2.5	-2.5
Inflation (%)	126.3	82.7	7.7	5.6	5.7	6.7	5.7	6.6	8.3
Poverty rate (%)	41.9	45.4	37.5	32.8	31	29.6	28.1	28.1	28.0
Extreme poverty rate (%)	19.7	20.3	14.7	13	12.1	11.6	11.3	11.7	12.0
Exports (% of GDP)	9.4	12.5	21.4	20.6	30.8	36.2	35.8	35.0	–

SOURCES: CEPALSTAT, CEPAL Cuadernos Estadísticos no. 37, World Bank World Development Indicators, and the IMF World Economic Outlook Database (October 2014 update). Fiscal data for the 1980s include the average for Argentina, Chile, Colombia, Brazil, Venezuela, Peru, and Mexico.
NOTE: Average growth for yearly groupings. Growth rates reflect geometric means.

TABLE 7.2 Sub-Regional GDP Growth Rates in South America
and Mexico, 1990–2014 (%)[a]

Region	1990s	2000–08	2009	2010	2011	2012	2013	2014
Latin America	3.1	3.6	−1.2	6.3	4.7	2.9	2.9	1.1
South America	3.0	3.9	−0.2	6.7	5.0	2.5	3.2	0.6
Mexico	3.5	2.4	−4.7	5.2	3.9	4.0	1.4	2.2

SOURCE: ECLAC, based on official figures.

NOTE: This chapter focuses on the economies of South America and Mexico, the largest contributors to Latin America's GDP, and examines the distinctive long-term economic performance among three of its broad groupings based on their main exports. The analysis of Central American economies has been left out because we considered that given their different sizes, export and productive structures, and even history, an in-depth analysis would require a far longer text.

[a] Average growth for yearly groupings. Growth rates for country groupings reflect geometric means.

price index dropped from a three-figure digit in the '80s, to two figures in the '90s, to 7.7 percent in the 2000s, and has gone even lower in recent years. In turn, and not unrelated, the fiscal deficit has declined from an average of −3.6 percent of GDP in the '80s to less than half in the following two decades. In 2009 it jumped to −2.8 percent as a consequence of the combined results of the recession and the compensatory, expansionary policies adopted to face the crisis (Bértola and Ocampo, 2012; Daude et al., 2013; De Gregorio, 2013; ECLAC, 2013c). Its subsequent increase pushed it to −2.5 percent in 2013, a higher but still enviable figure in the current international context.

This advance in economic matters has raised the standard of living of people in the region. Most importantly, it brought about a significant reduction of the incidence of poverty, including extreme poverty. Certainly, as Tables 7.2 and 7.3 indicate, the improvements in macroeconomic performance have not been the same throughout Latin America's subregions and individual countries. To varying degrees, such heterogeneity reflects differences in their productive structures, trade patterns, economic policies, incidence of external shocks, and even political events. Institutional factors may also affect their growth performance and advances in economic stabilization (De Gregorio, 2013).

In South America, the most dynamic economies in 2000–08 were the exporters of metals and minerals (Peru and Chile) and hydrocarbon exporters (notably Venezuela, Ecuador, and Colombia). The former group's real GDP expanded at an annual average rate of 4.8 percent, and the latter's at 4.5 percent, supported by a booming foreign demand that led to a steep rise in their world prices (ECLAC, 2013b; Céspedes and Velasco, 2012). On average, and

TABLE 7.3 Average GDP Growth Rates (%) in Latin America for Selected Economies, 1990–2014

Products and exporters	1990s	2000– 08	2009	2010	2011	2012	2013	2014
Metals and minerals	5.4	4.8	−0.2	6.8	6.1	5.7	4.8	2.1
Chile	6.4	4.2	−1.0	5.8	5.8	5.5	4.2	1.9
Peru	4.0	5.8	1.0	8.5	6.5	6.0	5.8	2.4
Agro-industrial products	3.9	3.6	0.2	9.5	8	0.9	3.5	0.9
Argentina	4.1	3.6	0.1	9.5	8.4	0.8	2.9	0.5
Paraguay	2.3	3.3	−4.0	13.1	4.3	−1.2	14.2	4.4
Uruguay	3.0	2.8	4.2	7.8	5.2	3.3	5.1	3.5
Exporters of hydrocarbons	2.4	4.5	−0.4	1.7	5.7	4.8	3.6	1.2
Bolivia	3.8	3.9	3.4	4.1	5.2	5.2	6.8	5.4
Colombia	2.7	4.4	1.7	4.0	6.6	4.0	4.9	4.6
Ecuador	2.0	4.6	0.6	3.5	7.9	5.2	4.6	3.8
Venezuela	2.1	4.5	−3.2	−1.5	4.2	5.6	1.3	−4.0
Major manufacturing								
Brazil	2.6	3.7	−0.2	7.6	3.9	1.8	2.7	0.1
Mexico	3.5	2.4	−4.7	5.2	3.9	4.0	1.4	2.1
Central America	4.8	4.5	0.0	4.9	4.7	4.4	4.4	4.9
Costa Rica	5.2	5.0	−1.0	5.0	4.5	5.2	3.4	3.5
Dominican Republic	6.1	5.0	0.9	8.3	2.8	2.6	4.8	7.3
El Salvador	4.6	2.6	−3.1	1.4	2.2	1.9	1.8	2.0
Guatemala	4.1	3.8	0.5	2.9	4.2	3.0	3.7	4.2
Honduras	3.3	5.0	−2.4	3.7	3.8	4.1	2.8	3.1
Nicaragua	3.4	3.5	−2.8	3.2	6.2	5.1	4.5	4.7
Panama	5.1	6.4	4.0	5.9	10.8	10.2	8.4	6.2
Cuba	−1.4	6.0	1.5	2.4	2.8	3.0	2.7	1.3
Haiti	0.0	0.5	3.1	−5.5	5.5	2.9	4.2	2.8

SOURCE: ECLAC, based on official figures.
NOTE: Average growth for yearly groupings. Growth rates for country groupings reflect geometric means.

up to 2014, the subgroups of exporters of metals and minerals and of hydro-carbons have shown the greatest resilience in the aftermath of the international financial crisis, though their dynamism has tapered in light of the downturn in global commodity prices. Influenced by the overall slowdown in global activity in 2014, the economies of South America and Mexico also showed subdued expansion (0.6 percent on average), and that of Venezuela declined sharply with a 4.1 percent contraction in GDP.

Brazil and Mexico expanded modestly in the '90s. In the years leading up to the 2009 crisis, Brazil grew somewhat faster (3.6 percent) but Mexico less so (2.4 percent). Both economies rebounded quickly, but their growth subsequently cooled off, casting doubts on their future role as drivers of regional expansion. Brazil's strong commercial ties to the Eurozone, the slowdown of its exports to China, and internal battles against corruption cloud its economic outlook. In 2014 Brazil narrowly escaped recession with 0.1 percent expansion, and, given the fall in global oil prices and the emergence of complex political corruption scandals, the outlook for 2015 remained dim. Mexico has embarked on a new wave of neoliberal reforms and, in the context of a slowdown of public and private investment and a complicated domestic political climate, has yet to see substantive progress in its quest for growth (IMF, 2014; ECLAC, 2013a, 2013c; Moreno-Brid, 2014). Despite efforts to reform the energy, telecommunications, and banking sectors, Mexico showed just 2.2 percent growth in 2014.

Latin America suffered high inflation in the '80s and early '90s, including hyperinflationary episodes in Argentina, Brazil, Bolivia, and Peru. Inflationary pressures began to ease later in the '90s, with changes of governments and economic policies (Bernanke, 2005). In the '80s, annual inflation moved up toward double digits. It declined in the second half of the '90s, in terms of both its average growth rate and the number of countries exhibiting two-digit rates. The reasons for such decline differ from country to country but include firmer commitment to fiscal and monetary discipline, stable or appreciated exchange rates, wage restraint, and trade openness (IMF, 2013a). The adoption of inflation targeting by many countries in the late '90s and early 2000s, combined with the absence of major external shocks, helped to keep inflation in check. From the early 2000s, average inflation dropped to 7.7 percent in the region, still higher than the 4.1 percent world average (IMF, 2013b). In more recent years, following the downturn in world commodity prices (particularly petroleum), inflation has been rather well contained within the targets of national authorities, with the recent exceptions of Argentina and Venezuela.

Turning to assess the region's fiscal performance, as Table 7.4 shows, the primary fiscal balance has been healthy across countries in recent years,

TABLE 7.4 Public Finance Statistics for Latin America as Percentage of GDP, 1990–2014

Products and exporters	Overall primary balance								Overall fiscal balance							
	1990s	2000–08	2009	2010	2011	2012	2013	2014	1990s	2000–08	2009	2010	2011	2012	2013	2014
Metals and minerals																
Chile	3.2	3.4	-3.9	0.0	1.8	1.2	0.0	-1.0	1.4	2.5	-4.4	-0.5	1.3	0.6	-0.6	-1.6
Peru	0.4	1.2	-0.2	1.3	2.1	2.4	1.5	0.6	-3.1	-0.7	-1.5	0.1	1.0	1.3	0.5	-0.4
Agro-industrial products																
Argentina	0.4	1.7	1.2	1.2	-0.1	-0.1	-1.4	-2.5	-0.9	-0.2	-0.7	-0.1	-1.9	-1.9	-2.6	-4.4
Paraguay	0.1	1.0	1.3	1.2	1.8	0.4	0.9	-0.1	-0.2	-0.2	0.1	1.2	0.7	-1.7	-1.7	-1.1
Uruguay	0.1	1.0	1.3	1.2	1.8	0.4	0.9	-0.1	-1.2	-2.7	-1.5	-1.1	-0.6	-1.9	-1.5	-2.3
Hydrocarbons																
Bolivia	-0.9	-1.4	-0.4	1.4	-0.2	2.7	2.0	-1.7	-3.1	-3.3	-2.0	-0.1	-1.2	1.8	1.4	-2.4
Colombia	-1.1	-0.7	-1.2	-1.2	-0.3	0.1	-0.1	-0.4	-2.6	-4.0	-4.1	-3.9	-2.8	-2.3	-2.3	-2.4
Ecuador	2.5	2.2	-3.5	-0.9	-0.7	-1.0	-4.5	-5.0	-0.5	-0.5	-4.2	-1.6	-1.6	-2.0	-5.8	-6.4
Venezuela	0.8	1.5	-3.7	-2.1	-1.8	-2.2	1.0	-0.2	-2.6	-1.4	-5.0	-3.6	-4.0	-4.9	-1.9	-2.5
Major manufacturing																
Brazil	1.0	2.2	1.2	2.0	2.2	1.9	1.5	-0.3	-2.6	-2.2	-3.4	-1.6	-2.4	-1.8	-2.7	-5.3
Mexico	2.8	0.2	-0.5	-1.2	-1.0	-1.1	-0.8	-1.2	-0.2	-1.4	-2.2	-2.7	-2.5	-2.6	-2.4	-2.9
Central America																
Costa Rica	0.5	1.7	-1.3	-3.0	-1.9	-2.3	-2.9	-3.1	-2.9	-2.0	-3.4	-5.1	-4.1	-4.4	-5.4	-5.6

(continued)

TABLE 7.4 *Continued*

Products and exporters	Overall primary balance								Overall fiscal balance							
	1990s	2000–08	2009	2010	2011	2012	2013	2014	1990s	2000–08	2009	2010	2011	2012	2013	2014
Dominican Republic	1.2	0.9	–1.3	–0.7	–0.1	–2.8	–0.4	–0.1	0.7	–0.1	–3.0	–2.6	–2.1	–5.2	–2.7	–2.6
El Salvador	–0.1	0.3	–1.2	–0.4	–0.1	0.5	0.6	0.8	–1.8	–1.7	–3.7	–2.7	–2.3	–1.7	–1.8	–1.6
Guatemala	–0.1	–0.3	–1.7	–1.8	–1.3	–0.9	–0.6	–0.4	–1.3	–1.7	–3.1	–3.3	–2.8	–2.4	–2.1	–1.9
Honduras	–0.4	–2.2	–5.3	–3.7	–3.2	–4.3	–5.8	–2.1	–3.5	–3.3	–6.0	–4.7	–4.6	–6.0	–7.9	–4.4
Nicaragua	0.9	–0.4	–0.7	0.3	1.5	1.5	1.0	0.6	–0.7	–1.9	–1.7	–0.7	0.5	0.5	0.1	–0.3
Panama	2.0	2.1	1.3	0.1	–1.1	–0.8	–2.0	–2.8	–1.0	–1.7	–1.4	–2.4	–3.3	–2.7	–4.0	–4.6
Cuba	–1.2	–2.6	–3.8	–2.2	–	–	–	–	–2.2	–3.6	–4.9	–3.6	3.0	6.7	1.9	–
Haiti	–1.5	–1.3	–0.7	0.5	1.9	2.0	–1.0	–0.5	–2.2	–1.9	–1.3	0.0	1.6	1.7	–1.4	–0.9

SOURCE: ECLAC, based on official national sources. Figures reflect balances for the central government, with the exception of Bolivia, for which figures reflect general government balances.

NOTE: Reflects arithmetic average for yearly groupings.

with the exception of Venezuela. Exporters of minerals and metals have tended to register a primary surplus in the whole period, except for 2009, when the recession and their countercyclical policy response to the crisis temporarily pushed it into deficit. Exporters of agro-industrial products have also achieved a primary surplus on average, although in recent years Argentina and Paraguay ran small deficits. The two manufacturing exporters, Brazil and Mexico, differ in their fiscal performance. Brazil rather systematically registered a primary surplus in the period analyzed here, while Mexico boasted a primary surplus in the '90s and in the 2000s, until 2009, when it expanded public expenditure in reaction to the crisis. Since then, it has had a deficit close to −1.0 percent of GDP.

The healthy diagnosis of Latin America's fiscal situation, derived from the evolution of its primary balance, changes when we examine the overall fiscal balance. For some groups of countries, the change is dramatic. Such contrasting evolution is not new in a region where public debt used to be very high. Recall that in the '80s, the massive fiscal adjustments in the region's primary balance in response to the international debt crisis were not reflected in their overall fiscal position. The rise in interest rates in world financial markets combined with the sharp depreciation of national currencies swelled the fiscal deficit. Moreover, on average, external public debt rose forty points to reach 75 percent of GDP, and surpassed 100 percent of GDP in Ecuador, Nicaragua, Peru, and Bolivia (Bértola and Ocampo, 2012; ECLAC, 2012). When it finally declined, this was due largely to the processes of restructuring and the resumption of economic growth.

IS LATIN AMERICA REALLY ON THE ROAD TO SUSTAINED DEVELOPMENT?

The prevalence of acute and somewhat asymmetric cyclical fluctuations in the growth path of Latin America's economies—and, on the other hand, the high burden of interest payments on public debt, which in some cases restrict fiscal space as they turn a solid primary balance into an overall fiscal deficit—is a cause for concern in the region. In this section, we analyze some of these issues in further depth. We start by examining the extent to which Latin America's renewed dynamism is helping the region catch up with the developed world. For this purpose, we examine the evolution of the gap between the GDP per capita of selected Latin American countries and that of the United States, both measured in constant U.S. dollars.

Chile and Peru are the only countries that have persistently reduced their gap vis-à-vis the United States during 1990–2013. The picture among hydrocarbon exporters is not favorable, with Colombia, Ecuador, and Bolivia showing minimum or no progress and Venezuela's persistent decline since 1990 only beginning to be reversed in 2003. Latin America's manufacturing powerhouses show very disappointing results in their aspirations to catch up. Mexico's gap is actually wider in 2013 than in 1990, and Brazil's shows no significant improvement. Notwithstanding the region's renewed dynamism in the 2000s, in general the gap in its income per capita vis-à-vis that of the United States is as wide as it was twenty-five years before, in 1990. However, as Berg et al. (2008) argue, closing the income gap requires long and sustained periods of high growth, not just isolated years of strong expansion.

Given the rather favorable overall picture presented so far of Latin America's progress on its fiscal and public debt fronts, it would be difficult to claim that currently, in the aftermath of the 2009 financial crisis, its fiscal performance is the binding constraint on its economic growth. But some caveats apply. The first includes countries with tax revenues at such low levels that they impede the state from adequately fulfilling its most basic functions to provide public goods. The second includes countries with markedly inadequate public investment, a crucial determinant of competitiveness, especially in a region with pressing and long-standing needs for infrastructure modernization, expansion, and upgrading. In this sense, there is consensus that the region's progress in its capacity to implement countercyclical policies must be matched by greater efforts to ensure that public investment is shielded as much as possible instead of being used as the preferred tool for fiscal contraction. A third and related issue concerns the dependency of fiscal revenues on exports of commodities whose prices may be very sensitive to external shocks. As evidenced in late 2014 and early 2015, with the worldwide decline in oil prices, this concern has become particularly pressing for some countries.

Across the region, low tax revenues and inefficient fiscal institutions have traditionally been a structural weakness and major constraint on Latin America's economic performance. The sources of fiscal revenues raise important questions regarding their long-term sustainability. The region's copious natural-resource bounty, in addition to its favorable contribution to exports, is a significant source of government revenue in many countries and has had increasing importance over the past decade (see Table 7.5). Indeed, in Mexico, a major petroleum extractor and producer, the amount of revenues from such resource exploitation rose from an already conspicuous 6 percent of GDP to 7.5 percent in 2009–11, on average, and grew further in 2013 to 8 percent of GDP. Bolivia and Ecuador, also important

TABLE 7.5 Fiscal Revenues from Natural Resource Exploitation in Selected Economies as Percentage of GDP

Country	1999–2001	2009–11	2012	2013	Change in 2013[a]
Bolivia	5.1	9.6	13.7	14.2	9.1
Venezuela	13.2	12.9	10.0	12.2	−1.0
Ecuador	6.3	13.5	14.7	12.1	5.8
Mexico	6.1	7.5	7.7	8.0	1.9
Colombia	1.2	2.4	4.4	5.1	3.9
Peru	0.2	1.6	3.3	2.8	2.6
Brazil	2.4	2.3	2.2	2.4	0.0
Chile	0.8	3.7	3.1	2.1	1.3
Argentina	0.0	3.0	2.8	1.8	1.8

SOURCE: ECLAC, based on official statistics.
NOTE: Average for yearly groupings.
[a] Compared to average for 1999–2001.

hydrocarbon exporters, saw a huge rise in their fiscal revenues derived from such exploitation. Such dependence makes fiscal performance highly vulnerable and limits countries' capacity to implement countercyclical policies in the face of adverse shocks in their terms of trade or export revenues (Fricke and Süssmuth, 2014).

A final comment on the scant capacity of fiscal policy to reduce the concentration of income may be useful. Although the region's tax systems are designed to be progressive, with marginal personal income tax rates of 25–40 percent for the highest income brackets, many factors work against this, including informality; tax evasion and avoidance; tax exemption regimes; weak, costly, inefficient systems of tax administration; and political economic considerations (ECLAC, 2015). To varying extents, future fiscal reforms in the region should aim at correcting these challenges to strengthen the contributions of fiscal policy to long-term growth. But if the fiscal structure is not the key binding constraint, what are the other possible restrictions?

Latin America's current account deficit underwent a substantial reduction in recent decades, going from an average of −2.4 percent of GDP in the 1990s to −0.3 percent in 2000–08. Since then it has been persistently increasing, reaching −2.6 percent in 2103. This recent deterioration of the current account has been particularly strong among exporters of metals and

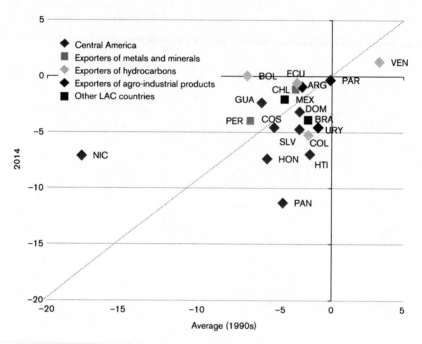

FIGURE 7.1   Current account balance for Latin American and Caribbean (LAC) countries, 1990–2014, as percentage of GDP. (Source: ECLAC, based on official figures.)

ARG = Argentina	COS = Costa Rica	HON = Honduras	PAR = Paraguay
BOL = Bolivia	DOM = Dominican	HTI = Haiti	PER = Peru
BRA = Brazil	Republic	MEX = Mexico	SLV = El Salvador
CHL = Chile	ECU = Ecuador	NIC = Nicaragua	URY = Uruguay
COL = Colombia	GUA = Guatemala	PAN = Panama	VEN = Venezuela

minerals, at close to four or five points of GDP. Among exporters of agro-industrial products, the shift between 2009 and 2013 was also noticeable: three points in Argentina and four in Uruguay (though not in Paraguay, where the current account went into surplus). The exporters of hydrocarbons did not register major changes in their current account balance in this period, except for Venezuela (five points).

By 2014, the current account surplus or the comfortably small deficit of the 2000–08 period had vanished and, in some cases, acutely deteriorated (see Figure 7.1). A matter for concern is that the deterioration of the current account balance since 2009 in relation to the '90s coincides with a slowdown in economic growth. It is clear that the commodity boom of 2003–08 and the improvement of the terms of trade enabled some countries in the region to grow at a higher pace without putting pressure on their

TABLE 7.6 Contributions of Demand to GDP Growth in Latin America as Percentage of GDP Growth, 1990–2013

	1990–2000	*2000–08*	*2010–13*
Final consumption	75.6	77.2	89.3
Government consumption	11.8	13.1	14.3
Private consumption	62.7	63.7	74.4
Gross capital formation	27.2	33.0	39.4
Gross fixed capital formation	22.5	28.4	31.2
Exports of goods and services	40.5	30.0	28.0
Imports of goods and services	−42.1	−36.4	−54.3

SOURCE: ECLAC, based on official national sources.
NOTE: Geometric average for yearly groupings.

current account balance. In other words, the commodity boom helped these economies temporarily alleviate the binding grip of the balance-of-payments constraint on their growth. Another factor to consider has been the increasing importance of remittances in the current account balance of many countries in the region. With regard to other factors in the balance of payments, in general, interest payments and profit repatriation are today less important than in the '80s and '90s. However, after the 2009 crisis, and looking forward into uncertain global economic conditions, the repatriation of dividends may become more important for the region. In the current context of volatile foreign exchange rates and with the imminent rise in interest rates in the United States with the winding down of quantitative easing, a potential net outflow of foreign capital in the near future may further underline the relevance of the balance of payments as a key constraint on Latin America's long-term economic growth.

To further explore the weight of the balance of payments on Latin America's long-term expansion growth, we examine the changing roles of the exports and other components of aggregate demand in GDP growth. As Table 7.6 shows, in the '90s exports provided a larger contribution (40.5 percent) than fixed capital formation (22.5 percent) to GDP growth. In 2000–08, perhaps paradoxically, the contribution of exports declined to 30 percent while that of fixed capital formation rose to 28.4 percent. This reflects the fact that while exports rose at an average annual rate of 4.5 percent (7.7 percent in the '90s), fixed investment increased at 5.5 percent

(3.8 percent in the '90s). In the postcrisis period, their relative contributions have so far continued the same trends. Thus, exports accounted for 28 percent of GDP growth and fixed investment for 31.2 percent, a reflection of the fact that the former have expanded at a slightly lower rate (3.9 percent) than the latter (4.0 percent).

Particularly worrying in the postcrisis economic performance of the region is the fact that for the first time in years, exports are expanding at a slower pace than the whole economy, a pattern that may draw the curtain on the era of export-led growth. Clearly, Latin America's exports will not expand in a much more dynamic way unless they start reversing their reprimarization pattern and diversifying to activities based on technologically intensive goods and services. Additionally, as the unadjusted trade balance's systematic deterioration shows, once the commodity boom has ceased, Latin America's imports cannot keep increasing at practically the same pace as in 2000–08 without leading to a severe problem in the balance of payments.

Another feature in the region's growth performance concerns consumption. Prior to 2009, private consumption contributed around 63 percent to GDP growth, and government consumption around 12 percent. In 2010–13 the contribution of private consumption increased by 10 points to an average of 77.4 percent, and the government's contribution augmented to 14 percent. As ECLAC (2013a, 2013c) argues, this shift reflects greater access to consumer credit, somewhat higher real wages, and a rise in formal employment in various economies. The evidence so far examined indicates that exports are no longer the engine of economic expansion in the region and, given the outlook of world trade, they will not be in the near future. It is unclear whether domestic demand will be able to pull the region onto a path of fast and sustained expansion. For this to occur, the region must adopt a development agenda firmly oriented toward reducing inequality and widening the domestic market. In addition, given the high income elasticity of imports, it must implement policies to induce investment oriented toward transforming the productive structure and multiplying its forward and backward linkages.

As the academic literature agrees, investment is the key determinant of economic growth. Its impact depends on its magnitude, efficient operation, and adequate orientation toward modernizing infrastructure and expanding productive capacities in activities that are subject to increasing returns, with strong domestic linkages, or that face dynamic demand in world markets (see ECLAC, 2012). As the data show, investment performance is a major challenge for the region. It is of concern that no Latin American economy has been able to allocate more than 25 percent of GDP to fixed capital formation, the proportion identified by UNCTAD, ECLAC, and other analysts as the minimum to ensure annual long-term rates of expansion of GDP over and above 5 percent. In other words, the accumulation dynamics are insufficient to generate major transformation in the region's infrastructure and productive capacities (ECLAC, 2013c). In the 2000s, there is evidence that foreign investment as well as domestic private investment shifted relatively away from large-scale infrastructure and manufacturing in favor of mining and non-tradable activities. The limited scale and scope of public-sector investment may also have significant impacts on the region's growth potential.

The disappointing behavior of labor productivity in the region is, in our view, not independent of the scant dynamism of investment. Given insufficient investment in infrastructure, plants, machinery, and equipment, there is no reason why labor productivity should rise to international standards. As Figure 7.2 illustrates, across all subgroups, and with the exception of Chile, labor productivity in Latin America has been persistently lagging behind that of the United States. Given this poor performance, on average the employed labor force in the United States is at least four times more productive than its counterpart in Latin America. The worst cases are Bolivia, Paraguay, Peru, and Ecuador, whose labor productivity is ten times lower than that of the United States. Troublingly, the region's major manufacturing exporters struggle with low and declining levels of labor productivity. By 2013, Mexico's labor productivity was not even a quarter of U.S. labor productivity, and Brazil's was less than 15 percent of the latter. In short, the region is not catching up with the United States in terms of either its GDP per capita or its labor productivity.

CONCLUSION

In its quest for high economic growth cum price stabilization, the region is no longer stuck on a long, frustrating, and ineffective path to sustained growth, as it was in the '80s and '90s. It has made major progress on the macro-stabilization front, lowering inflation, reducing fiscal deficits, and penetrating export markets. Yet Latin America—both individual countries and the region as a whole—is far from changing its development trajectory and commencing with a new development strategy. Its growth performance has still, with few exceptions, failed to reduce the income gap vis-à-vis the United States.

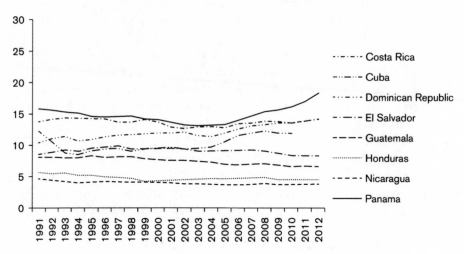

FIGURE 7.2A   Latin American labor productivity as a share of U.S. labor productivity, 1991–2012 (percentages).

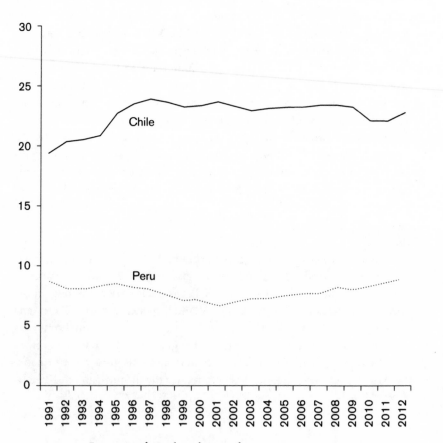

FIGURE 7.2B   Exporters of metals and minerals.

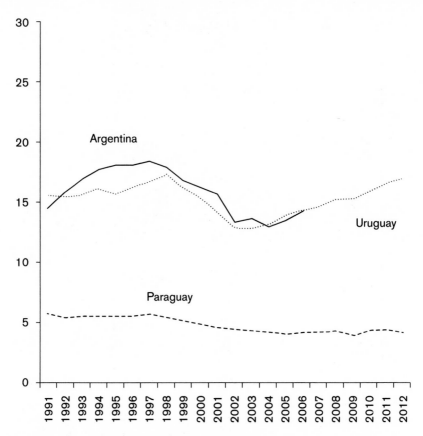

FIGURE 7.2C   Exporters of agro-industrial products.

The region's economic structure is marked by weak backward and forward linkages, scant innovation or high-technology-intensive processes, and an export performance dependent on natural resources cum favorable terms of trade. Gross fixed capital formation remains low. Weak fiscal revenues, the rather pro-cyclical orientation of fiscal policy, and, in some cases, a dependence on natural resource revenues, are important obstacles to improving infrastructure and boosting long-term economic expansion. Latin America's development faces both old and new constraints that pose key challenges for policy makers.

The first action needed is a process of structural transformation to strengthen the domestic backward and forward linkages of the region's productive matrix, and to promote investment and technology transfer in activities subject to increasing returns or facing dynamic demand in international markets. The second is a process to build a strong domestic market

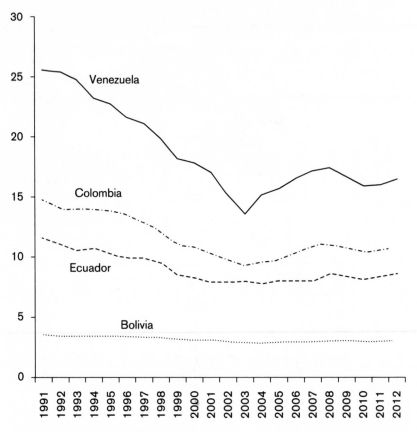

FIGURE 7.2D   Exporters of hydrocarbons.

to complement or substitute exports as the main engine of economic expansion. To achieve this entails strengthening fiscal positions to give more room to expand public investment, avoiding persistent appreciations of the real exchange rate, and removing the obstacles that hinder private investment, innovation, and technological upgrading (Ocampo, 2011; Moreno-Brid, 2014).

As a consequence, after 2009, in the context of a weaker global economy, the region's economic growth started to taper off at the same time that its overall balance-of-payments position deteriorated. Unfortunately, this subdued prospect for future growth appears to be the new normalcy in the region, with just 2.9 percent growth in 2013, 1.1 percent in 2014, and only 1.0 percent growth projected for 2015 (OECD, ECLAC, and CAF, 2014;

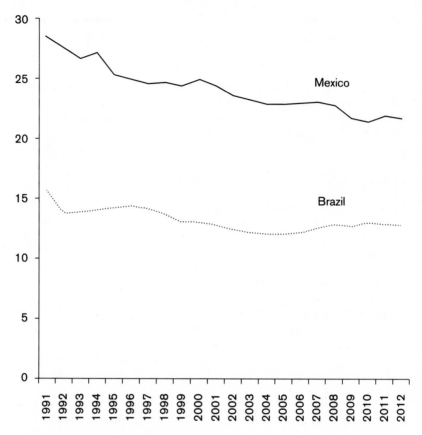

FIGURE 7.2E Major manufacturing exporters.

ECLAC, 2015). South America's prospects for 2015 look even dimmer, as growth is expected to be near zero for the year, given recessionary pressures in Venezuela and Brazil. Mexico's outlook also remains subdued, with growth not expected to reach more than 2.6 percent, according to forecasts from Consensus Economics (2015).

Long-term sustainable growth for Latin America as a whole and for the specific economies that make up the region requires a nuanced understanding of the heterogeneity of productive structures, institutions, labor markets, and societal norms, while providing room for changing global conditions and priorities. Sustained growth also requires cooperative action from both the public and private sectors to enact reforms and increase capacities. Whether governments and other relevant economic and political agents will be able to build the necessary consensus to implement a new sustainable growth agenda remains to be seen. ⌉

. . .

Juan Carlos Moreno-Brid is a professor of economics at the Universidad Nacional Autónoma de México. Stefanie Garry is an economic affairs officer in the Economic Development Unit at the Economic Commission for Latin America and the Caribbean in Mexico City, Mexico.

REFERENCES

Bárcena, A., and A. Prado (Eds.). (2015). "Neoestructuralismo y corrientes heterodoxas en América Latina y el Caribe a inicios del siglo XXI." Libros de la CEPAL, no. 132 (LC/G.2633-P). Santiago: Comisión Económica para América Latina y el Caribe (CEPAL).

Berg, A., J. Ostry, and J. Zettelmeyer. (2008). "What Makes Growth Sustained?" IMF Working Paper WP/08/59. Washington, DC: International Monetary Fund.

Bernanke, B.S. (2005). "Inflation in Latin America: A New Era?" The Federal Reserve Board. Speech presented at the Stanford Institute for Economic Policy Research Economic Summit, Stanford, CA, USA.

Bértola, L., and J.A. Ocampo. (2012). "Turning Back to the Market." In The Economic Development of Latin America since Independence. Oxford, UK: Oxford University Press.

Céspedes, L.F., and A. Velasco. (2012). "Macroeconomic Performance during Commodity Price Booms and Busts." IMF Economic Review 60(4). Washington, DC: International Monetary Fund.

Consensus Economics. (2015). "Latin American Consensus Forecasts. July 2015 Update." London: Consensus Economics.

Dabla-Norris, E., et al. (2013). "Benchmarking Structural Transformation across the World." IMF Working Paper WP/13/176. Washington, DC: International Monetary Fund.

Daude, C., A. Melguizo, and A. Neut. (2013). "Fiscal Policy in Latin America: Countercyclical and Sustainable at Last?" Working Paper no. 291. Paris: OECD Development Centre.

De Gregorio, J. (2013). "Resilience in Latin America: Lessons from Macroeconomic Management and Financial Policies." IMF Working Paper/13/259. Washington, DC: International Monetary Fund.

ECLAC (Economic Commission for Latin America and the Caribbean) (2012). "Structural Change for Equality." San Salvador: ECLAC.

———. (2013a). "Balance Preliminar de las Economías de América Latina y el Caribe 2013." Santiago: ECLAC.

———. (2013b). "The Current International Context and Its Macroeconomic Repercussions for Latin America and the Caribbean." Santiago: ECLAC.

————. (2013c). "Estudio Económico de América Latina y el Caribe 2013: Tres décadas de crecimiento económico desigual e inestable." Santiago: ECLAC.

————. (2015). "Proyecciones de América Latina y el Caribe, 2015." http://www.cepal.org/sites/default/files/pr/files/tabla._proyecciones_pib_america_latina_y_el_caribe.pdf.

Fricke, H., and B. Süssmuth. (2014). "Growth and Volatility of Tax Revenues in Latin America." World Development 54: 114–138.

Gutierrez, M. (2005). "Economic Growth in Latin America: The Role of Investment and Other Growth Sources." Macroeconomía del desarrollo. WP no. 6.

Hofman, A. (2001). "Long-Run Economic Development in Latin America in a Comparative Perspective: Proximate and Ultimate Causes." Macroeconomía del desarrollo. WP no. 6.

IMF (International Monetary Fund). (2012a). "Statement by the IMF Executive Board on Argentina." Press Release No. 12/30. February 1. Washington, DC: International Monetary Fund.

————. (2012b). "World Economic and Financial Surveys Regional Economic Outlook. Western Hemisphere: Rebuilding Strength and Flexibility." Washington, DC: International Monetary Fund.

————. (2013a). "World Economic and Financial Surveys Regional Economic Outlook. Western Hemisphere: Time to Rebuild Policy Space." Washington, DC: International Monetary Fund.

————. (2013b). "World Economic Outlook Database." Washington, DC: International Monetary Fund.

————. (2013c). "World Economic Outlook Update: Growing Pains." Washington, DC: International Monetary Fund.

————. (2014). "World Economic Outlook Update: Is the Tide Rising?" Washington, DC: International Monetary Fund.

Moreno-Brid, J. C. (2014). "Politica macroenomica para el desarrollo." Economía UNAM 32.

————. (2015). "Después de la Tormenta: Panorama económico de América Latina a cinco años de la crisis financiera internacional." Foreign Affairs Latinoamérica 15: 98–104.

Ocampo, J.A. (2009). "The Impact of the Global Financial Crisis on Latin America." CEPAL Review 97. Santiago: ECLAC.

————. (2011). "Macroeconomy for Development: Countercyclical Policies and Production Sector Transformation." CEPAL Review 104. Santiago: ECLAC.

————. (forthcoming). "Latin America in the Midst of the Global Quicksands."

OECD (Organisation for Economic Co-operation and Development). (2013). Statistics Database. Tax Statistics. Revenue Statistics in Latin America. Comparative Tables. Paris: OECD.

OECD and ECLAC. (2013). "Latin American Economic Outlook 2014: Logistics and Competitiveness for Development." Paris: OECD.

OECD, ECLAC, and CAF (Banco de Desarrollo de América Latina). (2014). "Perspectivas económicas de América Latina 2015: Educación, Competencias e Innovación para el Desarrollo." Paris: OECD.

Pérez Caldentey, E., D. Titelman, and P. Carvallo. (2014). "Weak Expansions: A Distinctive Feature of the Business Cycle in Latin America and the Caribbean." World Economic Review 3: 69–89.

Rojas-Suarez, L. (Ed.). (2009). "Growing Pains in Latin America: An Economic Growth Framework as Applied to Brazil, Colombia, Costa Rica, Mexico and Peru." Washington, DC: Center for Global Development.

Spillan, J. E., N. Virzi, and M. Garita. (2014). Doing Business in Latin America: Challenges and Opportunities. New York: Routledge.

8.   South America after the Commodity Boom

Martín Abeles and Sebastián Valdecantos

INTRODUCTION

The 2008–09 global financial crisis revealed a novelty in Latin American economic history: for the first time in many decades, an external shock of considerable magnitude did not provoke a massive balance-of-payments crisis, nor did it threaten the stability of local financial systems. At the same time, it revealed an unprecedented fiscal space for implementing counter-cyclical policies (CEPAL, 2012). For many analysts, it was these countercy-clical policies that made the region's "V-shaped" recovery in 2010 possible, with 6 percent annual growth immediately following the 1.3 percent contraction in 2009 (Gutiérrez and Revilla, 2010; Daude et al., 2010).

This unprecedented fiscal space is typically attributed to improved macroeconomic management during the period before the crisis, including prudent handling of tax resources and improved management of public-sector liabilities between 2003 and 2008.[1] Notwithstanding the improvement in public-sector solvency (particularly regarding external public debt) and the expansionary policies implemented in many countries in the region, there is a less self-indulgent interpretation that emphasizes the role of external factors in the region's recovery toward the end of 2009, in particular, the countercyclical reaction of the developed world and China.[2] As a result of this coordinated action, international prices for commodities—which had contracted by 47 percent, on average, in 2009—picked up almost entirely in just one year. This proved critical for South America's economic recovery.

This second interpretation is more consistent with the "balance-of-payments dominance" hypothesis (Ocampo, 2011), according to which the short-term economic dynamics of peripheral countries—those that do not issue a reserve currency—are largely determined by the external environment, which is shaped, in turn, by a range of possible exogenous shocks, including in terms of trade, liquidity in international credit markets, or the growth rates of trading partners. This interpretation also fits more closely with the empirical evidence.[3]

The importance of such exogenous shocks is evident in comparing the recent economic performance of South America with that of Mexico, Central America, and the Caribbean. The former recovered much more quickly than the latter following the 2008–09 crisis, in line with the rebound in international commodity prices. Mexico, Central America, and the Caribbean did not recover with the same speed, in large part due to their greater exposure to declining economic activity in the United States, but also because most of these countries do not benefit from the rise in international commodity prices as South American ones do. Once past the peak of the recovery in 2010, growth rates in South American countries declined steadily, from a 6 percent annual growth rate between 2004 and 2008 to around 1.4 percent for the period 2012–15. This decreasing trend put these countries in negative territory in 2015 (−1.1 percent) and for the 2016 projection (CEPAL, 2015b).

In this chapter, we aim to illustrate the causes underlying the deceleration trend in South American economies, with a particular emphasis on the external sector. Two working hypotheses inform our analysis. The first is that the key component of countercyclical policy, capable of reactivating aggregate demand and consequently the short-term level of economic activity, is fiscal policy (Arestis and Sawyer, 2003, 2004, 2010). This view diverges from the conventional approach, which typically identifies monetary policy as the countercyclical instrument par excellence. The conventional approach therefore dismisses the use of expansive fiscal policies in economic downturns, considering them ineffective (or even counterproductive).

The second hypothesis is that countercyclical fiscal space[4] depends, fundamentally, on the situation of the economy's external sector (Martner and Tromben, 2004; Pérez Caldentey, 2007; Abeles et al., 2013). The relationship between countercyclical fiscal space and the external sector tends to be related solely to the fiscal impact of certain exogenous factors, such as terms-of-trade dynamics, which can influence tax revenues, or the evolution of international interest rates, which can increase the cost of servicing external public debt. Yet what this second hypothesis seeks to underscore is that in developing countries, the relationship between countercyclical fiscal space and the external sector is eminently financial and is related to the limitations that peripheral countries face in issuing debt denominated in local currency in international financial markets.[5] This *structural* constraint, which reflects the imperfect substitution relationship between assets denominated in domestic currency and those denominated in an international reserve currency, comprises the key underlying determinant of balance-of-payments dominance.

From this perspective, the countercyclical challenge in boom times consists more in preserving a sustainable situation in the external sector in the medium term than it does in implementing countercyclical fiscal policy in the conventional sense. In the upward phase of Prebisch's "universal cyclical movement" (favorable terms of trade, high international liquidity, etc.), this involves maximizing efforts to tackle the typical sources of external vulnerability in Latin American countries: structural heterogeneity, which imposes a limit or *external constraint* on growth; and the tendency toward unsustainable external leverage. The focus of economic policy in the upward phase of the cycle should therefore be none other than that historically championed by various heterodox economic schools of thought in the region: the implementation of industrial policies aimed at a change (diversification) in the production structure and a more active regulation of cross-border capital flows. It is likely that the robustness of public finance depends as much on the effectiveness with which these policies can be implemented as on the state's good financial management per se.[6]

The chapter is organized as follows. After this introduction, the second section briefly describes the most recent Latin American growth phase (2004–08), distinguishing various national trajectories, and analyzes the specific nature of the South American deceleration of the following years, characterized by the worsening of current account deficits. The third section examines the underlying causes of this deceleration from the perspective of aggregate demand. The fourth section analyzes the fiscal reaction of countries in the region, noticing a fairly widespread countercyclical effort that helped mitigate—at least initially—the negative pressures emanating from the foreign front. The fifth section considers the overall evolution of the external sector in South American economies, including real and financial factors, in order to assess the state of countercyclical fiscal space. We find a generalized trend of increasing external vulnerability that may limit the capacity of governments to implement (or maintain) countercyclical fiscal policies capable of reversing current deceleration trends. The sixth section presents some concluding remarks, in which we highlight that the general increase in external vulnerability of South American countries stems from shortcomings that have historically conditioned the region's development—a heterogeneous and disjointed production structure—

TABLE 8.1 Growth in Latin America and the Caribbean

Weighted averages in percentage points

Regions	2004–08	2010	2011	2012	2013	2014	2015[a]	2012–15
South America	5.9	6.7	5.0	2.6	3.3	0.8	−1.1	1.4
Mexico, Central America, and the Caribbean	3.7	4.8	4.0	4.0	1.9	2.5	2.7	2.8
Latin America and the Caribbean	5.1	6.3	4.8	3.0	2.9	1.3	−0.4	

[a] Estimated (CEPAL, 2015b).

in addition to newer restrictions associated with increased foreign owner-ship of key assets (strong inward foreign direct investment) and a practi-cally unrestricted financial openness. Such conditions are likely to reinforce heterogeneity and relative backwardness, impeding a more autonomous exercise of economic policy.

ECONOMIC DECELERATION AND EXTERNAL DETERIORATION IN SOUTH AMERICA

The balance-of-payments dominance hypothesis is quite evident in the dif-ferent growth trajectories observed in the region. As shown in Table 8.1, South American countries recovered from the 2008–09 crisis much faster than Mexico, Central America, and the Caribbean, essentially because of the rebound in international commodity prices. The slow recovery of Mexico and Central American and Caribbean countries is explained by their greater exposure to the contraction in the level of economic activity in the United States, where growth was slow to regain its pace. It was only later, as of 2013, that growth rates for this group of countries began to more fully recover, in line with the recovery in the United States.[7]

South American countries show a different path. Growth rates rose from an average of 5.9 percent for the period 2004–08 to a peak of 6.7 percent in 2010 and fell continuously thereafter, averaging 1.4 percent for the period 2012–15. In this latter period, there was a marked declining trend: from 5 percent in 2011, to 0.8 percent in 2014, to −1.1 percent in 2015, and with a projection (at the time of this writing) of another year of negative growth for 2016 (CEPAL, 2015b).

TABLE 8.2 Growth in South America

In percentage points

Country	2004–08	2011	2012	2013	2014	2015[a]	2012–15
Bolivia	4.8	5.2	5.1	6.8	5.5	4.5	5.5
Paraguay	4.6	4.3	−1.2	14.2	4.4	2.9	5.1
Chile	5.5	5.8	5.5	4.3	1.9	2.0	3.4
Colombia	5.4	6.6	4.0	4.9	4.6	3.1	4.2
Peru	7.3	6.5	6.0	5.8	2.4	2.8	4.3
Uruguay	5.9	5.2	3.3	5.1	3.5	1.5	3.4
Argentina	7.5	8.4	0.8	2.9	0.5	2.0	1.6
Brazil	4.8	3.9	1.8	2.7	0.1	−3.5	0.3
Ecuador	5.3	7.9	5.2	4.6	3.8	0.4	3.5
Venezuela	10.5	4.2	5.6	1.3	−4.0	−7.1	−1.1

[a] Estimated (CEPAL, 2015b).

From this general deceleration pattern, it is possible to distinguish three different situations or groupings within South American countries (Table 8.2):

(1) countries where growth rates increased in the period 2012–15 compared to 2004–08 (Bolivia and Paraguay);

(2) countries where growth rates decreased in the latter period but continued to be at relatively high levels, at least in 2012 and 2013 (Chile, Colombia, Peru, and Uruguay); and

(3) countries where growth rates fell after 2010 or 2011 and continued to show very low growth rates, bordering on stagnation or, in some cases, recession (Argentina, Brazil, Ecuador, and Venezuela).

Even though, in statistical terms, Ecuador fits better in the second group, its recent economic performance and constraints seem to resemble more the countries of the third group.

The trend of the third group is significant for the performance of the region as a whole. This is, however, due more to arithmetic than to economic reasons. Argentina, Brazil, Ecuador, and Venezuela—growing, on average, 2.1 percent between 2012 and 2014, and declining −2.0 percent in 2015—together account for approximately 75 percent of South America's gross domestic product (GDP),[8] but they do not account for more than 8 percent of total export destinations for the other South American countries. The low levels of commercial and production integration in the region have, in this instance, reduced the induced or second-round effects associated with the weak performance of Argentina, Brazil, and, to a lesser extent, Ecuador and Venezuela.[9] In 2015, the average growth rate for this group fell into negative territory (−2.0 percent), largely due to the negative performances of Brazil (−3.5 percent) and Venezuela (−7.1 percent).

A similar deceleration pattern, though starting from somewhat higher growth rates in recent years, is observed in three of the four countries in the second group. Chile, Peru, and Uruguay grew at 5.8 percent, 6.5 percent, and 7.3 percent in 2011, respectively, and slowed to growth rates of 1.9 percent, 2.4 percent, and 3.5 percent in 2014. Colombia tended to diverge from the rest of the group as its growth rate continued to rise in 2014 but slowed in 2015. As a matter of fact, in 2015 the growth rates of these four countries tended to converge, with a maximum of 3.1 percent (Colombia) and a minimum of 1.5 percent (Uruguay).

Against this backdrop of falling growth rates, the situation of Paraguay and Bolivia seems exceptional. Bolivia managed to grow continuously from 2004 to 2015, with annual grow rates above 5 percent even after 2011. It was not until 2015, when the price of its main commodity exports dropped sharply, that its growth rate fell below the 5 percent threshold. Paraguay's growth dynamics seem to be explained by idiosyncratic factors, mainly by the drought of 2012[10] (which implied a negative shock for the real economy) and the subsequent recovery in 2013. In any case, these two economies do not account for more than 2 percent of South America's GDP (and account for less than 1.5 percent of the total export destinations for the remaining South American countries), so their superior growth did not have a strong impact on their neighbors. In 2015, the average growth rate for this group is expected (at the time of this writing) to have been 3.7 percent.

Along with this general economic slowdown, there has been an important deterioration in the current account on the balance of payments for South American countries, as shown in Table 8.3. In 2014, all countries except Bolivia, Paraguay, and Venezuela ran current account deficits. In a number of cases, deficits were larger than 4 percent of GDP (Colombia, 5.1 percent; Peru, 4.0 percent; Uruguay, 4.9 percent). This dismal external picture seems to have worsened in 2015, when all South American countries exhibited current account deficits. In line with the decline in commodity prices, seven out of ten countries saw their current accounts deteriorate with respect to 2014. Only Chile, Peru, and Uruguay improved, though

TABLE 8.3 Current Account Balance and Trade Balance in South America

In percentage points of GDP

Country	2004–08		2011		2012		2013		2014		2012–14	
	CA	X-M	CA	X-M	CA	X-M	CA	X-M	CA	X-M	CA	X-M
Bolivia	8.8	5.4	0.3	0.3	8.3	8.6	3.3	5.5	0.7	1.9	4.1	5.3
Paraguay	1.4	10.2	0.4	2.7	-0.9	1.6	2.2	5.0	0.1	2.6	0.5	3.1
Chile	1.9	9.6	-1.2	3.2	-3.6	-0.2	-3.7	-0.6	-1.2	1.6	-2.8	0.3
Colombia	-1.9	-0.8	-2.9	0.3	-3.2	-0.2	-3.4	-0.7	-5.0	-3.0	-3.9	-1.3
Peru	0.4	5.2	-1.9	4.1	-2.7	2.0	-4.4	-0.6	-4.1	-1.5	-3.7	0.0
Uruguay	-1.7	0.6	-2.9	0.2	-5.4	-2.5	-5.2	-2.1	-4.7	-1.6	-5.1	-2.1
Argentina	2.7	4.9	-0.7	1.9	-0.2	2.0	-0.8	1.2	-0.9	1.2	-0.6	1.4
Brazil	0.6	2.8	-2.1	-0.3	-2.3	-0.9	-3.4	-1.9	-3.9	-2.3	-3.2	-1.7
Ecuador	1.9	-0.2	-0.3	-2.4	-0.2	-1.5	-1.0	-2.1	-0.8	-1.3	-0.7	-1.6
Venezuela	12.6	13.6	7.7	10.2	3.7	5.8	2.4	4.8	4.3	3.2	3.5	4.6

SOURCES: CEPAL 2015b, IMF 2015.

NOTE: CA = current account of the balance of payments. X-M = trade balance.

they still remain in negative territory. The general situation was not expected to improve in 2016.

This trend is significant because, in a context of lower economic growth, one would expect deficits to decrease or at least not to increase. In line with the different growth patterns between country groups, the aggregate deterioration in the current account balance is mostly explained by the second group of countries (Chile, Colombia, Peru, and Uruguay) and the third group (Argentina, Brazil, Ecuador, and Venezuela)—those countries that showed a general economic deceleration trend.

Current account deterioration during an economic slowdown and with commodity prices at still relatively favorable levels[11] could signal cash-flow problems that reflect stock-flow inconsistencies associated with the level of external liabilities. However, generally speaking, it can be said that the deterioration in the current account is fundamentally due to the worsening of the balance of trade—which, in turn, was due to the fall in exports—and not to a rise in interest and/or dividend payments.[12]

Of course, there are various nuances within this general schema. While the balance of trade in goods remained positive in the first and third groups, the surplus disappeared in the second group. In the first group especially, but also in the second, current transfers (mainly remittances of migrant workers) account for a significant share of the credits on the current account; however, since they did not go through significant changes, they should not be accounted for as a source of the deterioration of the current account. In these two groups, there was also a decrease in the income account (i.e., interest and dividend net payments, a structurally negative entry in the current account for all countries in the region), which helped lessen the deterioration of the current account balance. Thus, it was the fall in the balance of trade that was the main cause of South America's poor external-sector performance. In seven of the ten countries analyzed (Argentina, Brazil, Chile, Ecuador, Peru, Uruguay, and Venezuela), the trade balance was the fundamental cause of the current account deterioration. For the region as a whole, the balance of trade in goods fell from a surplus of 7.7 percent of GDP (in 2011) to a deficit of 4.9 percent (in 2014), due mostly to Brazil. This deterioration can be predominantly attributed to the fall in exports, affecting the main exporters: Argentina, Brazil, Chile, Peru, and Venezuela. Those countries where exports had been increasing until 2014 (Paraguay, Bolivia, Ecuador, Colombia, and Uruguay) were not able to compensate for the decrease experienced by the larger economies. In 2015, however, all countries were affected by the same shock—the fall in commodity prices—leading to an average decrease of 21 percent in the value of total exports in South America.

CAUSES OF THE SLOWDOWN: AN ANALYSIS
OF AGGREGATE DEMAND COMPONENTS

Table 8.4 looks at the various components of aggregate demand and presents their contributions to GDP growth for each country during two periods (2004–08 and 2012–14).[13] Private consumption is, as expected, the most important component of aggregate demand for all countries in the region. Its trajectory tends to be endogenous, responding to the general level of economic activity. Likewise, investment tends to respond endogenously to economic growth, although in this case macroeconomic and political expectations can play a key role. Government spending and exports, on the other hand, are more exogenous variables in that they depend on policy decisions or other factors originating abroad. Thus, without neglecting changes in private consumption and investment, we begin with an analysis of the more exogenous components of aggregate demand (exports and government spending) and pay special attention to the evolution of the aggregate wage bill.

In the first group (Bolivia and Paraguay, countries where growth rates increased in the latter period), the contribution of government spending to aggregate demand growth between 2012 and 2014 increased significantly—doubling, on average—in relation to the previous period (2004–08). In Bolivia, government spending explained 0.6 percentage points of the 4.8 percent growth in aggregate demand between 2004 and 2008, rising to explain 1.1 percentage points of the 5.8 percent growth in aggregate demand between 2012 and 2014; and in Paraguay, the increase was from 0.5 percentage points of the 4.6 percent in 2004–08 to 1.0 percentage points of 5.8 percent in 2012–14. Investment's contribution to aggregate demand also increased in these countries. And there was a minor fall in the contribution by exports, which coincides with the deterioration in the international context.

The situation of the second group of countries (Chile, Colombia, Peru, and Uruguay) is the same as that of the first group, with the exception of Chile. There was an increase in government spending's contribution to aggregate demand growth, which mitigated some of the deceleration pressures coming from the external sector (Uruguay and then Peru were the most affected by this). As a result of slowing growth rates, there was a general fall in investment's contribution. This fall was particularly acute in Colombia, Chile, and Peru. In the latter two, the contribution of investment to aggregate demand growth fell by practically half. The relative contribution of private consumption increased in all cases, which is reasonable considering that income is less elastic than investment in response to the business cycle. In other words, when the economy contracts, both consumption

TABLE 8.4 Contributions to GDP Growth

In percentage points

Country	2004–08					2012–14				
	C	I	G	X	Y	C	I	G	X	Y
Bolivia	1.8	0.4	0.6	2.0	4.8	2.6	0.3	1.1	1.9	5.8
Paraguay	1.9	−0.3	0.5	2.5	4.6	1.9	0.1	1.0	2.8	5.8
Chile	2.9	1.3	0.5	0.8	5.5	2.9	0.1	0.4	0.5	3.9
Colombia	2.5	1.8	0.8	0.3	5.4	2.2	1.2	1.1	−0.1	4.5
Peru	2.6	3.0	0.7	1.0	7.3	2.8	1.5	0.8	−0.5	4.7
Uruguay	3.0	1.0	0.3	1.7	5.9	3.0	1.0	0.4	−0.3	4.0
Argentina	4.4	2.1	0.6	0.4	7.5	2.3	−0.7	0.4	−0.6	1.4
Brazil	2.5	1.2	0.7	0.4	4.8	1.4	0.1	0.2	−0.1	1.5
Ecuador	2.4	1.4	0.6	0.9	5.3	1.4	1.4	1.5	0.3	4.5
Venezuela	5.0	5.1	1.3	−1.0	10.5	n/d	n/d	n/d	n/d	0.9

SOURCE: CEPAL, 2015b.

NOTE: C = consumption. I = investment. G = government spending. X = exports.
Y = C + I + G + X. n/d = no data.

and investment are negatively affected (due to their endogeneity), but investment tends to fall more.

Contrary to the first two groups, in the third group (Argentina, Brazil, Ecuador, and Venezuela) the contribution of government spending to aggregate demand growth decreased, falling to practically zero (with the exception of Ecuador, which, from the point of view of fiscal activism seems to resemble Bolivia and Paraguay). This pro-cyclical bias was combined with an important decrease in the contribution of exports,[14] especially in Argentina.[15] There was also a strong contraction in investment's contribution, which became nil in Brazil and negative in Argentina. The deceleration in capital accumulation is, in part, a response to the endogeneity of investment decisions, particularly in Brazil. In Argentina, troubled foreign exchange markets and the corresponding macroeconomic uncertainty were also important factors in the decline of investment, the same as in Venezuela. In line with the severe economic contraction, there was a fall in consumption, although the contribution of consumption increased in relative terms. This implies that consumption was the only driving factor in these countries' growth during the slowdown.

In sum, the critical exogenous contractionary factor underlying the economic slowdown across South American countries is tied to the decreased dynamism of exports, which was accompanied by a fall in investment in Argentina and Venezuela and a complete stalling of investment in Brazil, Paraguay, and Chile. The main expansionary factor, on the other hand, was government spending—illustrating a somewhat unprecedented countercyclical mood. Even if—as will be shown below—countercyclical fiscal policies were insufficient to counter the contractionary pressures coming from the external sector, a discernible pattern between fiscal policy and growth comes to light: growth rates increased more (or decreased less) in countries that implemented larger fiscal stimuli to aggregate demand. This goes along the lines of our first working hypothesis—that fiscal policy is the key component of countercyclical policy.

THE ROLE OF COUNTERCYCLICAL FISCAL POLICY

In comparing 2004–08 with 2012–14, the countercyclical bias in the fiscal policy of South American countries becomes evident; however, the strength of this bias varies by country. To that effect, Table 8.5 shows the evolution of nonfinancial, public-sector primary government spending, public investment, and the resulting primary balance, each as a proportion of GDP. Countries are grouped according to their growth rates in recent years as in the previous sections.

As shown in the table, across the board, the share of primary government expenditure in GDP is greater in the second period than in the first. The two countries in the first group show significant increases here, which is consistent with their higher growth in recent years. Note, however, the case of Paraguay, where, despite a sizable increase in public expenditure between the two periods, government spending as a share of GDP remains at a relatively low level. In the second group of countries, public expenditure as a share of GDP increased, but to a much lesser extent. In Colombia, the share barely increased at all, though it was starting from a higher level than other countries in its group. The participation of the public sector in the Colombian economy (estimated on the basis of this indicator) is a bit higher than in Chile or Peru. However, within this second group, it is Uruguay where government spending as a share of GDP is greatest. In the third group of countries, there were important increases in Argentina, Ecuador,[16] and Venezuela; such was not the case in Brazil.

In addition, primary fiscal balances in all countries were lower in the period 2012–14 than in 2004–08; in some cases, this implied moving from fiscal surpluses to deficits. Within the first group, Bolivia was the only country to maintain a positive primary balance—though it has been falling

TABLE 8.5 Key Economic Indicators
In percentage points of GDP

Country	2004–08				2012–14				2014			
	Growth	Expenditure/GDP	Public investment/GDP	Primary surplus/GDP	Growth	Expenditure/GDP	Public investment/GDP	Primary surplus/GDP	Growth	Expenditure/GDP	Public investment/GDP	Primary income/GDP
Bolivia	4.8	35.9	7.6	2.2	5.8	48.6	12.1	0.5	5.5	54.0	13.3	-2.5
Paraguay	4.6	13.9	2.4	1.9	5.8	19.7	2.4	-1.7	4.4	19.8	2.3	-1.9
Chile	5.5	17.8	1.9	6.1	3.9	21.2	2	0	1.9	21.7	2.0	-1.0
Colombia	5.4	26.5	1.6	3.1	4.5	27.5	3.1	1.6	4.6	28.9	2.9	0.3
Peru	7.3	15.9	3.3	3.1	4.7	19.5	5.7	2	2.4	20.7	5.9	0.9
Uruguay	5.9	24.8	2.7	3	4.0	28.8	3.3	-0.1	3.5	29.3	3.4	-0.4
Argentina	7.5	18.6	0.6	2.8	1.4	29.4	1.2	-0.6	0.5	33.1	1.2	-1.0
Brazil	4.8	33.0	2.5	3.4	1.6	34.7	3.4	1.1	0.1	40.2	n/d	-0.6
Ecuador	5.3	22.8	5.2	3.3	4.6	41.9	11.5	-2.7	3.8	42.8	11.8	-4.2
Venezuela	10.5	32.9	0.3	2.1	1.0	42.5	0.2	n/d	-4.0	n/d	n/d	n/d

SOURCES: CEPAL and national institutes of statistics.

NOTE: n/d = no data.

systematically (to the extent that it has been exhibiting a deficit since 2014)—while Paraguay showed a significant reversal from surpluses to deficits. In the second group, primary surpluses in Chile and Uruguay disappeared; Colombia and Peru remained in surplus territory, though primary balances followed a decreasing trend as well. In the third group, Argentina, Ecuador, and Venezuela showed much larger decreases, which took them from surpluses to deficits. Brazil shared this trend, though with a smaller absolute change. The trend toward increasing fiscal deficits seems to have deepened in 2015, with only three countries showing an improvement in their public finances (Brazil, Ecuador, and Uruguay, the latter having succeeded in its attempt to restore its budget balance).

These results should be interpreted with caution, however, because the primary balance has a strong endogenous component related to changes in the economic activity level (which determines tax revenues). Therefore, this variable should be interpreted as an indicator more of results than of (an exogenous) fiscal impulse. To more reliably evaluate *deliberate* countercyclical action by governments, it is important to analyze public investment data, the third variable in Table 8.4.

In all countries, there is an increase in public investment as a share of GDP. Countries that registered an increase in growth in the period 2012–14 compared to 2004–08 (particularly Bolivia) are those where public investment increased the most. Increases in public investment are evident in the second group as well (with the exception of Chile), though they are smaller. The third group shows a similar dynamic, although in this regard Ecuador behaves more in line with the countries of the first group. However, it is important to note that (according to unofficial data) the growth of public investment seems to have stalled as commodity prices fell dramatically in 2014–15.

What is it that explains the greater expansive fiscal impulse of countries in the first group compared to the rest? In the case of the latter, was the less significant countercyclical reaction the result of autonomous decisions by governments or did structural constraints come first? This question is especially important in light of the reduction in primary balances and the persistent current account deterioration in recent years. If the external performance of a country determines its capacity to undertake countercyclical policies—our second working hypothesis—it would appear (a priori) that countries in the second and third groups found themselves in much worse external conditions than those in the first group as of 2012. We therefore turn to the analyses of these external conditions.

EXTERNAL VULNERABILITY AND SO FORTH

To analyze the external situation of South American countries, we examine three groups of variables. The first group can be called "structural flow" variables and includes indicators such as the balance of trade and the degree of "primarization" of exports. This group of indicators includes the components of the current account that do not depend on preexisting stock variables (e.g., external debt and the stock of foreign direct investment) but rather on the structural characteristics of the economy associated with its specialization profile, which determines the sustainable level of internal economic growth—as posited, for example, by Thirlwall (1979) and Rodríguez (1977).

The second group of variables includes "stock position" indicators. These reflect the financial economic situation in relation to the rest of the world and include all liabilities of the international investment position. Indicators in this group therefore range from the stock of short-term debt (public and private bonds and shares) to long-term agreements such as the stock of inward foreign direct investment and longer-term debt securities.

Last but not least, the third indicator is a measure of an economy's ability to access international financial markets: sovereign risk as reported by J.P. Morgan's Emerging Markets Bond Index (EMBI). This indicator is taken as a reflection of how a country is viewed in financial markets. It is not necessarily related to the variables previously mentioned ("structural flow" and "stock position" variables); however, at least in the short term, it tends to be associated with the international financial community's perception of domestic institutions or the "quality" macroeconomic management of a particular country. This variable is thus critical for short-term dynamics, because it is what allows countries to temporarily bypass the external financing constraints on growth by tapping international financial markets. This has been the rule in recent years in the majority of South American countries, which have run current account deficits since 2011.

Figure 8.1 presents an integrated view of these variables. The horizontal axis indicates "real vulnerability" (RV), which is proxied by the ratio between exports (X) of primary products (P) and the sum of all credits (C) on the current account (CA):

$$RV_t^i = \frac{X_t^{pi}}{C_t^{CA^i}}$$

where RV_t^i is the real vulnerability indicator of country i at time t, X_t^{pi} represents exports of primary products, and $C_t^{CA^i}$ represents credits on the current account. This ratio attempts to measure an economy's exposure to

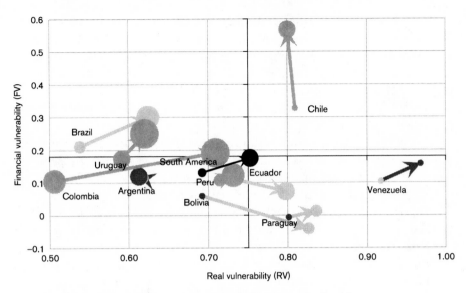

FIGURE 8.1 External vulnerability in South America.

fluctuations in international commodity prices. The higher the ratio, the more vulnerable the economy is considered to be to a negative shock in its terms of trade. On the graph, less diversified economies fall on the right-hand side, with Venezuela being the least diversified, followed by Chile, Bolivia, Ecuador, and Paraguay.

The vertical axis maps "financial vulnerability" (FV), proxied by the ratio between an economy's net debt (calculated as portfolio investment liabilities [PI] plus foreign direct investment [FDI] from the viewpoint of the international investment position minus international reserves) and GDP:

$$\text{FV}_t^i = \frac{\text{PI}_t^i + \text{FDI}_t^i - \text{Reserves}_t^i}{\text{GDP}_t^i}$$

where FV_t^i is the financial vulnerability indicator for country i at time t, PI_t^i is the stock of portfolio investment liabilities, FDI_t^i is the stock of foreign direct investment liabilities, and Reserves_t^i is the stock of foreign exchange reserves held by the central bank. GDP is measured at purchasing-power parity.

This ratio is a measure of the degree of leverage in an economy. The higher the indicator—increasing with a rise in external debt or a fall in international reserves—the more vulnerable an economy is considered to be to a negative shock in international liquidity. Paradoxically, in this case, economies that are more financially integrated into global markets (Brazil, Chile, Colombia, and Uruguay) show up on the figure in positions of higher relative vulnerability.

For each country, we present two observations: the first corresponds to the period before the crisis (2005–07 average) and the second corresponds to the period before the reversal of the commodity boom (2012–14 average). The figure includes two additional dimensions: the current account deficit and the degree of access to international credit markets. The size of the current account deficit is illustrated by the size of the dot: the larger the circle, the larger the current account deficit. The ability to access international credit markets is estimated by the EMBI and illustrated by the color of each dot (in this case, as reflected by the value for the EMBI in December 2014). Gray dots indicate full access to international credit markets (EMBI < 200), light gray indicates intermediate situations (EMBI range: 200–500), and dark gray indicates exclusion (EMBI {{!}} 500).

On average, South American countries moved upward and to the right in the period following the 2008–09 crisis, which implies increased vulnerability in both the real and the financial dimensions. There are, of course, variations within this trend. In the first group, both Bolivia and Paraguay increased their real vulnerability (exposing some structural inertia linked to natural-resource extraction) but reduced their financial vulnerability (indicating a relatively sound external position, due to either a low level of external debt, a high level of reserves, or a combination of the two). Deteriorations in the current account occurred in both cases. It is important to note, however, that in these two countries, access to international finance appears to have improved,[17] which increases the space for implementing countercyclical policies.

In the second group (Chile, Colombia, Peru, and Uruguay), most countries suffered deteriorations on the two fronts; Uruguay, the exception, reduced its external financial vulnerability.[18] Current account deterioration was significant for all four, with particularly large reductions in Colombia, Peru, and Uruguay. The strong devaluations in 2015 seem to portend a change in global conditions, which could make it harder for these countries to continue their growth based on international credit.

Finally, situations differ in Argentina, Brazil, Ecuador, and Venezuela. Argentina appears to have maintained constant levels of real and financial vulnerability. In the case of real vulnerability, the price effect of the increase in international commodity prices was compensated by a reduction of their share in Argentina's exports basket; in the case of financial vulnerability, its reserves fell sharply but its liabilities fell as well. Brazil, Ecuador, and Venezuela, on the other hand, experienced an increase in their external vulnerability. External vulnerability in Ecuador and Venezuela (both in levels and in variation) is concentrated in the real dimension, with oil exports explaining the majority of the credits on the current account. By contrast, the source of risks in Brazil seems to lie more on the financial side of vulnerability, allegedly due to massive inflows of short- and long-term capital flows. All four countries evidence deterioration of their current accounts and a worsening in international credit-market-access conditions, although in this regard, Brazil (even though it lost its investment-grade status in December 2015) still exhibited a more favorable situation than Argentina, Ecuador, and Venezuela.

In short, while six of the ten countries experienced an increase in both their real and financial vulnerabilities (Brazil, Colombia, Paraguay, Peru, Uruguay, and Venezuela), no country has managed to improve both of these dimensions simultaneously. Two countries reduced their real vulnerability but increased their degree of financial vulnerability (Chile and Argentina), while two others improved their financial vulnerability but increased their real vulnerability (Bolivia and Ecuador). In addition, it must be noted that the external positions of all South American countries worsened, as measured by the current account balance and illustrated by the larger dot size for 2012–14 compared to 2004–08 in Figure 8.1.

Behind the increase in real vulnerability also lies the commodity boom; commodity prices were, on average, 53 percent higher in 2012–14 than in 2005–07. Although commodity prices began to rise following the collapse of the "dot-com bubble," the exponential jump in prices that took them to record or near-record levels occurred between the end of 2006 and the collapse of Lehman Brothers in 2008. Between 2012 and 2014, prices plateaued at a high level. Real vulnerability combines both structural factors (such as the composition of the export basket, as in the case of Colombia) and situational factors (such as the evolution of international prices, as in most cases noted above). In the long term, structural factors are the decisive element; however, for short-term dynamics, one factor is not more important than another. Rather, it is the concurrence of both structural and situational factors that determines a country's degree of exposure to terms-of-trade volatility.

This is seen clearly from mid-2014 onward, when prices of primary goods fell abruptly, leading to a generalized deterioration in current account balances,[19] a reduction in fiscal space for countercyclical policies (a product of growing fiscal deficits or falling surpluses on one hand, and of increases in the EMBI on the other), large currency depreciations (on the order of 50 percent annually in Brazil and Colombia), and, as a consequence of all of the above, economic deceleration.

Behind the increase in financial vulnerability lies the loose monetary policy pursued by developed countries (mainly the United States) after the subprime crisis. South American countries, in particular financially integrated ones (Brazil, Chile, Colombia, Peru, and Uruguay), became an attractive destination for this excess international liquidity. Inflows not only involved short-term financial investment, which grew from 2.6 percent of GDP in 2004–08 to 3.7 percent in 2012–14, but also foreign direct investment. Indeed, from 2009 to 2014 the flow of inward foreign direct investment more than doubled for South America as a whole, to a large extent allocated to natural resources (CEPAL, 2015a).

Given that the majority of countries in the region tend to fall into a pattern of what has been defined as *debt-led growth*, the possibility of continued growth depends, fundamentally, on the will of international credit markets to provide the necessary financing. Using the EMBI as a proxy for market access, we find evidence of greater financial restrictions (higher EMBI) in seven of the ten countries: four in the third group (Argentina, Brazil, Ecuador, and Venezuela) and three in the second group (Chile, Colombia, and Peru). In the case of Argentina and Venezuela, EMBI levels are high enough to indicate exclusion from financial markets, which explains why these governments have faced harsher limits in implementing more intense countercyclical policies up to 2015. Even though neither of these two countries shows a highly negative current account balance, efforts to restore economic growth would imply running deficits that markets have not seemed willing to finance. By contrast, Brazil, Chile, Colombia, and Peru maintained access to international credit markets. However, the sharp currency depreciations during 2015, added to the uncertainty regarding the shift in the U.S. Federal Reserve's policy, indicate that the situation could change swiftly, forcing acute adjustment processes.

CONCLUSION

South American countries transitioned from export-led growth before the subprime crisis to debt-led growth afterward, as illustrated by the shift from a scenario of historically high growth rates along with current account surpluses (2004–08) to one of much slower growth rates and rising current account deficits. So called *debt-led growth* puts countries progressively at the whim not only of prevailing liquidity conditions in international credit markets but also of the predominant institutional vision of financial markets. This may imply that the capacity of South American governments to implement countercyclical polices to reignite growth and advance economic development depends fundamentally on the vision held by the international investor community.

Even though South American countries have increased their external vulnerability in recent years—as illustrated by their moving upward and to the right in the chart presented in Figure 8.1—their situation does not appear as risky from a historical perspective, compared, for example, to the end of the 1990s or to a large part of the 1980s. Throughout the 2000s, the region has increased its capacity to mitigate shocks from the external sector through the adoption of more flexible exchange-rate regimes and by improving its net international investment position (i.e., external debt reduction and reserve accumulation).

It is therefore unlikely that the new external environment will result in outcomes as traumatic as the financial crises provoked by destabilizing exchange-rate adjustments in the past. However, increasing external vulnerability can impose serious restrictions on governments' capacity to counteract downward pressures coming from abroad. As a result, there appears to be an inevitable convergence toward a "new normal"—or a "new mediocre," as some analysts have pointed out—characterized by lower growth rates and limited space for implementing countercyclical policies to reestablish growth.

The information presented in this chapter suggests that South American countries did not manage during the boom years to advance a process of structural change that would allow them to diversify their exports, in order to reduce their exposure to fluctuations in international prices. This is evidenced by the increase in real external vulnerability. Countries also failed to make significant advances regarding financial account regulation. In many cases, indiscriminate financial openness seems to have led to "too much" external leverage, jeopardizing subsequent growth. This is evidenced by the increase in financial external vulnerability.

There is, of course, a political-economy side to this juncture. In fact, there may exist a somewhat perverse relationship of reciprocal interdependence between the difficulties in implementing policies and advancing necessary institutional transformations for structural change, on one hand, and the deregulation/liberalization of the capital account on the balance of payments on the other. In a context of free-flowing international capital (i.e., of indiscriminate international financial integration), as is currently the case for most countries in the region, the type of policy that may support economic development—be it an increase in taxes on high-income sectors to fund public education, state exploitation of mineral resources to foster diversification and prevent resource depletion, fiscal stimulus targeted toward specific industries, or the establishment of a minimum wage policy for the sake of equity—can be seen, in practice, *conventionally* (i.e., by the international investor community) as a policy that puts into question the fiscal solvency of the state or its institutional "quality," therefore resulting in penalties in the valuation of debt securities or, in the extreme case, sheer credit rationing. It is also for this reason—to avoid the *ideological* interference in the viability of specific development policies—that, aside from the analytical concern over macroeconomic sustainability, historically both Keynesianism and structuralism have called for a more resolute regulation of cross-border capital flows than the one that currently prevails in the region (Keynes, 1933; Crotty, 1983).

In a context of free capital mobility, the type of policy necessary to maintain or reestablish access to external financing in order to resume higher growth rates tends to be anathema to development, involving the retreat of ("interventionist" or "statist") institutions that lie at the basis of successful late-industrialization success stories. Now, past the peak in international commodity prices, in an environment of growing external vulnerability, governments are likely to be forced to signal that their national efforts to restart growth will be limited—or at least will not be rooted in any progressive institutional reform of the state—under penalty of being cut off entirely from external financing sources. So long as regulation of international capital flows fails to be seriously considered, the ever-elusive external financing may be occasionally available to finance growth, but not development.

• • •

Martín Abeles is at the Economic Commission for Latin America and the Caribbean in Buenos Aires, Argentina. Sebastián Valdecantos is a research associate at the Universidad Nacional de Mar del Plata and invited professor at the Universidad Nacional de San Martín.

NOTES

1. It is worth noting, however, that some studies do not share this perspective and suggest instead that fiscal management in the majority of Latin American countries maintained its typical pro-cyclical bias in the precrisis period (IDB, 2008; Ocampo, 2009). According to this perspective, improvements in the aforementioned indicators are due to propitious external conditions

between 2003 and 2008 (favorable exchange rates and increased global liquidity), particularly for South American countries.

2. In the same vein, it is worth remembering the (also unprecedented) countercyclical stimulus by the International Monetary Fund in which it allocated U.S. $250 billion in special drawing rights for member countries in the third quarter of 2009.

3. Raúl Prebisch (1946) put forth a similar line of thinking—that there exists a "universal cyclical movement" that has its epicenter in developed countries and spreads to the periphery through real and financial channels (terms of trade and international liquidity cycles, respectively).

4. We define *countercyclical fiscal space* as the capacity of states to obtain the necessary financing to increase or maintain a level of public spending that sustains aggregate demand in the face of a reduction in the level of economic activity.

5. Even if countries managed to issue debt in local currency—as has been the case recently in Latin America—new forms of external vulnerability may arise, as pointed out in Kaltenbrunner and Painceira (2015).

6. This does not mean that the centrality of tax policy and the design and execution of government spending should be ignored in any development agenda. Rather, it suggests the preeminence of the external sector for fiscal policy.

7. Various Central American and Caribbean countries even benefited from the reversal of the upward trend in international commodity prices (as most of them are net importers of these commodities).

8. This is why, for example, between 2012 and 2014 the growth rate for South America differs significantly if it is calculated by the simple average (3.7 percent) versus the weighted average (2.1 percent).

9. However, it is worth mentioning that this situation may affect Argentina and Brazil, given that both countries are relatively important export destinations for each other: Brazil is the destination for 21.6 percent of all Argentine exports, and Argentina accounts for 8.1 percent of all Brazilian exports.

10. In Paraguay, the agricultural sector accounts for 25 percent of GDP.

11. Though not as high as between 2006 and 2011, commodity prices were still at historically elevated levels, at least until the first semester of 2014.

12. This is consistent—as will be evident in the following section—with the fact that the exogenous component of aggregate demand underlying the most serious contractionary pressures is that associated with the demand for exports.

13. In breaking down aggregate demand into its four components, we distribute imports between private consumption, investment, and exports—rather than netting imports entirely from exports as is typically done. This way, we obtain *net* private consumption (of imports), *net* investment, and *net* exports. Government expenditure is excluded from this adjustment, as it mostly consists of wages. Such an adjustment assumes that all components of aggregate demand, with the exception of public spending, have an important requirement for imports, not just exports as the conventional analysis tends to presuppose.

14. Constant prices are used in estimating contributions to aggregate demand growth. Therefore, exports can generate a negative contribution to real growth, even when the country shows a trade surplus.

15. In Venezuela, the contribution of exports to aggregate demand growth continued to be negative. However, since the size of its negative contribution fell between the two periods, the *change* in exports' contribution is positive.

16. To the extent that this increase is associated with international oil prices—Ecuador's most important export—it is highly likely that government spending's contribution to GDP will fall significantly in 2015.

17. For example, Bolivia issued sovereign bonds for U.S. $500 million in 2013, whereas Paraguay issued debt for U.S. $1 billion in 2014.

18. With respect to real external vulnerability, Colombia stands out; its large increase is explained by the fact that oil export volumes nearly tripled between the two periods analyzed. On the side of financial vulnerability, Uruguay is the exception, in that most of its foreign liabilities are concentrated in the "other investments" account of the international investment position, which is not included in our indicator. Taking these liabilities into consideration, Uruguay's financial vulnerability has also increased.

19. At the time of this writing, it is estimated that the deficit for the region as a whole has increased from −3.0% in 2014 to −3.3% in 2015.

REFERENCES

Abeles, Martín, Juan Cuattromo, Pablo Mareso, and Fernando Toledo (2013), "Sector externo y política fiscal en los países en desarrollo. La experiencia de América Latina ante la crisis internacional de 2008–2009," CEFID-AR, Documento de Trabajo no. 48, March.

Arestis, Philip, and Malcolm Sawyer (2003), "Reinventing Fiscal Policy," Journal of Post Keynesian Economics, 26, pp. 3–26.

——— (2004), "On Fiscal Policy and Budget Deficits," European Journal of Economics and Economic Policies: Intervention, 1, pp. 61–74.

——— (2010), "The Return of Fiscal Policy," Journal of Post Keynesian Economics, 32, pp. 327–346.

Bernat, Gonzalo (2015), "Tipo de cambio real y diversificación productiva en América del Sur," Serie Estudios y Perspectivas, no. 43. Oficina de la CEPAL en Buenos Aires: CEPAL.

CEPAL (2012), "Cambio estructural para la igualdad: Una visión integrada del desarrollo," Trigésimo Cuarto Período de Sesiones de la CEPAL, San Salvador, August 27–31, 2012.

——— (2015a), "La inversión extranjera directa en América Latina y el Caribe" (LC/G.2641-P), Santiago.

——— (2015b), "Preliminary Balance of the Economies of Latin America and the Caribbean" (LC/G.2655-P), Santiago.

Crotty, James (1983), "On Keynes and Capital Flight," Journal of Economic Literature, 21, pp. 59–65.

Daude, Christian, Ángel Melguizo, and Alejandro Neut (2010), "Fiscal Policy in Latin America: Countercyclical and Sustainable at Last?" Working Paper 291. Paris: OECD Development Centre.

Eichengreen, Barry, Ricardo Hausmann, and Ugo Panizza (2002). "Original Sin: The Pain, the Mystery and the Road to Redemption," paper presented at a conference on Currency and Maturity Matchmaking: Redeeming Debt from Original Sin, Inter-American Development Bank.

Gutiérrez, Mario, and Julio Revilla (2010), "Building Countercyclical Fiscal Policies in Latin America: The International Experience," World Bank Policy Research Working Paper 5211.

IDB (Inter-American Development Bank) (2008), "All That Glitters May Not Be Gold: Assessing Latin America's Recent Macroeconomic Performance." Washington, DC: IDB.

IMF (International Monetary Fund) (2015), "World Economic Outlook: Adjusting to Lower Commodity Prices." October. Washington, DC: IMF.

Kaltenbrunner, Annina, and Juan P. Painceira (2015), "Developing Countries' Changing Nature of Financial Integration and New Forms of External Vulnerability: The Brazilian Experience," Cambridge Journal of Economics, 39, pp. 1281–1306.

Keynes, John M. (1933), "National Self-Sufficiency," Yale Review, 22, pp. 755–769.

Martner, Ricardo, and Varinia Tromben (2004), "La sostenibilidad de la deuda pública," Revista de la CEPAL 84 (December).

Ocampo, José Antonio (2009), "Latin America and the Global Financial Crisis," Cambridge Journal of Economics, 33, pp. 703–724.

——— (2011), "Macroeconomía para el desarrollo: Políticas anticíclicas y transformación productiva," Revista de la CEPAL 104 (August).

Pérez Caldentey, Esteban (2007), "Debt in CARICOM: Origins and Consequences for Growth and Economic Development," Business, Finance & Economics in Emerging Economies, 2, pp. 97–143.

Prebisch, Raúl (1946), "Memoria: Primera reunión de técnicos sobre problemas de banca central del continente americano," Banco de México, pp. 25–26.

Rodríguez, Octavio (1977), "Sobre la concepción del sistema centro-periferia," Revista de la CEPAL.

Thirlwall, Anthony (1979), "The Balance of Payments Constraint as an Explanation of International Growth Rate Differences," Banca Nazionale del Lavoro Quarterly Review.

9. China in Latin America

Social and Environmental Lessons for Institutions in a Commodity Boom

Rebecca Ray and Kevin P. Gallagher

INTRODUCTION

Latin America's recent commodity boom brought a sharp increase in social conflict and environmental degradation. Driven by trade and investment with China, the boom was concentrated in petroleum, mining, and agriculture—sectors historically linked to environmental and social conflict. With some notable exceptions, Latin American governments have fallen short of mitigating these risks. Moreover, as the boom cools and Latin American economies slow, regional governments face pressure to "streamline" approvals for new export and investment projects, stymieing civil society's work of holding governments and foreign firms accountable.

While China should not be blamed for most of Latin America's environmental and social problems, it is important for China to mitigate the impacts of its overseas activities, to maintain good relations with host countries and reduce the risks of international investment. Some Chinese firms have demonstrated an ability to reach best practices in these arenas, but overall they lack the experience or policies to manage their impacts in the region. It is in the interests of the Latin American and Chinese governments, as well as Chinese firms, to put in place the proper social and environmental policies in order to maximize the benefits and mitigate the risks of China's economic activity in Latin America.

These results stem from our work with the Working Group on Development and the Environment in the Americas, a multi-university effort coordinated by the Center for Transformation Research (CENIT) in Argentina, the Research Center of the University of the Pacific (CIUP) in Peru, Boston University's Global Economic Governance Initiative (GEGI), and Tufts University's Global Development and Environment Institute

(GDAE). Comprised of an aggregate regional analysis and eight country studies conducted by university-based researchers from across the hemisphere, the study asked two research questions. First, to what extent has China independently driven environmental and social change in Latin America? Second, to what extent do Chinese investors in Latin America perform differently from their Western and domestic counterparts?

CHINA AS A DRIVER OF SOCIAL AND ENVIRONMENTAL CHANGE IN LATIN AMERICA

China is now the top export destination for South American goods, and second only to the United States for the entire region. In 1993, China consumed less than 2 percent of exports from Latin America and the Caribbean (LAC), but by 2013 it accounted for 9 percent. However, that importance was quite uneven across different export sectors. As Figure 9.1 shows, over the past decade China nearly tripled its share of total LAC exports, more than tripled its share of extractive exports, and nearly doubled its share of agricultural exports. But its demand for manufactured LAC exports has remained at about 2 percent of LAC's manufacture exports.

As a result, LAC exports to China have become heavily concentrated in extraction and agriculture. As Figure 9.2 shows, over the past five years, extraction alone accounted for more than half of all LAC–China exports. This stands in contrast to overall LAC exports, which are much more diverse. Nor does this composition reflect that of Chinese imports, which are dominated by manufactured goods. Instead, this composition reflects a strategic, commodities-driven relationship between China and the LAC region.

Chinese investment in LAC has been similarly concentrated in primary sectors. Figure 9.3 shows the sector distribution in the past five years of foreign direct investment (FDI) from mergers and acquisitions and from greenfield projects, respectively. Among greenfield projects, China's difference is most visible in new infrastructure projects (the $40 billion Nicaragua Canal project represents most of the greenfield investment shown here; dollar values throughout this chapter are U.S. dollars). Among mergers and acquisitions, over two-thirds of investment has been in extraction (specifically the oil and gas sector), a sharp contrast to overall mergers and acquisitions, where extraction represents just 15 percent.

Employment Creation

LAC–China exports support fewer jobs per $1 million because of their heavy concentration in extractive industries. Figure 9.4 compares the labor

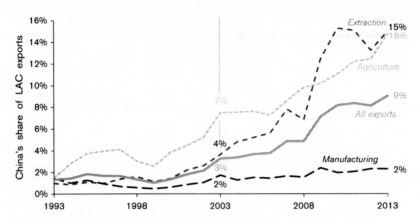

FIGURE 9.1   China's share of exports from Latin America and the Caribbean (LAC) by sector, 1993–2013. (Source: Ray and Gallagher, 2015.)

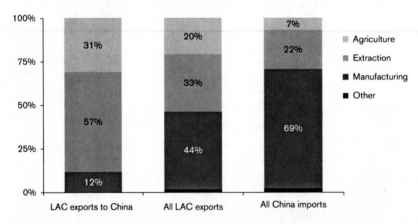

FIGURE 9.2   Trade basket composition for Latin America and the Caribbean (LAC) and China by market, 2009–2013. (Source: Ray et al., 2015.)

intensity of LAC overall economic activity, overall exports, and exports to China. Total exports have remained fairly stable, supporting between fifty and sixty jobs per $1 million. Exports to China, however, have fallen by over a third in the number of jobs they support for every $1 million, from nearly seventy in 2002 to fewer than forty-five in 2012.[1]

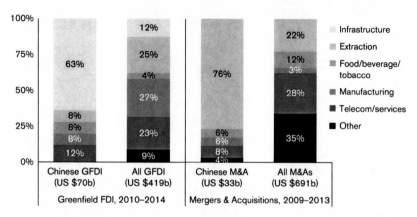

FIGURE 9.3 Sector distribution of foreign direct investment (FDI) inflows to Latin America and the Caribbean for the most recent five years. (Source: Ray et al., 2015.)

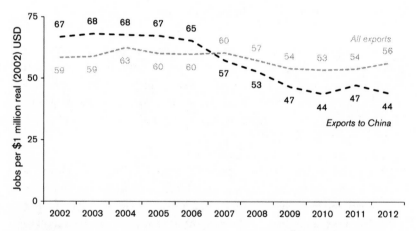

FIGURE 9.4 Jobs supported by overall economic activity and exports in Latin America and the Caribbean, 2002–2012. (Source: Ray et al., 2015.)

Environmental Impacts

The high concentration of extractive and agricultural products among LAC exports to China gives them a heavier environmental footprint than other exports. This section looks more closely at two environmental impacts, one global (greenhouse gas emissions) and one local (water use and contamination).

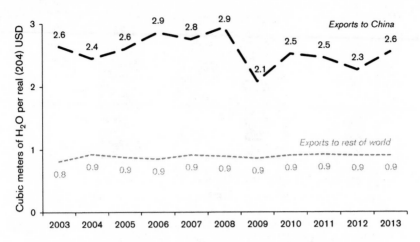

FIGURE 9.5 Water intensity of Latin American and Caribbean exports to China and the rest of the world, 2003–2013. For full methodology, see Ray (2017). (Sources: Authors' calculation using water intensities from Mekonnen and Hoekstra, 2011a, 2011b, 2012; commodity price data from FAO and the World Bank; export basket composition from UN Comtrade.)

As Figure 9.5 shows, LAC exports to China have used over twice as much water as other LAC exports: two to three cubic meters per dollar to produce, compared to less than one. The water intensity levels shown here include both the use of clean water ("blue" and "green" water footprints for groundwater and rainwater, respectively) and water contamination (the "gray water" footprint).

Taken together, the data in Figures 9.4 and 9.5 have important implications for social and environmental conflicts. Our case studies show that the most common causes of conflict surrounding Chinese investment in Latin America were water and jobs. The disproportionate use and contamination of water by oil wells, mines, and plantations for export to China can endanger local communities' traditional livelihoods of small-scale agriculture, ranching, and fishing. But these same wells, mines, and plantations create very few new jobs to make up for this loss of income. In the context of this double squeeze on local communities, it is important for Latin American policy makers to set and enforce appropriate environmental standards and continue to prioritize diversification away from production of raw commodities for export.

As Figure 9.6 shows, LAC–China exports have also consistently caused more net greenhouse gas (GHG) emissions than other LAC exports. Figure 9.6 measures *net* GHG emissions in CO2 equivalency, including agricultural sources of methane and the elimination of natural carbon sinks through defor-

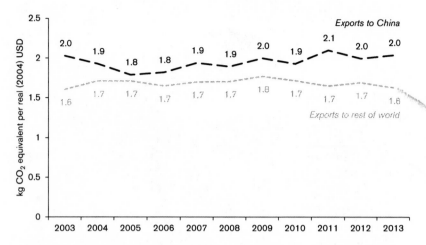

FIGURE 9.6 Net intensity of greenhouse gas emissions from overall economic activity and exports in Latin America and the Caribbean, 2003–2013. For full methodology, see Ray (2017). (Sources: Authors' calculation using GHG intensity data from Peters et al., 2011; commodity price data from FAO and the World Bank; export basket composition from UN Comtrade.)

estation and the clearing of the Brazilian *cerrado* grasslands. In LAC, land-use change is one of the most important factors in net GHG emission changes, accounting for about 41 percent of the region's total in 2010 (FAOStat, no date). Our case study of China's relationship with Brazil shows that exports to China are a statistically significant driver of deforestation in the Brazilian Amazon, together with the total soybean-planted area. In turn, China has been an important driver in the expansion of the soy area: in 2013 China accounted for three-fourths of Brazil's oilseed exports (Fearnside and Figueiredo, 2015).

In terms of deforestation, Figure 9.6 actually understates the GHG emissions from LAC's relationship with China; while it accounts for deforestation directly linked to exports, it does not account for the most important cause of deforestation, namely roads, canals, and railroads to move those products to ports. Research by Philip Fearnside et al. (2013) shows that access roads are the most important cause of Amazonian deforestation, as they open the forest to new human settlements and interrupt animal migration patterns. Thus, in order to adequately account for the GHG impact of the "China boom" in Latin America, it is important to include not just exports to China but also Chinese-financed roads, canals, and railroads, as well as dams to provide power to mines and oil fields.

Figure 9.7 shows South America's most biodiverse areas and indigenous territories, with Chinese-financed infrastructure and FDI projects. The

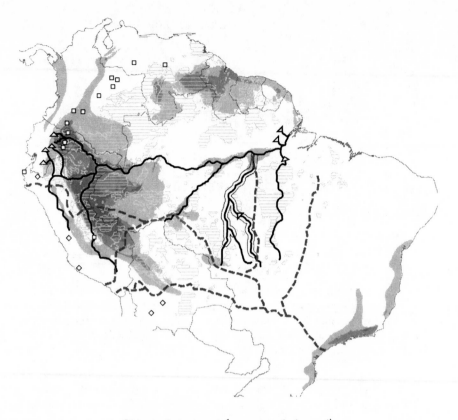

Chinese investment (current and planned):

- - - - Railways
≡≡≡ Commerical waterways
△ Dams
◇ Mines
□ Oil concessions

High-biodiversity areas:

High biodiversity in 4 species
groups: mammals, birds,
amphibians, and plants

3 groups
2 groups
1 groups

Indigenous territory

Major rivers

FIGURE 9.7   Chinese investment, high-biodiversity areas, and indigenous territory in Latin America. "High biodiversity" is defined as the top 6.4 percent of South American land area for species richness. Note that the mines and some oil concessions are already in operation, whereas the railway locations are approximate because most plans for those are not yet final. (Source: Ray et al., 2015.)

BOX 9.1 CHINESE LOANS FOR LAC OIL

Much has been made in the press about Chinese loans that are repayable in oil. However, while the form of these loans may be novel, their impact is nothing new.

In loans for oil, a Chinese development bank lends money to an oil-producing LAC country, which agrees to ship oil in return to Chinese oil companies. These companies then divert part of their payment for the oil to the bank for the loan's repayment. The oil is sold at market prices; if the oil price rises, the loan will get repaid more quickly, and vice versa. Finally, the contracts involve more oil than needed to pay the loans: the remaining money goes back to the borrowing country.

As in all loans, the lender and borrower agree to interest rates and repayment periods, as well as the quantity of oil to be shipped. However, future oil prices are unknown, as is the share of each oil shipment that will go to repay the loan. The result is similar to a loan payable in U.S. dollars for an oil-producing country: the borrower exports oil and repays their debts from the proceeds. Finally, as long as there is a world market where a country can exchange oil for dollars, there is no additional risk that low oil production will endanger repayment. In such a case, the country can buy oil on the world market and have it shipped to China. For more on these loans, see Gallagher et al. (2012).

biodiversity of these areas is reflected in the various shades of gray, with the darkest gray patches (present only in eastern Ecuador and the northern extreme of Peru) representing areas with the highest biodiversity. Indigenous territories are indicated by stripes.

As Figure 9.7 shows, two major Chinese investments may pose serious risks to highly biodiverse areas and indigenous territories in the Amazon basin: the western half of the Twin Ocean Railway and oil fields in eastern Ecuador. The Twin Ocean Railway is still in its planning stage, so it does not yet have a finalized path. Two possible routes exist for its western end: one through northern Peru and another through southern Peru. The northern route crosses into Brazil through indigenous territory, which also boasts very high biodiversity. The southern route largely avoids this sensitive region. The final choice of route for this railway will be crucial in determining its environmental impact.

The other major Chinese investment in highly biodiverse land is oil development in eastern Ecuador, much of which also occupies traditional indigenous territory. The southernmost two Chinese oil concessions in

Ecuador are new, and their contracts have not yet been finalized. If these concessions go through, the terms of their contracts will be extremely important for both their social and environmental impacts. These concessions are in addition to official Chinese financing for oil production by Ecuador's state-owned oil company PetroEcuador, some of which are to be repaid with shipments of oil (see Box 9.1).

LATIN AMERICAN MARKET SHARE AND POLICY SPACE

As shown in Figure 9.1, LAC exports to China are heavily concentrated in primary commodities. In fact, just four commodities—iron, soybeans and similar oilseeds, refined copper, and copper ores and concentrates—account for over two-thirds of that export basket. However, as Table 9.1 shows, the LAC region commands a sizable share of the Chinese market in those commodities. For example, the region represents over half of China's imports of copper ores and concentrates and nearly half of China's imports of soybeans and similar oilseeds.

Because of LAC's market power in these top exports to China, the region has room to enforce environmental and social protections on copper mining and production, or on the deforestation impacts of soybean production, even if it results in somewhat higher prices, without being easily replaced as a supplier for China. Similarly, LAC is responsible for over half of the world's (and China's) unrefined copper but less than one-third of refined copper. If the region prioritized the development of downstream industries with higher value added, there is no other source of unrefined copper that could take the place of LAC's exports.

Rising to the Challenge: Social and Environmental Safeguard Innovations

Facing this upsurge in sectors linked to high environmental and social risks, several Latin American countries have developed important policy responses to minimize these risks. Three of the most innovative of these responses are Brazil's new environmental oversight measures, Ecuador's new labor standards, and Peru's transparency measures and indigenous protections.

Brazil dramatically enhanced the enforcement power of its environmental regulations in 2008, without changing current environmental laws themselves. Instead, the Central Bank of Brazil changed its rules to no longer allow public bank loans to operations with unpaid environmental fines. Fines can be postponed through appeals, but this more proactive approach has immediate effect.

TABLE 9.1 Market Share of Latin America and Caribbean (LAC) for Top LAC–China Export Commodities

Country	Iron (ores and concentrates)		Soybeans and other oilseeds		Copper (refined)		Copper (ores and concentrates)	
	World imports	China's imports	World imports	China's imports	World imports	China's imports	World imports	China's imports
Argentina	–	–	7%	10%	–	–	3%	
Brazil	26%	16%	25%	34%	1%	1%	3%	1%
Chile	1%	1%	–	–	21%	27%	32%	28%
Mexico	–	–	–	–	1%	1%	2%	6%
Peru	1%	1%	–	–	2%	2%	15%	17%
Other	–	–	5%	1%	–	–	–	–
LAC total	28%	18%	37%	45%	25%	31%	57%	51%

SOURCE: Ray and Gallagher (2015).

Ecuador enacted a series of labor protections in 2008 and 2010 that form one of the most progressive labor packages in the region for the nation's petroleum sector. In 2008, Ecuador strictly curtailed the use of subcontracted labor, limiting it to "complementary" work such as security and custodial services. The 2010 Hydrocarbon Law further boosted labor protections in the oil and gas sector, by requiring foreign investors to hire Ecuadorean workers for 95 percent of unskilled and 90 percent of skilled jobs. Moreover, it required profit sharing with all employees, including contract workers. Together, these laws eliminated two of the most important sources of labor conflicts facing Chinese (and other international) investment projects across the LAC region: the use of foreign laborers, and differences in the labor conditions between directly hired and subcontracted employees working at the same project.

Peru has made important strides in transparency and indigenous rights over the past decade. Peru joined the Extractive Industries Transparency Initiative (EITI) in 2007, and in 2011 it became the first country in the Americas to be declared compliant within that framework. Under EITI, the Peruvian government and participating companies publish detailed reports of revenue flows related to the extractive industries, available online. Furthermore, the Peruvian government assigned staff to encourage participation among non-participating companies. Starting in 2014, three major Chinese companies confirmed their involvement in the process: Shougang, China Minmetals, and China National Petroleum Corporation (CNPC). Also, in 2011 Peru became the first LAC country to enact legislation to implement International Labour Organization (ILO) Convention 169, recognizing indigenous communities' right to prior consultation on new developments that directly affect them or their traditional territories. These two measures put Peru in a leadership position regionally for public participation in the resource boom.

Progress under Fire: Challenges to Existing Protections

High commodity prices associated with the China boom empowered local mining and agricultural interests, including investors and sectoral ministries. As the commodity boom cools, Latin American governments face declining GDP growth, and regional governments face pressure from these newly empowered sectors to curtail environmental and social safeguards to streamline new investment projects. To that end, Peru has recently curtailed the authority of the Environment Ministry over the approval and supervision of extractive projects. Bolivia nearly enacted similar changes, but these were resisted between the draft and final versions of the new Mining Law (Saravia López and Rua Quiroga, 2015; Sanborn and Chonn, 2015). In Brazil, Chinese demand has enriched and empowered the "ruralist" voting block, representing large landholders in Congress (Santilli, 2014; Smeraldi, 2014). It has mounted an effort to roll back the new Central Bank rules cited above, which have proved useful in strengthening enforcement of environmental safeguards.

THE PERFORMANCE—AND INCENTIVES—OF CHINESE INVESTORS IN LATIN AMERICA

Our research shows that Chinese firms do not perform significantly worse in relation to domestic or other international firms. In fact, despite relatively weaker levels of regulation at home in China, and a fledgling set of guidelines for overseas companies, case studies have found some instances of Chinese firms outperforming their competitors, especially with proper incentives from governments and civil society. We have examined eight case studies in depth, in eight LAC countries: Argentina, Bolivia, Brazil, Chile, Colombia, Ecuador, Mexico, and Peru. This section explores lessons from each of these case studies. Overall, they show that Chinese firms are flexible, able to adapt to new environments and perform to local standards. However, several of the cases show that as these investments continue to expand, major challenges still lie ahead.

Among these Chinese firms is one that our case studies examine in three different Latin American countries: Sinopec. The case studies show that Sinopec has had vastly different experiences under different regulatory regimes and with different incentives. Sinopec's labor relations in Argentina and its environmental performance in Ecuador have been more positive than either in Colombia.

Sinopec's labor challenges in Colombia have involved the local community action boards, which are common in rural Colombia and control oil employment. Allegations abound of local authorities trading jobs for favors or fees, or unfairly favoring workers from other areas over local workers, but regional Labor Ministry officials state that these complaints have not been formalized for fear of endangering the very employment positions they involve. The Colombian national government is considering removing hiring authority from community action boards, but the proposal faces vigorous opposition by the boards themselves, unsurprisingly. In contrast, Sinopec faces no such issues in Argentina or Ecuador, because of the regulatory framework in each country. In Argentina, Sinopec has signed an agreement with the local government ensuring that all workers will have had residency in the Santa Cruz province for at least two years prior to their hiring. In Ecuador, oil-sector labor is tightly regulated, as discussed above.

Environmentally, Sinopec has a better record in Ecuador than most of its competitors, with fewer local protests over spills than any of its competitors, either foreign or domestic. This record is partly due to the incentives it faces there: it bought oil concessions that were initially owned by Chevron and therefore receive a great deal of attention. Sinopec's ability to maintain a low profile has been key to its ability to continue operations for nearly a decade. In contrast, the attorney general of Colombia cited Sinopec in 2014 for never having paid $500,000 in promised investment in land conservation to ensure clean water for a local community. These two cases show the importance of establishing—and enforcing—an effective regulatory framework for international investment. Fortunately, Colombia appears to be taking this to heart, as its 2014 environmental finding and the recent proposed change in labor regulation show.

Other positive outcomes in the case studies show that Chinese investors are capable of living up to high standards, especially when the proper incentives are in place. These case studies show the importance of cooperation between governments, investors, local communities, and Chinese regulators in creating those incentives. This cooperation can be especially helpful in the areas of oversight by lenders, community engagement at the outset of projects, and training investors in compliance with local laws.

Incentives from Home: The Role of Lender Oversight

China should be credited for enacting guidelines for its overseas economic activities. When Western countries were at middle-income status, such guidelines were not on government radar screens. Other middle-income countries (like Brazil, discussed above) prevent public lending to *domestic* projects with outstanding environmental fines, and *multilateral* lenders have long required borrowers to meet environmental performance standards. But these kinds of standards for *outbound* international investment set China ahead of its middle-income-country peers. Nonetheless, China is a relative newcomer to international investment, and its environmental and social safeguards still lag behind those of the traditional multilateral lenders.

China has three levels of safeguards for outbound investment. First, the Ministry of Commerce (MOFCOM) has voluntary "Guidelines for Environmental Protection in Foreign Investment and Cooperation" for all investors, regardless of whether they are public or private and how they are financed. While these are not binding, they carry moral authority for state-owned enterprises (SOEs; Tao, 2013). For bank-financed projects, the China Banking Regulatory Commission has "Green Credit Guidelines" for all Chinese banks that finance investment projects abroad, which include requiring investments to meet host-country and international environmental laws. Finally, state-owned "policy banks" that fund overseas interests in the name of the Chinese government, the China Development Bank and the Export-Import Bank of China, have developed safeguard practices for projects within their portfolios.

Table 9.2 compares Chinese guidelines to those of major multilateral lenders: the World Bank, the International Finance Corporation, and the Inter-American Development Bank. While the Chinese lenders and regulators have fewer requirements than the multilateral lenders, there is one notable exception: only the Chinese policy banks require ex-post environmental impact assessments.

The regulations shown in Table 9.2 represent a major step forward for Chinese lenders, but those lenders still face steep challenges in enforcement. For example, without a grievance policy, lenders may not know about violations of other requirements like international environmental laws. Furthermore, even compliance with a host country's law—arguably the simplest of the requirements in Table 9.2 to enforce—can be challenging if local governments are not enforcing their own laws. For example, in the Sinopec case in Colombia discussed above, the attorney general cited not only Sinopec but also the national environmental licensing agency, for not enforcing its own regulations. In that type of situation, it is not clear that MOFCOM has the grounds to claim that Sinopec has violated their guidelines. Latin American civil society groups have begun educating communities about China's environmental and social safeguards; but without a formal method for receiving and investigating complaints, banks have little immediate incentive to follow up on any communication they receive. Given the difficulty in policing investor behavior abroad, Chinese lenders could benefit from approaching Latin American civil society and governments as partners in holding investors accountable, perhaps through introducing a formal grievance mechanism.

The Importance of Community Engagement

Our case studies show that an investor's willingness to work with governments and communities from the outset of their project, especially when deciding where to build, is one of the most important aspects of establishing positive community relations. Three examples highlight this lesson particularly well: Chinalco's Toromocho copper mine in Peru, the Jungie tin mine

TABLE 9.2 Chinese and Multilateral Regulations Compared

Regulations	Multilateral lenders			Chinese banks and regulators			
	WB	IFC	IDB	MOFCOM[a]	CBRC	CDB	Ex-Im
Ex-ante environmental impact assessments	X	X	X	X		X	X
Project review of environmental impact assessments	X	X	X			X	X
Industry-specific social and environmental standards	X	X					
Require compliance with host country's environmental regulations	X		X	X	X	X	X
Require compliance with international environmental regulations	X				X		
Public consultations with affected communities	X	X	X	X			X
Grievance mechanism	X	X					
Independent monitoring and review	X						
Establishing covenants linked to compliance	X	X	X				X
Ex-post environmental impact assessments						X	X

SOURCES: China Banking Regulatory Commission, 2012; Gallagher et al., 2012; Leung and Zhao, 2013; State Forestry Administration, 2010.
NOTE: WB = World Bank. IFC = International Finance Corporation. IDB = Inter-American Development Bank. MOFCOM = China Ministry of Commerce. CBRC = China Banking Regulatory Commission. CDB = China Development Bank. Ex-Im = Export-Import Bank of China.
[a] MOFCOM policies are voluntary.

in Bolivia, and Andes Petroleum in Ecuador. Each case illustrates the importance of government incentives and assistance in the negotiations.

In Bolivia, China's Jungie Mining and the local Alto Canutillos mining
cooperative formed a joint venture to mine tin in Tacobamba in 2010.
Although the mine is not in the high-biodiversity areas shown in Figure
9.8, it does lie within threatened land: the Tropical Andes Biodiversity
Hotspot.[2]

Before operations began, surveys showed that the local community was
opposed to the establishment of a processing plant and tailings dam in
Tacobamba. In response, the state-owned COMIBOL mining company
donated land over twenty-five miles away for the facility, in Agua Dulce,
Villa de Yocalla, where a public consultation showed that the community
welcomed it. This move required cooperation between the investors, the
government, and the local community, but it prevented a major potential
source of conflict (Saravia López and Rua Quiroga, 2015).

In Peru, a Chinese SOE, Chinalco's Toromocho mine, also borders the
Tropical Andes Biodiversity Hotspot, as shown in Figure 9.9. In 2007, Chinalco
committed to relocating the 5,000 residents of the existing town of Morococha
to make way for the mine construction. Morococha is a mining camp with
badly contaminated water and soil from decades of nearby mining operations.
While the old Morococha had communal latrines and a limited water supply,
"Nueva Morococha" boasts a modern water and sanitation system. Perhaps
most importantly, the move was overwhelmingly voluntary and the product
of dialogue and negotiation between community members, local authorities,
the central government, and the investor—considered the first example of
voluntary, participatory community relocation in modern Peruvian history.
While it has not been without problems (for example, Chinalco offered each
family a title to its new home, but the municipality has been delayed in issuing
them) and there continue to be a number of holdouts, it represents a step forward in Peruvian mining community relations (Sanborn and Chonn, 2015).

Community consultation has not gone so smoothly in Ecuador, where
Andes Petroleum (a joint venture between Chinese SOEs Sinopec and
CNPC) won two new concessions in 2014. As shown in Figure 9.7, Ecuador
is the only South American country where major Chinese investments exist
in an area with extremely high biodiversity as well as traditional indigenous
territory (shown in more detail in Figure 9.10). Andes Petroleum's respect
for social and environmental safeguards is thus especially important, perhaps more so than any other Chinese investments in LAC. Until now, Andes
has had better community relations than its competitors (including
Ecuadorean SOEs), with fewer protests due to contamination or unfulfilled

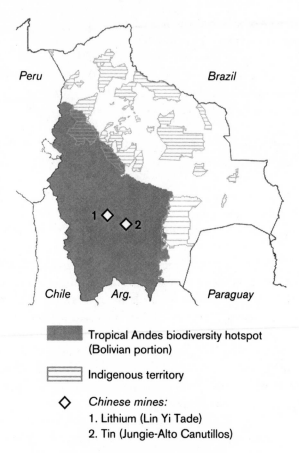

FIGURE 9.8   Biodiversity hotspot, indigenous territory, and Chinese mines in Bolivia. (Source: Ray et al., 2015.)

social obligations. But its real challenge lies ahead: its expansion is beginning acrimoniously, without the proper community consultation.

Ecuadorean law requires the Secretary of Hydrocarbons (SHE) to seek majority approval within the affected communities: the Sápara and Kichwa indigenous nations, whose authority over developments in their territory Ecuador recognized by joining ILO Convention 169. However, instead of seeking majority approval of the Sápara and Kichwa communities, SHE merely signed an agreement with the Sápara president. SHE also opened temporary outreach offices in the affected area, and it claims that 16,469 people participated in workshops or submitted comments—about one-fourth of the local adult indigenous population, or about one-eighth of the

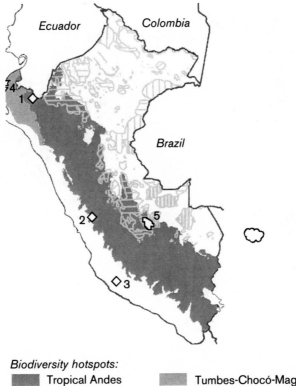

Biodiversity hotspots:
███ Tropical Andes   ▒▒▒ Tumbes-Chocó-Magdalena

Indigenous territory:
▨ Unrecognized   ☰ Recognized, not set aside
▥ Reserve, set aside   ⦀ Reserve (proposed)

◇ Chinese mines:
  1. Rio Blanco copper, molybdenum mine (Zijin group)
  2. Toromocho copper mine (Chinalco)
  3. Marona iron mine (Shougang Corporation)

Chinese oil concessions:
  4. Talara oilfield, blocks 6 & 7 (CNPC)
  5. Lot 58 (SAPET, CNPC subsidiary)

FIGURE 9.9   Biodiversity hotspots, indigenous territory, and Chinese mines and oil concessions in Peru. (Source: Ray et al., 2015.)

Current concessions (as of 2006)
Upcoming concessions (as of 2014)

High-biodiversity areas:
High biodiversity in 4 species groups:
mammals, birds, amphibians, and plants
High biodiversity in 3 species groups
2 groups   1 groups

Indigenous territory:
Not officially recognized
Recognized and set aside

FIGURE 9.10   Chinese oil concessions, biodiversity, and indigenous territory in Ecuador. (Source: Ray and Chimienti, 2015.)

total adult population in the new concession blocks. Sápara and Kichwa community leaders mounted an international struggle to reclaim authority over their traditional lands and reject all oil development there. The possibilities for Andes Petroleum to establish a positive relationship with the local community are extremely slim at this point, with good-faith negotiations between the government and the local community almost impossible (Ray and Chimienti, 2015).

Government–Firm Relations: The Importance of Outreach and Learning

Another important venue for cooperation between investors, governments, and civil society is in training new arrivals on local regulations and customs. Recent examples in Peru, Argentina, and Mexico show that this is a promising area that Latin American governments are just beginning to explore.

In March 2014, Chinalco's Toromocho mine project in Peru (noted above for its community relocation process) suffered a major setback when the Environment Ministry ordered it to halt operations following a leak of acid wastewater. The problem was generated by unexpectedly heavy rainfall, which Chinalco had not taken into account. After the cleanup, which happened within a few days after rapid action by regulators and Chinalco, the Association of Chinese Companies in Peru asked the Environment Ministry to organize a series of conferences for all of their members about Peru's environmental regulations. This was an opportunity for the government to address environmental concerns in a proactive way as well as to form working relationships with environmental safety personnel at the investing firms, and to lay the groundwork for future cooperation.

Argentina is a unique case: negotiations over oil royalties and environmental and social commitments happen at the provincial level, which gives local civil society groups more access to the negotiators. Small business groups, for instance, have successfully pressed for foreign oil companies to develop more linkages with local suppliers. For example, Pan American Energy—a joint entity of China National Offshore Oil Corporation (CNOOC) and British Petroleum (BP)—has developed the "SMEs of Golfo San Jorge" program to build capacity for small businesses and incorporate them into Pan American Energy's supply chain. This kind of cooperation requires provincial government help to connect recently arrived foreign investors with local organizations. Another important opportunity for training in Argentina involves more experienced and more recent investors—in this case, CNOOC and Sinopec. Our case study shows that

CNOOC has a better environmental record than Sinopec, partly because CNOOC partners with BP, which has a long history of foreign investment and global scrutiny of its environmental record. Even though both CNOOC and Sinopec are Chinese SOEs, one benefits from its cooperation with more experienced investors while the other does not. Argentina can help bridge these differences by facilitating training, where new arrivals can learn from their more experienced peers.

The Mexico case study is another situation where training may be useful. Generally speaking, the Golden Dragon copper tube manufacturing company has abided by environmental and labor law and has even introduced energy-efficiency innovations. Nonetheless, it has run into labor difficulties due to cultural barriers. One major obstacle springs from Chinese managers' unfamiliarity with Mexican customs. Chinese minimum wages are quite low, and workers compensate by working long hours. Mexican workers tend to be less willing to work on weekends and holidays. Golden Dragon has historically required work on those days and has not compensated workers appropriately for overtime, largely because they are not accustomed to workers expecting that time off. These cultural differences between Golden Dragon's Chinese and Mexican workers are unlikely to be resolved without being specifically addressed, because the two groups of workers do not speak the same language. But they are the types of misunderstandings that can be addressed straightforwardly with training to ensure that Chinese investors respect Mexican labor laws.

POLICY RECOMMENDATIONS

Our study shows that Latin America's China-led commodity boom has accentuated environmental and social conflict. Although Latin American governments, Chinese firms, and civil society can be credited for some innovations during the China boom, the benefits of China-led trade and investment have come with significant environmental and social costs. These costs can be reduced by the concerted action of Latin American governments, the Chinese government and Chinese firms, and civil society in both regions.

Latin American Governments

For Latin America to benefit from this commodity-led growth, Latin American governments will need to invest more of the windfall into social and environmental protections. Meanwhile, civil society organizations will need the freedom to hold governments and investors accountable. Our case studies found numerous examples of Latin American governments developing innovative policy responses to the China boom. Ecuador's labor laws, Bolivia's implementation of community consultation, and Peru's leadership on transparency stand out as particularly important policy steps. There is room for Latin American civil society groups to take advantage of these examples to push for higher standards everywhere.

Chinese oil companies have shown in Ecuador that they are capable of operating with almost entirely Ecuadorean staff. Bolivia has shown that it is possible for Chinese mining companies and local SOEs to collaborate to honor communities' decisions about where processing plants should be located. Peru has shown that Chinese mining and oil companies can adopt high levels of transparency. Latin American civil society and government can push for these standards to be adopted in countries that do not yet have them, knowing not only that these standards are reasonable, but that Chinese investors are perfectly capable of reaching them.

This progress is being threatened, however, by the very sectors enriched by the China boom, such as mining ministries and large landowner voting blocs. For example, regulatory reforms in Peru are cutting back the Environment Ministry's oversight of extractive projects, without putting in place safeguards to prevent conflicts of interest in the approval process. In Brazil, the progress in environmental law enforcement faces strong resistance from the "ruralist" landowner voting bloc that has benefited so much from China's demand for soy. Proposed labor-law protections for oil workers in Colombia may not go through because of pressure from the community action boards that have been the target of so many abuse complaints. It is crucial for Latin American governments to hold the line against these deregulation efforts.

Specifically, we recommend that Latin American governments prioritize the following actions:

- Enforcing and upgrading environmental and social protections.
- Joining the EITI and encouraging Chinese firms to participate.
- Implementing ILO Convention 169 (which most Latin American governments have signed) by requiring prior consultation of indigenous peoples regarding developments that affect their interests and welfare.
- Requiring foreign investors to hire local workers wherever possible, and limiting the use of subcontracted labor.

- Spearheading collaboration between ministries, civil society, and foreign investors to seek informed consultation before extractive projects begin, and to address local concerns in good faith.

- Investing in capacity building for local businesses and encouraging foreign investors to incorporate them into their supply chains.

- Developing mechanisms for local and Chinese governments and local civil society to collaborate in holding Chinese investors to the standards in China's guidelines and local regulations.

- Creating opportunities for new foreign investors to learn local regulations and customs from governments, civil society, and more experienced investors.

- Defending the capacity of civil society organizations for networking and other opportunities to serve as monitors of the social and environmental behavior of firms and governments alike.

China and Chinese Investors

Mitigating the social and environmental impacts of Chinese investment overseas helps Chinese firms and the Chinese government better assess risk and expand market share. Driving the China boom in LAC are billions of dollars in Chinese investment in mines, oil and gas fields, dams to power them, and railways to get the products to port. These projects will take years to begin operation and additional years to break even. In order to reach that point, Chinese investors will need to mitigate risks to these projects' longevity, especially risks of environmental damage or social conflict that could jeopardize their relationships with host countries.

Our case studies show that Chinese firms are capable of meeting—and beating –environmental and social standards set by their host countries. We have found some instances of Chinese investors outperforming their local and international competitors, especially when given appropriate incentives and regulatory frameworks. China has taken important steps toward providing incentives for Chinese investors to act with corporate social and environmental responsibility. Making these processes more transparent is paramount to success, allowing Chinese companies, Latin American governments, and civil society to better understand the true benefits and risks of various investments. Overseeing investor behavior abroad is extremely difficult without the collaboration of host-country governments and civil society. For that reason, we recommend that China and Chinese investors prioritize the following actions:

- Disseminating and implementing existing social and environmental guidelines among Chinese firms in the Americas.
- Making social and environmental guidelines more transparent for company representatives, governments, and civil society.
- Upgrading current guidelines with independent monitoring, a formal grievance process, enforcement mechanisms for investors who fall short of the standards, and other safeguards that have become commonplace among other major foreign investors across the globe.
- Participating in transparency programs in their host countries, such as the environmental reporting requirements in Colombia or the voluntary EITI program in Peru.
- Establishing working relationships with Latin American governments and civil society groups to learn the local regulations and customs.

Civil Society

Policy improvements like these—on both sides of the Pacific—will only be enhanced by the participation of civil society:

- Non-governmental organizations could benefit from expanding their networks to monitor new economic actors in their region and link with their counterparts in China, and across the region and world, to bring further attention to these issues.
- Academic research and workshops can help derive a more empirically based understanding of these complex issues and serve as a neutral space where governments, companies, and civil society can dialogue. Academics can also form international networks to compare findings with other analyses and disseminate their work more widely.
- Academic researchers and universities can also play a role in promoting educational and cultural exchange, joint research, and training for governments and other members of civil society.
- Non-governmental, academic, and other organizations can collaborate with governments and companies to learn best practices and lessons from past mistakes.
- Business-to-business collaborations such as the association of Chinese enterprises in Peru can meet to learn best practices and pending regulatory changes.

- The press could contribute by moving beyond general discussions of the China–Latin America economic relationship to more empirical reporting to hold governments and firms accountable.

CONCLUSION

This project underscores the importance—and the promise—of collaboration between governments, Chinese investors, and Latin American civil society. The most successful stories uncovered here involve these groups cooperating: Bolivia's successful community consultation process, Chinese companies in Peru joining the EITI program, and CNOOC's development of local small-business suppliers in Argentina. China needs Latin American governments and civil society as their eyes and ears for the implementation of their guidelines for overseas investors. Chinese investors need Latin American governments and civil society to teach them local regulations and customs, to prevent environmental and social conflicts from erupting. Latin American governments need Chinese investors and local community groups to work together to find solutions that work for everyone. It is imperative for all stakeholder groups to establish working relationships, in order for the China–Latin America relationship to have the greatest benefit and the least risk.

· · ·

Rebecca Ray is a predoctoral fellow at Boston University's Global Economic Governance Initiative (GEGI) at the University of Boston. Kevin P. Gallagher is codirector of GEGI.

NOTES

1. It is worth noting that Figure 9.5 includes only direct rather than indirect employment. Direct labor intensity across the region has an average of 60.1 jobs in agriculture, 11.6 jobs in extraction, and 71.8 jobs in manufacturing for every U.S. $1 million output in each sector. Estimates of indirect employment vary dramatically, even within each sector. According to the World Input-Output Database (Timmer, 2012), for every dollar of output, extraction creates about twice as much demand for upstream (indirect) industries as agriculture in Brazil, only about a third as much in Mexico, and about three-fourths as much in non-OECD countries. Based on these estimates, it is highly unlikely for the total (direct and indirect) employment from extraction to rival the other sectors shown here in terms of employment generation.

2. *Biodiversity hotspots* are defined as areas with at least 1,500 endemic plant species that have lost at least 70 percent of their original habitat. For more

on biodiversity hotspots, and on the Tropical Andes hotspot specifically, see Zador et al. (2015).

REFERENCES

China Banking Regulatory Commission (2012). "Green Credit Guidelenes," accessed January 20, 2015, http://www.cbrc.gov.cn/chinese/files/2012 /E9F158AD3884481DBE005DFBF0D99C45.doc.

Donabauer, Julian, Andrés López, and Daniela Ramos (2015). "FDI and Trade: Is China Relevant for the Future of Our Environment? The Case of Argentina." Boston: BU Global Economic Governance Initiative Working Paper 2015–2. http://www.bu.edu/pardeeschool/files/2014/12/Argentina1.pdf.

FAO (no date). "FAO Food Price Index," UN Food and Agricultural Organization, accessed January 20, 2015, http://www.fao.org/worldfoodsituation /foodpricesindex/en/.

FAOStat (no date). UN Food and Agricultural Organization, accessed January 20, 2015, http://faostat3.fao.org.

Fearnside, Philip, and Adriano Figueiredo (2015). "China's Influence on Deforestation in Brazilian Amazonia: A Growing Force in the State of Mato Grosso." Boston: BU Global Economic Governance Initiative Working Paper. http://www.bu.edu/pardeeschool/files/2014/12/Brazil1.pdf.

Fearnside, Philip, Adriano Figueiredo, and Sandra Bonjour (2013). "Amazonian Forest Loss and the Long Reach of China's Influence," Environment, Development and Sustainability, 15, pp. 325–338.

Gallagher, Kevin P., Amos Irwin, and Katherine Koleski (2012). "The New Banks in Town: Chinese Finance in Latin America." Boston and Washington, DC: BU Global Economic Governance Initiative and the Inter-American Dialogue. http://www.bu.edu/pardee/files/2013/07/The-New-Banks-in-Town_English.pdf.

Hoekstra, A. Y., and M. M. Mekonnen (2012). "The Water Footprint of Humanity," Proceedings of the National Academy of Sciences, 109, pp. 3232–3237.

Leung, Denise, and Yingzhen Zhao (2013). "Environmental and Social Policies in Overseas Investments: Progress and Challenges for China." Washington, DC: World Resources Institute Issue Brief. http://www.wri.org/sites /default/files/pdf/environmental_and_social_policies_in_overseas_ investments_china.pdf.

Mekonnen, M.M., and A.Y. Hoekstra (2011a). "National Water Footprint Accounts: The Green, Blue and Grey Water Footprint of Production and Consumption." Value of Water Research Report Series no. 50. Delft, The Netherlands: UNESCO-IHE.

———. (2011b). "The Green, Blue and Grey Water Footprint of Crops and Derived Crop Products," Hydrology and Earth System Sciences, 15, pp. 1577–1600.

———. (2012). "A Global Assessment of the Water Footprint of Farm Animal Products," Ecosystems, 15, pp. 401–415.

Peters, Glen, Jan Minx, Christopher Weber, and Ottmar Edenhofer (2011). "Growth in Emission Transfers via International Trade from 1990 to 2008," Proceedings of the National Academy of Sciences USA, 108, pp. 8903–8908.

Ray, Rebecca (2017). "The Panda's Pawprint: The Environmental Impact of the China-led Re-primarization in Latin America and the Caribbean." Ecological Economics 134, 150–159.

Ray, Rebecca, and Adam Chimienti (2015). "A Line in the Equatorial Forests: Chinese Investment and the Environmental and Social Impacts of Extractive Industries in Ecuador." Boston: BU Global Economic Governance Initiative Working Paper. http://www.bu.edu/pardeeschool/files/2014/12/Ecuador1.pdf.

Ray, Rebecca, and Kevin P. Gallagher (2015). "China-Latin America Economic Bulletin—2015 Edition." Boston: BU Global Economic Governance Initiative Discussion Paper 2015–9. http://www.bu.edu/pardeeschool/files/2015/02 /Economic-Bulletin-2015.pdf.

Ray, Rebecca, Kevin P. Gallagher, Andrés López, and Cynthia Sanborn (2015). "China in Latin America: Lessons for South-South Cooperation and Sustainable Development." Boston: BU Global Economic Governance Initiative. http://www.bu.edu/pardeeschool/research/gegi/program-area /chinas-global-reach/chinas-global-reach-environment-and-development /working-group/.

Rudas Lleras, Guillermo, and Mauricio Cabrera Leal (2015). "Colombia and China: Social and Environmental Impact of Trade and Foreign Direct Investment." Boston: BU Global Economic Governance Initiative Working Paper. http://www.bu.edu/pardeeschool/files/2014/12/Colombia1.pdf.

Sanborn, Cynthia, and Victoria Chonn (2015). "Chinese Investment in Peru's Mining Industry: Blessing or Curse?" Boston: BU Global Economic Governance Initiative Working Paper. http://www.bu.edu/pardeeschool /files/2014/12/Peru2.pdf.

Santilli, Márcio (2014). "Ruralismo de fronteira," Instituto Socioambiental, February 27. http://www.socioambiental.org/pt-br/blog/blog-do-ppds /ruralismo-de-fronteira.

Saravia López, Alejandra, and Adam Rua Quiroga (2015). "An Assessment of the Environmental and Social Impacts of Chinese Trade and FDI in Bolivia." Boston: BU Global Economic Governance Initiative Working Paper. http:// www.bu.edu/pardeeschool/files/2014/12/Bolivia1.pdf.

Schatan, Claudia, and Diana Piloyan (2015). "China in Mexico: Some Environmental and Employment Dimensions." Boston: BU Global Economic Governance Initiative Working Paper. http://www.bu.edu/pardeeschool /files/2014/12/Mexico1.pdf.

Smeraldi, Robert (2014). "Para sair da estaca zero," Folha da São Paulo, February 26. http://www1.folha.uol.com.br/opiniao/2014/02/1417853-roberto- smeraldi-para-sair-da-estaca-zero.shtml.

State Forestry Administration (2010). "A Guide on Sustainable Overseas Forests Management and Utilization by Chinese Enterprises," January 26. http://www.forestry.gov.cn/portal/main/s/224/content-401396.html.

Tao, Hu (2013). "A Look at China's New Environmental Guidelines on Overseas Investments." Washington, DC: World Resources Institute. http://www.wri .org/blog/2013/07/look-chinas-new-environmental-guidelines-overseas-investments.

Timmer, Marcel P. (2012). "The World Input-Output Database (WIOD): Contents, Sources and Methods," WIOD Working Paper no. 10. http://www .wiod.org/publications/papers/wiod10.pdf.

UN Statistics Division (no date). UN Comtrade Database, accessed January 20, 2015, http://comtrade.un.org/.

Water Footprint Network (no date). "WaterStat: National Water Footprints," accessed January 20, 2015, http://www.waterfootprint.org/?page = files /WaterStat.

World Bank (no date). "GEM Commodities," accessed January 20, 2015, http:// data.worldbank.org/data-catalog/commodity-price-data.

World Resources Institute (no date). "Climate Analysis Indicators Tool 2.0," accessed January 20, 2015, http://cait2.wri.org/.

Zador, Michel, et al. (2015). "Ecosystem Profile: Tropical Andes Biodiversity Hotspot." Critical Ecosystem Partnership Fund. http://www.cepf.net /SiteCollectionDocuments/tropical_andes/Tropical_Andes_Profile_Draft .pdf.

10. Some Concluding Thoughts

Esteban Pérez Caldentey and Matías Vernengo

New institutionalists who follow the work of Douglass North, such as Acemoglu and Robinson (2012),[1] tend to view institutions as human-created restrictions that structure human relations. These restrictions can be formal (e.g., rules, laws, and constitutions) or informal (e.g., behavioral norms, social conventions, and self-imposed conduct codes). For new institutionalists, institutions are essentially a set of designed incentives that have important economic outcomes. Further, institutions are often related to the reduction of transaction costs.[2] Finally, this view tends to emphasize that the adoption of Western-style institutions—often associated with private property, prudent macroeconomic policies in the economic arena, the normal functioning of markets, the rule of law, and democratic institutions, thereby providing some degree of political stability—would be sufficient to promote economic development. These institutions would provide the environment for rational, profit-maximizing economic agents to invest in human and physical capital and would thus lead to catching up with advanced economies.[3]

These views have a long tradition in economic development and have basically been used to suggest that Latin America fell behind as a result of its inability to promote the development of this institutional framework. A weak state incapable of protecting property rights and the rule of law, and populist governments unwilling to pursue prudent macroeconomic policies or abide by democratic principles, are then often seen as the deep causes of Latin American backwardness.[4] Note, however, that this new institutionalist perspective, which has come to dominate views on the institutional framework required for economic development, seems to take a page out of eighteenth-century social contract literature (in spite of its clear utilitarian affiliation) and presupposes a sort of state of nature devoid of institutions. The maximizing behavior of rational economic agents, assumed as natural by neoclassical economists, presupposes the existence of certain norms of behavior, or, in other words, some sort of institutional framework.[5] The same can be said about the nature of markets: they somehow seem to exist in nature, and the only thing needed for societies to take advantage of them is to get the state out the way.

It is plausible, then, to think that even if Western-style institutions were developed and policies to promote them in Latin America were widely implemented, one would find neither that the behavior of economic agents conforms to the prescribed conceptions of mainstream neoclassical economics, nor that selfish behavior responsive to market incentives would lead to growth and to catching up with the advanced economies. Also, it is well known, at least since Polanyi (1944), that markets do not arise naturally and that they are deeply embedded in society. The state has a fundamental role in setting markets and shaping the rules that allow for their existence.

The chapters in the first part of this volume look at some of the analytical limitations of the mainstream view of the relation between institutions and economic development. There is a certain agreement that the range of institutions that are accepted by the new institutionalists is too narrow, often centered on the supply side of the economics spectrum. Further, there is a belief that in Latin America the requirements of late industrialization have imposed persistent balance-of-payment problems that require more than clear rules and prudent macroeconomic policies to promote development. The role of industrial policy is then seen as being crucial, and institutions associated with them must play an important role. Medeiros suggests, in chapter 2, that state intervention is necessary to build coherent industrial policy to provide technological dynamism.[6] In chapter 4, Centeno and Ferraro argue, by looking at specific institutions in Brazil and Chile, that given the tradition of presidential supremacy in the region, experts should play a more prominent role and be somewhat guarded from executive abuse. It seems that the state must play a role, but not all types of state intervention might be adequate, and the role of experts is also crucial.

Pérez Caldentey and Vernengo suggest, in chapter 3, that beyond the state-versus-market ideology, a crucial role in the development of the institutional framework in the region was its persistent specialization, from colonial times, in the production of commodities.[7] In that sense, the idea is that successful economic development would require the design of institutions that promote the change in the pattern of specialization in the region. In chapter 5, Portes and Nava develop this theme further and seek to determine what makes certain institutions developmental. They try to provide a rigorous quantitative understanding of institutional design and evolution, which allows for cross-country comparisons, and show that some institutions (e.g., tax authorities) have played an important developmental role in the region, while that has not been the case for institutions that provide social services for the population.

While the contributions in the first part of the book look at the limitations of a narrow definition of developmental institutions based exclusively on the theoretical tenets of neoclassical economics, trying to go beyond both neoclassical economics and economicism itself, the chapters in the second part analyze the continuous problems of economic development in the region after the end of the commodity super-cycle. The effects of reprimarization and premature deindustrialization—often seen as related to the new patterns of international integration, in which China has played an outsized role—are central. These are particularly important because they hinge on the ability to promote technological dynamism and reduce the balance-of-payments problems that remain at the center of the inability to catch up.

The chapters in the second part cover similar ground in many ways and tend to reinforce the analytical views discussed in the first part. In particular, it seems clear that in the post-commodity-boom period, in a more integrated world—which now includes low-wage, manufacture-exporting countries in Asia—the prerequisites for closing the gap with advanced economies include institutional development that encourages competent bureaucracies with the technical capacity to promote a transformation of the structure of production, technological dynamism, and the lifting of external constraints, all with a long-term, sustainable perspective. Latin American economies have failed not because they lacked Western-style institutions, though at times they did. They fell behind because they failed to keep up with the permanent institutional evolution that has kept advanced economies at the forefront of technological innovation.

NOTES

1. The extent to which the new institutionalist views can be seen as building on the old institutionalism of Thorstein Veblen and his followers is beyond the scope of this work.

2. A typical example would be money, which is seen as an institutional arrangement created to reduce the transaction costs associated with the double coincidence of wants in market exchanges. Note that in this view, money is essentially a means of exchange and a veil that does not affect real economic transactions. Alternatively, Keynesian authors tend to suggest that money is a social relation that emerges from the imposition by an authority, often the state, of a unit of account that allows for economic calculation. In other words,

without a unit of account, large-scale economic activity is precluded, and one cannot understand real economic activity as separate from its monetary dimension. In one view, the institution develops spontaneously to facilitate the functioning of the market, while in the other it can only arise as the outcome of social relations that reflect the ability to impose a common framework for valuation. For the different views on money as an institutional arrangement, see Ingham (2004).

3. These views always permeated mainstream views on economic development and were codified by Williamson (1990) as the infamous Washington Consensus.

4. See, for example, the essays in Haber (1997) as representative of this conventional approach.

5. Evidence on the evolution of human behavior suggests that the conventional neoclassical notion of rationality tied to individual gain may underestimate the role of cooperation. Cooperative behavior may have provided an evolutionary advantage to early humans and may have been a precondition for the species' own physical survival (see Morris, 2010).

6. Also, Medeiros notes that there is a danger in assuming that the only role for the government is getting prices right. In that respect, the new developmentalist literature that emphasizes the importance of getting the real exchange rate right may be misguided.

7. In more precise terms, the current development strategy in Latin America relies on commodity exports, mostly in South America, and on the export of cheap labor—directly through immigration or indirectly associated with low-value-added manufacturing exports—in Central America and Mexico. See Pérez Caldentey and Vernengo (2010).

REFERENCES

Acemoglu, D., and Robinson, J. (2012), Why Nations Fail. New York: Crown.
Haber, S. (1997), How Latin America Fell Behind: Essays on the Economic Histories of Brazil and Mexico, 1800–1914. Stanford, CA: Stanford University Press.
Ingham, G. (2004), The Nature of Money. London: Polity Press.
Morris, I. (2010), Why the West Rules. New York: Farrar, Straus and Giroux.
Pérez Caldentey, E., and Vernengo, M. (2010), "Back to the Future: Latin America's Current Development Strategy," Journal of Post Keynesian Economics, 32, pp. 623–644.
Polanyi, K. (1944), The Great Transformation. Boston: Beacon Press.
Williamson, J. (1990), "What Washington Means by Policy Reform," in J. Williamson (ed.), Latin American Adjustment: How Much Has Happened? Washington, DC: Institute for International Economics.

Index